Kate Howarth was born in Sydney in 1950 and grew up in the suburbs of Darlington and Parramatta, and far western New South Wales. She was forced to leave school at fourteen and an eclectic career followed; she has been a factory worker, an Avon lady, corporate executive and restaurateur, to name a few. At the age of fifty-two she began writing her memoir, *Ten Hail Marys*, which in 2008 was shortlisted for the David Unaipon Award for Indigenous writers. She is connected to and proud of her Aboriginal heritage.

To Dearest Astrid, with much Love, from Kate.

TEN HAIL MARYS

a memoir

kate howarth

UQP

First published 2010 by University of Queensland Press
PO Box 6042, St Lucia, Queensland 4067 Australia

www.uqp.com.au

Typeset in 11.5/16 pt Janson Text by Post Pre-press Group, Brisbane
Printed in Australia by McPherson's Printing Group

This project has been assisted by
the Commonwealth Government through
the Australia Council, its arts funding
and advisory body.

Cataloguing-in-Publication Data
National Library of Australia
Howarth, Kate Lesley Kay
    Ten hail marys
    ISBN 9780702237706 (pbk)
    ISBN 9780702237928 (pdf)
    Howarth, Kate Lesley Kay, 1950 – childhood and youth.
    St Margaret's Hospital (Sydney, NSW).
    Abandoned children – New South Wales – Biography.
    Unmarried mothers – New South Wales – Biography.
    Unmarried mothers – Institutional care – New South Wales – Biography.
    Women, Aboriginal Australian – Biography.
305.89915

Inside front cover (*clockwise from top left*): Granny (*seated*) and Mamma; Aunty Shirley,
Uncle Stan and baby Adam; Granny and Pop; Kate, eighteen months old.
Inside back cover (*clockwise from top left*): Kate and Adam; Kate and Pixie;
Adam, seventeen months old; Kate and John on their wedding day.
Throughout *Ten Hail Marys* names have been changed to protect the
privacy of certain individuals.

University of Queensland Press uses papers that are natural, renewable
and recyclable products made from wood grown in sustainable forests.
The logging and manufacturing processes conform to the environmental
regulations of the country of origin.

To my dear departed friend
John 'Pumpy' Scipione

Preface

It was a bitterly cold July morning when, a few years back, a fall from a train turned my life on its ear. Left with injuries that meant I was unable to run my business, I faced almost total financial ruin. My mobility was severely hampered but I decided to make the best of being completely housebound. I borrowed my daughter's computer and followed the advice of friends who for some time had been encouraging me to 'write the book' about my life.

Two years later I gave the manuscript to my trusted friend John Scipione. When he'd finished reading it, he asked why I'd skimmed over my experiences in St Margaret's Home for Unwed Mothers.

'I kept the baby,' I replied. 'Where's the story in that?'

My flippant response was a deliberate cover-up for a part of my life that I found very difficult to talk about. Not since the day I walked out of that godforsaken hospital had I told the whole story to anyone. This was partly because I didn't think anyone would believe me, but also because each time I recalled those events they inevitably evoked memories that left me melancholy for days.

John asked whether I knew that between 1998 and 2000 there had been a parliamentary inquiry into adoption practices. These years coincided with the long period of convalescence after my accident, when I'd been plunged into one of the bleakest periods of my life. I lived on painkillers and never left the house, turned on a television or read a newspaper. Little wonder I had never heard of the inquiry or its outcome.

From the internet I accessed the transcripts of evidence taken at the Parliamentary Inquiry into Adoption Practices 1950–1998, which began in Sydney on 19 October 1998. When I read the evidence, given under oath, from Sister Antoinette Baldwin, the spokesperson for the Sisters of St Joseph who ran St Margaret's Home for Unwed Mothers, I was outraged. Her evidence was largely anecdotal. She had not worked with the unmarried mothers and had had no involvement in implementing hospital policy. In fact, she had not worked at St Margaret's Hospital at all from 1962 to 1972, when the highest number of adoptions had taken place. Moreover, the good sister's words were totally at odds with my experience of being an unwed mother at St Margaret's.

In her opening address, Sister Antoinette, a neonatal nurse during the 1980s, said she felt the need to speak for the babies who were given up for adoption as she thought during the inquiry there had been an expression of the 'pain of one-sided bonding'. She apologised to the mothers for causing them any more pain by sharing her experience of the suffering of the tiny babies on the days the relinquishing mothers were discharged from the hospital. She went on to say, 'We saw the pain of separation that the babies also experienced, they would become restless and unsettled for that day.' *

---

* A full transcript of Sister Antoinette's evidence to the Parliamentary Inquiry into Adoption Practices 1950–1998 can be found on the internet at www.parliament.nsw.gov.au

As if rubbing salt into wounds, her subsequent evidence at the parliamentary inquiry would have left all the children adopted through St Margaret's feeling devastated that their mother had other options and didn't take them:

> It is my understanding that if a mother expressed a wish to keep her baby or changed her mind about adoption she would then receive the same treatment as any other mother who was keeping her child and was discharged from the hospital post-delivery. I understand that they were given some assistance but I do not know what form that assistance took. I understand it was practical help with baby clothes and equipment for the baby.

Earlier, in their submission to the inquiry, the Sisters of St Joseph stated: 'Between 1952 and 1966 girls who changed their minds could stay at the Home for six to twelve months, where they could have the baby cared for while they tried to find employment and accommodation.'

When the inquiry asked Sister Antoinette how many girls took this opportunity she replied: 'Anecdotally I know some did . . . I do not know how many and I do not know how much it was encouraged. I just know that it was a policy.'

This conflicts with evidence later taken from Sister Antoinette when she told the inquiry that 'adoption was seen as the only viable alternative in a society that did not condone single mother-hood nor offer any assistance to the mother struggling to raise her infant alone.'

Like most other young mothers of that time, I would imagine, I was not aware of my rights when it came to any proposed adoption of my baby. Under the *Child Welfare Act 1939*, adoption agencies were required to advise on the support, both monetary and material, that was available to a woman not wanting to adopt out her child.

Evidence taken from Dian Wellfare – the secretary of Origins Inc, the support group initiated in 1995 that was instrumental in bringing these matters before the parliamentary inquiry – exposed the many myths and well-kept secrets surrounding the viable options that, prior to 1973, were available for unmarried mothers wishing to keep their babies. According to Wellfare, the monetary assistance was only one dollar less than the Widow's Pension. Section 27 also made provision for other practical help, including accommodation and day care for the child while the mother worked.

Dian Wellfare also brought to the inquiry's attention the fact that the *Child Welfare of New South Wales 1959 Social Work Training Manual* states:

> When all of these aids have been made known and rejected and the mother still desires to surrender the child for adoption, the full import of surrendering the child is explained. Only when the mother still insists does the department's officer prepare the form of surrender.

It is generally assumed that financial assistance by way of the Supporting Mother's Benefit was not available until the Labor government introduced it in 1973. However, all Gough Whitlam did was change the name of a benefit that already existed. By concealing the availability of this assistance, the adoption agencies essentially railroaded unmarried mothers into the only direction offered to them.

Although I refused to relinquish my baby for adoption, had I known that this support was available things would have played out for me very differently.

But this was not, as Sister Antoinette put it, just about society 'not condoning single motherhood and not offering assistance to a mother struggling to raise her infant alone'. What was in operation was a brutal, heartless adoption industry with market pressures to locate 'healthy newborn' babies for infertile couples. As a result, the operators withheld information about viable alternatives to adoption and totally disregarded the human suffering that was inflicted on the mother and the child. Many people profited, including doctors, lawyers and St Margaret's Hospital itself, which enjoyed its reputation for being able to run on a shoestring. With an unpaid workforce of fifty or more unmarried mothers at any given time, it would have been easy to stay in the black. This is not to mention any adoption fees that may have been received. I don't imagine anyone believes that healthy newborn babies were simply given away.

In its final report, *Releasing the Past*, the inquiry stated that, from the 98,578 single unwed mothers who gave birth between 1950 and 1998, it had not been able to take evidence from one who actually kept her baby. Even had I known at the time that this inquiry was taking place, I probably would not have seen any real point in relating my story. In fact, it was not until I had accessed the transcripts of evidence that I realised how relevant my experience was.

My story tells of what happened when a young girl refused to surrender her child for adoption, and the extraordinary tactics of intimidation she was subjected to before, during and after the birth. But in order to write about this, I realised that I would have to go back more deeply into my past. My story demanded some explanation of how the events of my childhood and adolescence had impacted on me and given me the determination – unusual for the times – to pit myself against family, society and church, all of whom had various reasons for wanting me to 'relinquish' my child.

In telling my story, I do not want to create any misunderstandings that might suggest I believe the mothers who had their babies taken from them at birth were weak. On the contrary. If not for the unusual circumstances of my early life, I doubt that I would have been able to withstand the pressure, which at times was considerable, without breaking. As it was, I very nearly couldn't.

I hope that my story adds another voice to those of the mothers and their children seeking recognition. It would be gratifying if it goes even some way towards redressing what has happened and opening the door for compensation – even an apology – for the suffering that was inflicted by the adoption industry. It is simply not good enough to dismiss the practices that were the order of the day by saying 'mistakes were made' when basic codes of human decency and existing laws designed to protect mother and child during the adoption process were breached.

1

Out of a bottle

'Who's that lady?' I asked, pointing to the attractive dark-haired woman next to Uncle Ringer in a group photograph.

I was about five years old and helping Mamma clean the glass on the photographs on her sideboard. The photo I'd picked up had been taken at Aunty Lorna and Uncle Bill's wedding.

'That's your mother.'

'But you're my mother.'

'I'm not your mother, Phyllis is.'

I just stared at Mamma, trying to understand what this meant.

'She didn't want you,' Mamma said, as if anticipating an obvious question. 'She was going to throw you over the balcony,' she added, before gently placing the photograph onto a clean lace doily.

Phyllis was Mamma's daughter, and at this age I was still too young to work out that this meant Mamma was my grandmother and that her youngest sons were not my brothers, as I had thought, but my uncles.

So if I am not Katie Carlton, who am I? I wondered.

At night, when the adults were sitting around talking after dinner, I'd sit quietly, soaking up information like a sponge and trying to piece it all together to see where I fitted in. From what I could gather, before the outbreak of World War Two, Mamma and Bill Gresham, her first husband, and their four children, Leslie, Stan, Phyllis and Daphne, lived in Nyngan, in central New South Wales. As the work in the bush dried up they were forced to relocate to the 'big smoke' and moved into Raglan Street, Chippendale, in Sydney. Bill Gresham, my grandfather, was never more to me than a photograph of a handsome sandy-haired man in a slouch hat in the bottom of Mamma's wardrobe. Uncle Les lied about his age and followed his father into the army and they both went off to war. Uncle Stan, who was only fourteen at the time, had to forgo his calling into the priesthood and go to work to help Mamma with the younger girls.

It seemed that Phyllis was the wild child in the family. She hated school and at thirteen was declared 'uncontrollable' by the Albion Street Children's Court, and sent to the Sisters of the Good Shepherd, a Catholic home for wayward girls at Strathfield with a fearsome reputation.

When she was fifteen Phyllis got her father's consent to marry Ray Howarth, a baker from Nyngan, who was more than twice her age. The marriage was short-lived and Ray disappeared from the scene.

At eighteen Phyllis became pregnant. There was always some contention in the family as to who the father was. Aunty Lorna, Mamma's sister, told me that Phyllis tried everything to get rid of me, including sitting in a hot bath drinking gin, but I refused to budge. So she went dancing and partying for as long as she could squeeze her growing belly into a corset. By Christmas 1949 Phyllis was housebound and climbing up the walls. It was almost impossible for her and Mamma to be in the same room without pulling each other's hair out.

'She looks ready to drop it at any tick of the clock,' Mamma said one morning to Aunty Lorna, who had slept on the lounge after an all-night drinking session with Phyllis.

Sydney in January 1950 was hot, humid and one of the wettest months on record. Storms raged across the city, causing floods and cutting power to thousands of homes. The rain pelted down, drowning out the radio as Mamma tried to tune in to the horse-races in Melbourne. Phyllis was more agitated than usual, pacing the floor, chain-smoking and cursing all the angels and saints for her predicament. She knew not to look to her mother for help or sympathy.

'I'm going to call an ambulance,' Uncle Stan, Phyllis's older brother, said when she started screaming the house down at about three o'clock in the afternoon.

The ambulance arrived with sirens blaring. They had a hell of a job getting Phyllis onto the trolley – she didn't want to go to hospital and tried to fight everyone.

'Take us to the nearest maternity hospital,' Uncle Stan said, getting into the back of the ambulance and taking Phyllis's hand.

At first the admissions nurse at King George V Hospital in Camperdown wasn't going to admit Phyllis because she wasn't booked in to the maternity ward and didn't have a doctor. Uncle Stan, who is about five feet four inches in his socks and weighs 110 pounds wringing wet, is normally a mild-mannered man, but when he's had enough he'll let you know.

'You bloody will take my sister. She's not having this baby on the street!'

Having a baby at King George V Private Hospital was a privilege usually reserved for people with double-barrelled surnames and a pedigree going back to the colonial squattocracy. God knows what the other patients and staff made of a mob of black-fellas rocking up to visit one of our own, in a private room, to have a stickybeak at the new bub.

'She was sitting up like Lady Muck, ordering the staff around,' Uncle Stan told me one time, chuckling at the audacity of his feisty sister.

Being tied down with a baby didn't fit Phyllis's lifestyle. I was nine months old when Aunty Daphne stepped in and stopped Phyllis throwing me over the front balcony. Phyllis took off that night without leaving a forwarding address. I stayed with Mamma, who, as soon as she got a good look at me, said, 'This baby will have to go to hospital.'

That meant I was probably close to death's door. I had pneumonia. When I came home from hospital it was still uncertain whether I would make it, and Uncle Stan was nervous because I hadn't been baptised.

'We can't let this baby die with a mortal sin on her soul,' he said, bundling me into a blanket and taking me around to St Benedict's Church on Broadway, a short walk from Raglan Street, where I was christened and baptised a Catholic. Uncle Stan was a devout Catholic and took his role as my godfather very seriously.

By 1953 Mamma's second husband, Fred Carlton – Kev, Robbie and Dan's father – was gone for good. Fred was by all accounts a drunken no-hoper who liked to throw his weight around. He was last seen running into the back lane after Granny, Mamma's mother, had up-ended a pan of sausages over his head, hot fat and all. This left Mamma with four children to support. Aunty Daphne had left home to marry Jack McCarthy. Uncle Leslie was away fighting in another war, and no one had heard from Phyllis. Things would have become pretty grim if Uncle Stan had not postponed his marriage to his fiancée, Shirley, to stay home to help Mamma look after his three younger brothers and me.

Uncle Stan was a wool dyer, and, although he worked long hours at the Alexandria Woollen Mills, he was a keen gardener. Our backyard was only small but every inch of dirt grew something. Flowers, vegetables and fruit trees were all clumped in together and thrived, and Uncle Stan even grew things in tin cans with holes cut in the side. A profusion of jasmine climbed up and over the outside dunny and choko vines twisted their way along the top of the paling fence. Surrounded by the colour and fragrance of lemon trees and roses, I'd amuse myself for hours drawing pictures with sticks of charcoal from the wood-fired stove in the kitchen onto the concrete path that ran from the back door to the gate leading to the laneway. On the hottest days the jasmine helped to mask the stench from the open-pan toilet.

When it was too wet to play outside, and if Mamma was in a good mood, we'd play a game I called horsey. Mamma would pull up a chair to the stove in the kitchen and take a breather from the endless housework. She'd cross her legs and I'd straddle the outstretched leg and say 'giddy up'. Then slowly her leg would rock me up and down, like the carousel ponies at Luna Park.

'Do you want to go faster?' Mamma would say, taking a drag on her cigarette.

'Yes,' I'd reply, grabbing hold of her knee with both hands.

'Where did Katie come from?' she'd ask.

'I came out of a beer bottle,' I'd say, quickly shooting back my stock-standard reply.

Mamma would throw her head back in peals of laughter, causing her leg to pump up and down a little faster.

'What's Katie going to be when she grows up?' she'd ask.

'A prostitute,' I'd jump in, barely giving her time to finish the sentence. Then I'd hold on for the ride of my life as Mamma's whole body shook with laughter. It took all of my strength and concentration not to fall off and crash into the hot stove.

I was trained to repeat these responses like an organ grinder's monkey but had no idea what was so amusing. For years I had nightmares about being trapped in the long neck of an amber glass bottle.

One night I went to sleep at Raglan Street and woke up in a soaking wet bed next to my cousin Jimmy, Aunty Lorna's son, who was about my age and still wet the bed every night. Aunty Lorna, Uncle Bill, and their three kids, Elaine, Denise and Jimmy, lived in a rambling old weatherboard house in Lansdowne Street, Merrylands. Aunty Lorna's parents, Granny and Charlie 'Pop' Higgins, were also living with them.

Although Aunty Lorna and Mamma were sisters, you'd never know to look at them. Aunty Lorna had warm brown eyes. Her skin was the colour of Nestlé's milk chocolate and as soft as her best leather handbag. Mamma's skin was almost milky white and she had piercing blue-grey eyes that flashed like steel blades when she was angry.

Aunty Lorna could swear like a trooper and had a reputation for being able to drink ten sailors under the table. She had a shocking temper and flogged her kids if they didn't do as they were told. Even Uncle Bill copped the odd black eye, but she never so much as raised her voice to me. Sitting on Aunty Lorna's lap was like snuggling into an over-stuffed feather-filled lounge, and when Mamma was around it was the safest place to be.

'Leave the kid alone, she's only a baby,' Aunty Lorna would say, holding me close to her soft warm body.

Mamma and Aunty Lorna were not the only key women in my life during these early years. Granny had her part to play as well.

Born Elizabeth Harriet Wood, she was known to the Bogan community of Nyngan as Lizzie Higgins, but to the family she was just Granny. She was a tiny woman, shorter than five feet in heels. She couldn't even reach the clothesline without standing on a crate. It was my job to pass her the pegs.

By 1954 her hair had turned to silver and after a lifetime of physical hard work her hands were still as soft and strong as her heart. It was Granny's job to take care of Denise, Jimmy and me while the other adults went to work. Elaine was much older than we younger kids and was already at school. Granny was rarely seen without a duster or a broom in her hands and her kitchen always smelled of just-baked bread or fruit pies.

Like all kids of the 1950s we played outdoors and found ways to amuse ourselves with ordinary things. The junk that people threw into the stormwater drains that snaked through the backblocks of Merrylands provided an endless supply of raw material. The mulberry tree that dominated the backyard at Aunty Lorna's was the focal point of most of our games. Even after gorging ourselves, the plump berries continued to fall like rain, creating a squishy purple carpet that stained our feet up to the ankles.

Granny never hit us, but she was strict, and a cake of Sunlight soap was always at hand to wash out the mouth of any kid using bad language.

'Okay you kids . . . it's time for your bath,' Granny called from the back door one evening. As usual, Denise started acting up. Granny came running down the steps, with a dog collar in her hand.

'Right, you little bugger,' she said, grabbing Denise by the back of her dress. 'If you want to smell like the dogs, you may as well live with them.'

Granny attached the collar around Denise's neck. Denise bucked like a heifer as Granny tied her up next to the kennels.

Denise howled for ten minutes, setting off all the dogs in the street. Granny didn't release Denise from the chain until she had promised to never make a fuss taking a bath again.

Granny's fanatical cleanliness, which went way beyond being neat and tidy, had another purpose.

'If you kids aren't clean a whitefella in a big black car will take you away,' she warned.

I used to think Granny said this just to scare us into taking a bath, until the day a black car pulled up in front of Aunty Lorna's house while we were having lunch.

Granny looked through the curtains. 'Quick!' she said, gathering up our plates and glasses and putting them into the sink. 'Katie, get under the house and stay there until I tell you.'

Around lunchtime, most Saturdays, a truck from the Vauxhall Inn would pull up in front of the house. Uncle Bill would help the driver roll a large wooden keg of beer around the back and set it up in the outside laundry. Aboriginal people weren't allowed to go into hotels in those days, or even be sold alcohol at all. But Uncle Bill had red hair and freckles, so it was his job to order the grog.

When Aunty Lorna had a party we kids were allowed to stay up late. I hated the smells that came with adults, especially of beer and cigarettes, so I went to bed and lay awake listening to 'old leather lungs' Frankie Laine singing 'Jezebel' over and over again. It was only a matter of time before someone started a blue. Voices would be raised, followed by a scuffle and the sound of breaking glass.

'If youse want to fucking kill each other do it outside.' Aunty Lorna's booming voice could be heard above the commotion.

Although the music would be turned down, so as not to disturb the neighbours, the party wouldn't be over until the keg had been drained. The next morning the house always looked like a bomb had hit it. People just lay where they had fallen. The stink of stale booze and cigarettes repulsed me.

Granny was a Salvation Army officer and Sunday was the Lord's Day. She'd put on her navy blue uniform with the burgundy trim and silver buttons on the jacket. She'd comb her hair before putting on the bonnet and tying the long taffeta ribbons into a generous bow under her chin. Checking herself in the hall mirror, and satisfied that she looked her best, she would gather up her Bible and tambourine.

'I'm off now, love,' she'd call out to Aunty Lorna, who'd be looking like she'd passed out at the kitchen table.

Granny would walk down the hallway, vigorously shaking her tambourine over the head of anyone blocking her way as she went out to praise the Lord.

2

The new place

Aunty Lorna's house was about a two-mile walk to the Granville pool. In summer Uncle Bill would give Jimmy, Denise and me enough money to get through the turnstiles, and we'd pack a few peanut butter sandwiches for lunch. There was a water bubbler at the pool if we wanted a drink.

By Christmas, my skin was the colour of Nugget Brown boot polish, and the man at the pool called me a 'bloody little half-caste'. He wouldn't let me through the turnstile until Jimmy told him I was his cousin.

When we got back from the pool one day there was a fancy black car parked in front of Aunty Lorna's house. We hesitated, and then figured the car was probably too flash to be anyone from the government rounding up kids.

The man who owned it was introduced to me as Uncle Buster. He was a friend of Mamma and had been sent to take me to our new place at Herne Bay. No one had told me we were moving, let alone why, but that wasn't unusual. Mamma and the boys had

10

moved to our new place while I was at Aunty Lorna's. I hoped they had remembered to take 'Cockie', our sulphur-crested cockatoo.

Aunty Lorna had packed my things into a small cardboard box. She walked me out to the car.

'Bye, Katie darlin',' she said, lifting me up and into the passenger's seat. She pushed a button down and slammed the door shut.

As the car took off I started to feel very nervous. Granny had drummed it into us to never get into a car with strangers and I had forgotten 'to go' before we left. I pressed my legs together and hugged the cardboard box on my lap.

Uncle Buster lit up a cigarette.

'May I put the window down a bit, please?'

'It's going to rain. The inside of the car will get wet,' he said, blowing the smoke in my direction.

Aunty Lorna had forgotten to tell Uncle Buster that I vomited if I didn't have a window down. She'd found that out for herself the hard way one night when we were coming home from Bullen's Circus in a taxi.

Uncle Buster's car rocked from side to side. Heavy rain pounded the windshield. Thunder and lightning seemed to be clashing in unison. I closed my eyes and concentrated as hard as I could, trying not vomit or pee on the nice leather upholstery.

'Here we are,' he said at last, turning left through a set of high wire gates.

Here we are where? This place didn't look like anywhere we'd live. There were no proper houses. No grass or trees, just dirt and rows of strange looking buildings. Uncle Buster pulled up in front of one of them and tooted the horn.

'G'day, Buster. Come inside, we're just about to have tea,' Mamma called from the doorway.

I unlocked the car and scrambled to the ground. Dodging

potholes filled with muddy water, I ran for the door. 'Uncle Stan,' I whispered, jumping up and down like I had ants in my pants, 'where's the dunny? I need to go.'

'It's at the end of the row,' he said, and handed me a few sheets of toilet paper.

The communal toilets at Herne Bay defied description. Human waste was smeared on the corrugated iron walls and cigarette butts floated in the pee all over the floor. It said a lot for the other people living here. I shivered with disgust as I walked barefoot in the filth. There was a cold-water tap outside the toilet block so I rinsed my hands and feet.

Back inside, the rain pounded the iron roof and everyone was shouting to be heard above the din. An assortment of buckets, pots and pans caught the water pouring in through the gaping holes in the roof of the hut. Except for the pot plants Uncle Stan had brought from Raglan Street and Cockie screeching, 'You old bastard!', nothing felt like home.

Herne Bay was a kind of halfway house for immigrants arriving from England and Europe as well as people like us, who were waiting for government-assisted housing to become available. We were a bubble and squeak of humanity at various stages of disloca-tion, all tossed into a hellhole on the edge of the swampy marshes along the Georges River, a breeding ground for millions of mos-quitoes. It didn't matter how hot it was, you had to sleep under a sheet or get eaten alive. Uncle Stan brought home some mozzie coils that filled the hut with smoke. It stank to high heaven, but at least it kept the mozzies away.

If these blood-sucking parasites weren't enough to push the New Australians to the edge of despair, they could always count on the insults and abuse from the locals.

'Ungrateful Pommie bastards.'
'Bloody whingeing Poms.'
'Go back where you came from, you bloody New Australians.'
'Go home, stupid bloody wog.'
'Speak English, you are in Australia now.'
These were the more kindly remarks.

One afternoon I came home for lunch and there was a vaguely familiar person sitting at the table. He was wearing a uniform with a green beret stuck in the epaulet on the shoulder.

'Hello, Katie darlin'.'

'Uncle Les?' I asked shyly.

He smiled. 'You remember me?'

When Uncle Les went away I was just a toddler. But he was the spitting image of his father, Bill Gresham, especially in the khaki uniform. Uncle Les had just returned from Korea, where Mamma said he had been fighting the 'yellow peril'.

'What was the war like, Uncle Les?' I asked.

'We don't talk about the war,' Mamma said sharply, handing me the cutlery to set the table.

Uncle Les unzipped his duffle bag. 'This is for you, Katie. It has come all the way from Korea.'

He handed me a small brown paper parcel. It was so exciting to get a present when it wasn't even Christmas.

'Oh, thank you, Uncle Les!'

I thought I was going to burst with joy when I saw the yellow pyjamas with the little red bird embroidered onto the pocket.

'They're pure silk,' he said, and smiled.

I ran my hand over the fabric. It was as soft as butterfly wings. That night, after my bath, I got into the yellow silk pyjamas. I was busy admiring myself when something reflecting in Mamma's dressing table mirror caught my eye. I turned and stared at the hole, which was the size of a threepence. An eyeball was staring back at me. I jumped down from the bed and ran from the room. Mamma always kept a packet of Bandaids in the kitchen drawer. I used one to cover the hole.

At the end of our row of huts was a park. The long grass was crawling with snakes and if you didn't want to step on a brown one and end up dead, it was smart to beat a path to the swings by thumping a stick onto the ground.

One day when I was at the park, a new boy turned up. He wasn't watching where he was going as he kicked around a black-and-white ball and dumped right into me, nearly knocking me off my feet.

'Hey, why don't you look where you're going?' I said, shoving him back.

'Sorry. My name's John Heywood,' he said, without taking his eye off the ball.

It was apparent from his accent and pale skin that he was British, and he had the skinniest little chicken legs I'd ever seen.

'I'm Katie, would you like to come to my place for lunch?'

'Will it be alright with your mum?'

There was no need to ask permission. I was always bringing strays home. Cats, dogs, kids – it didn't matter. If they looked half-starved I took them back for a feed and Mamma never complained.

This day the front door was locked, which was unusual. And Uncle Stan was acting very strangely.

'You can't come in yet,' he said in his nervous voice.

After about five minutes he called out, 'Alright, you can come in now.' He unlocked the door.

Uncle Stan was incapable of telling a lie or being sneaky in any way. His voice and mannerisms always gave him away. He was up to something alright.

'Mamma, this is John, he's a new kid. He's from England.'

Mamma made us some Vegemite sandwiches and poured us a glass of homemade ginger beer. She was as sweet as pie and I was relieved that she didn't tell the joke going around that the safest place to hide a quid was under a Pommie's towel.

The next day Uncle Stan came home with a real Christmas tree, which we all helped to decorate. But we were never told the fanciful stories about a fat man in a red suit who came from the North Pole.

'Santa Claus is a pagan story,' Uncle Stan said.

As with most kids, curiosity got the better of us, so when Uncle Stan and Mamma went shopping, Dan and I went looking for the Christmas presents. Mamma's wardrobe was at an angle in the bedroom and, although I couldn't pull it out, I could see through the crack between the wardrobe and the wall. My breathing stopped when I spotted it – a child-sized china dresser, similar to Aunty Daphne's. Never daring to imagine that it would be for me, I wondered what little girl was going to get such a wonderful gift.

On Christmas morning Dan and I raced to the tree and there was the dresser, too big to waste wrapping paper on.

'That's for you, Katie,' Uncle Stan said with a giggle.

He must have known that a gift like this was going to blow my socks off. Giving presents always gave Uncle Stan such joy. He was beaming as he watched my wide-eyed reaction. I thought I was going to die of happiness as I opened the little doors and smelled the new wood.

Then he handed me a parcel that was wrapped. 'This is your Christmas and birthday present,' he said.

As my birthday was so close to Christmas, I always got a

combined gift. But Uncle Stan still gave me a card on my birthday, so it didn't feel like just another day.

I sat down on the floor and slowly removed the paper, being careful not to tear it for later use as drawer liners. Inside was a box. My hands trembled as I lifted the lid. Then all I could do was stare gobsmacked at the beautiful doll with dark curly hair, just like mine. Her eyes, with long lashes resting above her chubby cheeks, were closed as if she were sleeping. Her soft blue velvet dress had little white roses embroidered into the bodice, and on her feet was a pair of white leather shoes with tiny silver buckles and white cotton socks. As I lifted her gently from the box, her sparkling blue eyes opened and she said 'Mum-ma'. I called her Mary and she became my closest confidante. I told her all of my secret dreams. One day we would live in a great big beautiful house by the sea and travel to faraway places and be rich like princesses.

By the end of December, with the hottest months of summer still to come, the residents at Herne Bay were already at their wits' end. By February, with no let-up from the heatwave, people were dropping like flies. The sound of ambulance sirens became commonplace, as the elderly and babies were rushed to hospital with heat exhaustion.

One morning a letter arrived. Mamma looked excited as she ripped open the envelope.

'Oh, you little ripper!' she yelled, dancing around the room and waving the letter in the air.

I thought we must have won the lottery or something. It was as good as winning the lottery to learn that our new house at Parramatta was ready. Aunty Lorna and her brood were going back to the bush, and Granny and Pop Higgins were coming to live with us.

3

A fresh start

As the last of the furniture was loaded onto the back of the truck, Mamma and Uncle Stan swept and mopped like there was no tomorrow, wanting to make sure we left the hut at Herne Bay cleaner than we found it. Two taxis arrived. Mamma, Kev, Robbie, Dan and I took one. Uncle Stan, Granny and Pop Higgins travelled in the other one, along with Cockie and all the other the goods and chattels that were too awkward to pack or wouldn't fit onto the truck. Although I was glad to be leaving Herne Bay, saying goodbye to my friend John made me very sad.

I watched him waving to me until we turned the corner. Then he was gone. I remember thinking that this must be what it feels like when someone dies. I couldn't hold back my tears.

'Look at her! Only five years old and she's bloody boy crazy already,' Mamma said.

It was raining steadily as we left Herne Bay after lunch that Good Friday. I was sitting in the back seat of the cab. Kev wouldn't let me sit next to the window. Mamma sat up the front beside the driver and chain-smoked as she read aloud from a letter she had received from her sister Aunty Vera, who still lived in Nyngan.

'Oh well the good news is the bloody drought's broken,' she said, passing us the photographs Aunty Vera had sent of our cousins sitting in a rowing boat outside the butcher's shop on Nymagee Street.

Good Friday, the holiest day on the Christian calendar, was the biggest day at the Royal Easter Show. The pubs were closed and the show was the only place where people could get a drink. Double-decker buses, packed with people coming and going from the showground at Moore Park, were bumper to bumper, choking the roads in all directions.

Suddenly I felt very cold. Goose bumps ran down my arms and my stomach started churning. It caught me by surprise when we hit a sudden bump in the road.

'Oh Christ! Mamma, Katie's chucked up,' Kev said, shoving me away from him.

'Stop the bloody car!' Mamma said, sounding exasperated. She'd been studying the form guide, hoping to pick a few winners in tomorrow's horseraces at Rosehill, which was always a very serious business.

Mamma got out of the cab, holding the newspaper over her head to protect her new perm from frizzing in the rain. She went around to the boot and came back with two towels. With a puddle of vomit in my lap I was afraid to move.

'Don't just sit there,' she said, opening the door.

The contents of my lap spilled onto the bags on the floor.

'Here, clean yourself up,' she snapped, handing me a towel. She reached into the back of the cab and pulled out the bag that had copped the worst of it.

*

As soon as the taxi pulled up in front of our house in Jeffrey Avenue, the boys jumped out and headed for the bushland at the end of the street. I was keen to see the inside of the house; the bush could wait.

The housing settlement at North Parramatta had just been completed and the landscape was as bare as a plucked chook. Water mixed with clay ran in torrents down the sloping front yard, spilling onto the footpath. The stormwater drains couldn't cope, and the force of the water lifted the heavy steel grates from the drains and tossed them around like they were made of sponge rubber.

We had a brand spanking new house that no one had ever lived in, a blank page onto which our story would be written. But the first thing Mamma noticed about our new house was the green guttering. She was very superstitious about green.

'Green is bad luck,' she always said, and for her it was a self-fulfilling prophecy.

Mamma put the shiny brass key into the lock and there it remained for the next nine years.

'Oh look, Stan, we'll be able to get another table and chairs in here,' she said when she inspected the kitchen.

This was important to Mamma, as we always had a stream of blow-ins from the bush and no one was ever turned away. Mamma was in raptures. She ran her hands over the laminated bench tops and pulled on the chrome door knobs of the overhead cupboards, which were stiff and smelled of new paint. Overcome, she wiped away the tears as she continued to inspect our new home.

I was fascinated by the inside, flushing toilet. I'd have to stand on the rim of the toilet to flush until I was tall enough to reach the chain, but that was a small inconvenience for not having Dan the pan man's truck stinking up the neighbourhood with its putrid load that slopped all over the road.

The beautiful knotted pinewood floors were eventually covered with ghastly grey and gold linoleum that was freezing cold in the winter, and in the intense heat of summer smelled like a newly laid bitumen road. The petrol fumes were so strong they made my eyes water, and with so many smokers in the house it was a miracle we weren't blown to buggery.

Uncle Stan had his work cut out trying to get a lawn going. He had tons of topsoil delivered and had just finished sowing the whole front yard when we had another downpour, which lasted several days. All of his hard work washed down the drain in rivers of dark-brown liquid mud. He was frustrated, but not beaten. The next weekend he took a spade to the bush at the end of the street and came back with a hessian bag stuffed with kikuyu runners. Uncle Stan could get Paddle Pop sticks to flower in wet cement, and before we knew it our garden became one of the most admired in the street.

Aunty Daphne's husband, Uncle Jack, built a chicken coop for us in the corner of the backyard and gave us one of his roosters. That put him in Mamma's good books for a while.

For all the improvements in our material conditions, some things didn't change. Mamma was still very moody and unpredictable. The leather belt still hung from a nail behind the kitchen door. Kev still beat the crap out of me at every turn.

Dan – still referred to as the menopause baby – and I were enrolled into Parramatta North Public School. I started in kindergarten and Miss Jones, our teacher, seemed very nice.

'Good morning, class. This is Kay, she is a new girl! Let's all make her feel welcome,' Miss Jones said, standing beside me as I faced the class. 'Kay, why don't you tell the class where you came from,' she suggested kindly with an encouraging smile.

'I came out of a beer bottle,' I replied.

Miss Jones sucked in a deep breath. The kids in the class stared.

'Yes, well tell us what are you going to be when you grow up?' she said, hoping to find safer ground.

'I'm going to be a prostitute,' I said proudly, with chin up, and shoulders back.

Every kid in the class looked stone faced. It was as if I was speaking a foreign language. Miss Jones's startled expression remains indelibly printed on my mind. This was the moment when I realised that 'prostitute' was a word I should never repeat.

A couple of days before Christmas I was helping Mamma clean out our wardrobe. She tossed a photograph onto the bed. It was of the Western Suburbs football team, known as the Magpies. Mamma picked it up and pointed to a good-looking, dark-haired man in a black-and-white jersey, sitting with his arms folded across his chest.

'That's your father, Ray Burgess,' she said offhandedly.

This was the first time anyone had ever mentioned that I had a father. I was terrified of Mamma and never dared to speak back to her, even to ask a simple question, like, 'Then how come my name is Howarth?'

There was something very different about our family – that much I'd figured. But I couldn't put my finger on it at the time. Apart from Ellie Laughton, who lived down the road, Mamma never got involved with any of the neighbours. She'd say hello if she passed them on the street, but that's where the association ended. She wouldn't visit Gloria Hartley's house at all. It was the filthiest house in the street and Mamma had no time for dirty people.

'Lazy bastards,' she'd say. 'Water's free and soap's cheap.'

With few exceptions, our neighbours lived hand-to-mouth and kids were always knocking on the door for a cup of this or that, or some Bex powders or ciggies until pay day. We never borrowed from the neighbours. What we didn't have, we went without.

Mamma took special pride in having the healthiest kids in the neighbourhood, and I seemed to be particularly immune. I never suffered any of the childhood maladies like measles, mumps or tonsillitis. I used to wish I'd get tonsillitis so I could eat ice cream and jelly for breakfast. To make sure our bowels were clean, once a month Mamma made us line up for a dose of Epsom salts. The carry-on from Dan was the only time I ever saw her get cranky with him.

'Don't be such a bloody sook, it doesn't taste that bad.' One day she threatened him with the strap. That got him motivated

The thing I hated most about taking Epsom salts was that we had to wait around until it worked before we'd dare go out to play. There wasn't a lot of warning once the tummy rumbles started.

Our house faced west and every afternoon, winter or summer, Granny and Pop used to sit on the front step with a cup of tea, watching the sun go down. Some neighbours thought they were better than us for some reason and would walk past the house without saying hello to Granny and Pop. Some even looked down at the ground, quickening their pace.

'They think their shit doesn't stink. Well, they can kiss my arse,' Mamma said.

If anyone had bothered to ask me if I was happy I probably would have said yes. I knew plenty of girls who were really miserable, especially those who fathers were doing them, as Mamma put it. Gillian Welsh, who lived across the street from us, was terrified of her father, but she never uttered a word about what he did to her. I went over to her house after church one day and found Mr Welsh sitting on the back step. He was still wearing the suit he wore to church, his eyes were closed and the front of his pants was open. He was clutching his old fella in one hand and his missal in the other.

'Good morning, Mr Welsh!' I said, startled. Not knowing what else to do, I took a deep breath and jumped right over his out-stretched legs, hoping I wouldn't trip and fall into his lap.

Mamma had a friend we had to call Uncle George, but who was truly worthy of his nickname 'the big noise'. There was something very creepy about Uncle George, and I kept my distance. He was a tall, massively built man with acres of pink flesh and a shiny, totally bald head, who liked to eat boiled pigs' trotters with his hands. Why this disgusting man was welcomed into our home was ever a mystery to me.

One day I found myself alone in the house with Uncle George. I was standing in front of Mamma's dressing table applying some red nail polish to my pathetic fingernails, which I'd chewed to the bone. I felt the gush of warm air on the back of my neck and looked up to see his reflection in the mirror. He was naked except for a pair of big white saggy underpants and was leering at me. I tried to get away but he grabbed me. I dropped the open bottle. Nail polish spilled all over Mamma's dressing table.

'Give Uncle George a little kiss,' he said, slobbering.

His stinking hot breath sent shivers down my back. Fear gripped me; I knew that he was going to do something awful. We wrestled as he tried to get his hand down my pants. I couldn't scratch him and punches to his body were useless. Then I remembered what Robbie had told me to do if I was ever grabbed by a man. I clenched my fist into a tight, hard ball and punched Uncle George in his privates as hard as I could.

'You fucking little bitch!' he groaned, falling to his knees and clutching himself.

I bolted for the door and without looking back ran over the road to the safety of Ellie's house.

That night I got a belting with the leather strap for ruining the top of the dressing table. I didn't dare tell Mamma what had happened. I didn't think she would believe me, and even if she did she'd find some way to blame me and I would get a bigger hiding than the one I'd already got.

One afternoon Aunty Daphne and Uncle Jack came over for a visit. They had moved from Strathfield to Baulkham Hills, which was closer to Jeffrey Avenue.

'Pack some things, Katie. You are coming to stay with us for a while,' Aunty Daphne said.

I didn't need to be asked twice. I loved going to Aunty Daphne's even more than I loved going to Aunty Lorna's. Aunty Daphne and Uncle Jack didn't have any kids, and I got to sleep in my own bed.

4

Out at the farm

'Someone ought to put a bullet in that mongrel,' Mamma said, every time Uncle Jack's name was mentioned.

To outsiders Aunty Daphne and Uncle Jack would have appeared to be the perfect couple. Aunty Daphne was a petite brunette with impeccable manners, and when she laughed it sounded like music playing. Uncle Jack was what Mamma called a 'ladies' man', and when he flashed that gold-toothed smile even she melted and called him Johnnie.

It was a moonless night when we left Mamma's place to go to Jack and Aunty Daphne's new house at Baulkham Hills. Aunty Daphne let me have the window seat and I sat forward, craning my neck to see over the dashboard. Coronation Street was a bumpy dirt road that snaked its way around sandstone boulders and massive gum trees. In the headlights I could see we had come to a dead end with a high ornate gate across the road. Just before the gate we turned into a driveway. It was getting spookier by the minute as we drove deeper into the bush. If there was a house here it was well hidden from the street. Aunty Daphne took a torch from the glove box.

'Watch where you are walking, Katie. There are still a few snakes about,' she warned, leading the way.

Uncle Jack got out of the car without saying a word and disappeared into the blackness. He always checked on his dogs before going indoors.

'You rotten thing,' Aunty Daphne muttered, throwing all her weight against the heavy door as it scraped across the floor. A hard tug on a cord inside the doorway turned on the single light globe, which provided barely enough visibility to see through the gloom. One sniff told me this was the kitchen. The ceiling was so high I had to bend over backwards to see the tops of the windows.

'Your bedroom is at the end of the hallway,' Aunty Daphne said, handing me the torch.

I shone the torch down the long dark hallway. A hallstand stood about halfway down, stacked with long coats and hats – a perfect hiding place for a boogieman. I took a deep breath and made a dash for it. My heart was pounding as I stood on tiptoes, grappling for the light cord. I coughed at the fumes and squinted at the unexpected brightness of the freshly painted white walls and ceiling. Even some of the furniture had been painted white, which was typical of Aunty Daphne. Once she had a paintbrush in her hand she'd keep going until she ran out of paint. I got into my pyjamas and ran back to the kitchen.

Aunty Daphne had made me a cup of Milo, with real milk. When I'd finished it, Uncle Jack handed me a brand new toothbrush.

'Take good care of your choppers,' he said. 'You won't get any more.' Uncle Jack gave me that cheeky grin and wiggled his eyebrows. 'Did you find the gozunder?' he asked.

I was puzzled.

'The pot under your bed,' he explained. 'If you need to pee in the night. Would you like to come to live with us?' he asked then.

No one had ever before asked me whether I would like to do something. I was thinking about my answer when Aunty Daphne cut in.

'You've been enrolled into Baulkham Hills Public School. You'll start after the holidays.'

When I was very small I always wanted to stay with Uncle Jack and Aunty Daphne. Aunty Daphne thought she couldn't have children and Uncle Jack had told me they'd wanted to adopt me when I was a baby, but Mamma wouldn't have a bar of it.

'He's not going to get you,' was all she said when I asked her why they couldn't adopt me, which made me wonder if I was up for grabs for someone else.

The next morning I was awake with the dawn. It was too early to get up so I lay in bed listening to the new sounds. A cow mooed close to the house. Then a rooster crowed.

Maybe this is a real farm, I thought, excited at the prospect of riding a real horse.

The clock in the kitchen struck six times and I thought I could hear voices, which meant someone was up already.

Uncle Jack was sitting at the table, sipping tea from his favourite bone china cup and listening to the weather forecast on the radio. I froze at the door and waited. Uncle Jack raced pigeons, so knowing what the weather was going to do was very important. One of the few times he ever raised his voice to me was when I was moving around and gabbing while the weather forecast was on. When the radio station switched to playing music, Aunty Daphne, who had been standing like a statue by the stove, served Uncle Jack's breakfast onto a plate and brought it to the table. She waited on Uncle Jack hand and foot and he never once said please or thank you.

'Good morning, Aunty Daph and Uncle Jack,' I said cheerfully, hoping to lighten up the tension in the air.

Aunty Daphne's lips were swollen, but she smiled with her eyes and nodded.

'G'day, kiddo. Lassie is having pups,' Uncle Jack said, and he smiled. There were two things that made Uncle Jack happy – a pigeon that clocked in a good time, and one of his bitches having pups.

I shivered with delight at this news. Lassie was a champion blue heeler, with many blue ribbons from the Royal Easter Show. I knew they weren't going to be pets, but the thought of having little fat puppies around until they were sold was very exciting.

Uncle Jack finished his breakfast in silence, locked the telephone, put the key into his pocket and left for work. After I'd helped with the washing up, I got out of Aunty Daphne's way and went exploring.

'The rooms at the side of the house are out of bounds. We've laid rat traps,' she called after me.

So long as I was back for lunch Aunty Daphne didn't mind where I went. She knew I could be trusted not to go near Uncle Jack's work shed or snooping into places I had no business poking my nose into.

On rainy days I got to help with the housework. My favourite job was polishing the timber floor in the ballroom. Aunty Daphne would tie old woollen jumpers to my feet and smear the soles with beeswax.

'Okay, off you go,' she'd say.

I'd slide around the room, spreading the polish, pretending I was an ice-skater on a vast lake. Aunty Daphne came behind me with the electric polisher, buffing the floor to such a high shine that I could hardly walk on it without slipping over and landing on my bum.

Against one wall in the ballroom was a heavily carved pianola, with stacks of tattered cardboard boxes on top containing music scrolls. Sometimes Aunty Daphne would thread a paper scroll onto the brass roller. I was too small to sit on a seat and work the pedals with my feet, so I had sit on the floor under the keyboard and push them up and down with my hands to get the music playing.

Uncle Jack was a plumber with his own business and when he was working locally he'd come home for lunch, so it was too risky for Aunty Daphne to dance. But on the days when he took a packed lunch, Aunty Daphne would do her stretching exercises holding the back of a chair. I'd go to my room and lie down on my belly to pull out what she called her *en pointe* pink satin ballet shoes from the hiding place under the wardrobe.

'You keep an ear out for Uncle Jack's car,' she'd say, lacing the satin ribbons around her ankles.

For some reason Uncle Jack didn't like Aunty Daphne dancing, which seemed very strange to me because she had been a ballerina when he met her. Besides, Uncle Jack was always singing and whistling, and was as good, if not better, as anyone on the radio.

One day I was sitting under the keyboard and pushing the pedals flat out. Aunty Daphne had tucked the skirt of her floral house dress into the legs of her pants, and was whirling and twirling like Tinker Bell from *Peter Pan*, getting faster and faster in time with the music. She sprang high into the air, ending with the full splits flat onto the floor. I thought I heard Uncle Jack's car door slam.

'Uncle Jack?' I said, scrambling up.

'It's him!'

Her hands trembled as she untied the satin ribbons and handed me the shoes. 'Here, Katie, take these to your room and hide them. Quickly! He'll kill me.' She straightened her clothes as she ran down the hallway.

We both made it back to the kitchen seconds before Uncle Jack came into the house.

He pulled out a chair and sat down without saying a word. He looked at me, but didn't smile or speak.

'I heard music,' he said after a while.

Aunty Daphne was at the sink, her back to him.

'Look at me when I speak to you, Daphne,' he snapped, sounding like Mamma when she was about to strike.

'It was me, Uncle Jack,' I jumped in. 'I was playing the pianola. Aunty Daphne said it was okay.'

Uncle Jack wasn't an easy person to fool. The next morning, Aunty Daphne had a purple bruise under her eye and dragged her feet as she moved slowly around the kitchen. I was racked with guilt that I hadn't heard the car coming.

Over the years, although Aunty Daphne would have as many black eyes as she had odd cups and saucers in her kitchen cupboards, only she knew the real horrors of her existence after dark and behind closed doors. But her isolation was apparent to me even as a small child. There were no neighbours close by. Uncle Jack had the only car and locked the telephone every morning before he went to work. Aunty Daphne could receive calls but she couldn't call anyone except 000 in an emergency.

5

Bundles of trouble

Although Uncle Jack was nearly old enough to be Robbie's father, they were great mates and this infuriated Mamma no end. I liked Robbie when he came to Mitchell Farm; we laughed and had fun like a real brother and sister. He would never dare to hit me in front of Uncle Jack or Aunty Daphne, like he did openly at Mamma's. One of our favourite things was playing 'war games'. We'd ambush each other with rotten fruit fired from handcrafted sling-shots. Uncle Jack made us pea-shooters from long, thin copper pipe. The ammunition was a bag of dried corn and pigeon pellets. These were deadly, and it was pure luck that we didn't take an eye out.

Uncle Jack and Robbie liked to go shooting, and once, on the way home from a trip to the Burragorang Valley, Uncle Jack hit a kangaroo. The impact didn't kill the roo outright, so he got out of the car and took his rifle from its bag. A shot rang out. He came back holding a little joey, which he'd taken from the dead mother's pouch. It was the most adorable little creature. I carried

Joey around in Aunty Daphne's red Regal 'bucket' handbag, and fed him with a baby's bottle. When he got bigger and started eating grass, we played chasings in the orchard. He even came to me when I called his name. One day Uncle Jack's dogs ripped him to pieces. I was inconsolable. To cheer me up, Uncle Jack said I could have one of Lassie's puppies, which were due in a few weeks.

'I've finished your jumper,' Aunty Daphne said one night, handing me the jumper she'd made from the wool of several jumpers I'd grown out of.

'It's a bumblebee!' I squealed.

The jumper had yellow and black horizontal stripes with red mohair sleeves. I loved that jumper, and it was a battle to get it off me and into the wash. One day Aunty Daphne didn't sort the washing properly and the bumblebee jumper ended up in the boiling copper with the sheets and several of Uncle Jack's white shirts. The red wool ran, sending everything pink. Aunty Daphne burst into tears.

'I'm sorry, Katie,' she sobbed. 'I've ruined your jumper.'

The ruined jumper would be the least of her worries when Uncle Jack saw his shirts.

After a period of being the new kid in the weird jumper, I started to settle in to Baulkham Hills Public School. I earned the praise of my teacher for doing the neatest 'J' in running writing. This was the first time anyone had praised me for anything. It was just a letter of the alphabet written in chalk on the blackboard, but I felt ten feet tall. I had made a new best friend too, Lily Cheung. Lily's family owned the market garden on Coronation Street, and she was the first girl to become my friend. After school we played with our dolls and had tea parties in the garden, things I never got to do with boys.

*

'Pack your things, Katie. You're going back to Mamma's tonight,' Aunty Daphne announced one afternoon when I got home from school.

That was how it was for me; I just seemed to get moved around like a piece of furniture. I didn't get to say goodbye to my teacher, or to Lily.

When I got back to Mamma's she was in a foul mood and straightaway started pumping me for information.

'Does he hit her in front of you?'

'No,' I told her. And it was true. I'd never seen Uncle Jack hit Aunty Daphne. Although I'd figured out that she was copping plenty after I went to bed. I knew that whatever I told Mamma, it would make things worse for Aunty Daphne, but when I refused to say anything, Mamma turned on me like a viper.

'He only wants you for your cherry, and when you're old enough he'll take it.'

I had no idea what this meant, but there was something nasty in the way she said it. In her mind, saying nothing was the same as taking sides with Uncle Jack. But it was Aunty Daphne I wanted to protect.

'You old bag,' I muttered, walking away.

The next thing Mamma had me by the hair and was slapping me around the head. She dragged me into the kitchen and got the strap from behind the door. She was going berserk, hitting me as hard as she could, screaming and swearing at the top of her voice. She stopped to catch her breath and I bolted.

It was getting dark by the time I reached the Bull & Bush Inn at Baulkham Hills, so I made a reverse-charge call to Aunty Daphne from the public phone opposite the pub.

'Mamma was belting me so I ran away,' I babbled.

'Where are you?'

I told her.

'Uncle Jack is at the Bull & Bush, but you can't go in there. Walk down to the corner of Coronation Street and wait at the bus stop,' Aunty Daphne instructed. 'When you hear his car, wave him down. He'll see you.'

Hours seemed to pass before I heard the distinct sound of Uncle Jack's Ford Fairlane. I jumped up and waved frantically so he wouldn't miss me in the dark.

'G'day, princess,' he said, smiling. It must have been apparent to him why I was standing out there in the middle of the night, because he didn't ask me.

The next day was Saturday and Uncle Jack showed me Lassie's eight gorgeous puppies. They still had their eyes closed, and he held good to his promise that we would keep one. I named her Bonnie, after her mother, Bonnie Blue Lassie.

After lunch he drove over to Mamma's, leaving me with Aunty Daphne.

'The old girl said you can stay for the weekend, but I have to get you back for school on Monday,' he said when he got back, tossing a bag of my favourite lollies, black jelly beans, onto the table.

That night Uncle Jack went to the pub after dinner and Aunty Daphne and I settled in to listen to the serials on the radio. Our favourite was *The Adventures of Philip Marlowe*. They were detective stories that scared the wits out of both of us. We were holding hands during a particularly gripping scene, when a loud shot rang out. We nearly jumped out of our skins; it sounded like it was close to the house. Aunty Daphne raced to Uncle Jack's rifle stock for a gun. She didn't have any bullets and probably didn't know how to use it, but an intruder wouldn't know that looking down the barrel of a 303. We turned out the light and sat huddled in a dark corner. A short time later we heard Uncle Jack's car and relaxed.

'You rotten cunts!' we heard him shouting. 'I'll fucking kill you!'

Aunty Daphne grabbed the torch and we ran from the house. We found Uncle Jack in the dog enclosure. He was sitting on the ground with Lassie in his arms. There was so much blood and Lassie wasn't moving. *Someone has stolen the puppies*, was my first thought. I checked the box where they slept and they were gone. I heard a tiny whimper behind me and spun around. The puppies, all eight of them, were hanging from the fence by their necks with wire. They were all very still except for one, which was struggling for life. I ran to the pup and lifted it up to take its weight. Aunty Daphne took the wire from around its neck.

'It's Bonnie,' I cried, cradling the dying pup in my arms.

'She won't make it, Katie,' Aunty Daphne said, before going over to Uncle Jack to try to comfort him. He didn't push her away.

I took Bonnie to bed with me and stayed awake all night praying to the Virgin Mary. I had learned all the prayers when I made my First Holy Communion, and Uncle Stan told me that if I were ever in real strife to pray to the Virgin Mary. I said the Ten Hail Marys over and over again until I fell asleep. The next morning Bonnie was still breathing, but she was very weak. Aunty Daphne warmed some milk and I fed her though an eye dropper. I didn't go out to play that day. I nursed the pup to keep her warm and gave her tiny feeds throughout the day. That night I had to go back to Mamma's.

'She is going to be okay, Katie,' Aunty Daphne said reassuringly. 'I'll take care of her for you.'

When I got back to Mamma's she didn't say a word about my running away. I told her what had happened to Lassie and the pups.

'He'd have plenty of enemies,' she sneered. 'It was probably the husband of one of the sluts he shags.'

For a week I called Aunty Daphne every day, reverse charges from a phone box, to get an update on Bonnie.

'She's doing fine, her eyes are open and she is snuggling into your old bumblebee jumper.' Aunty Daphne never threw anything away that could be used for another purpose, and the thought of Bonnie snuggling into my favourite jumper made me very happy.

The next time I saw Aunty Daphne was when she came to visit Mamma.

'How come your belly is so big?' I whispered to Aunty Daphne when we were alone in Mamma's bedroom. I thought she had been eating too much chocolate.

'I'm having a baby,' she told me excitedly.

'How do you get a baby?' I asked, thinking I wouldn't mind a real baby myself.

'You are too young to know yet. When you're a bit older I'll tell you all about the birds and the bees.'

Mamma told me later that Aunty Daphne had to have several operations before she could become pregnant. Following a seventeen-hour labour, Steven John McCarthy tried to come into the world feet first and Aunty Daphne was nearly carried out of the delivery room the same way. An emergency caesarean left her with scars on her abdomen that would have done Jack the Ripper proud.

Not long after Stevie was born, I was sent back to Mitchell Farm.

'That mongrel won't let the baby sleep in their room and Daphne's terrified the rats will get to him,' Mamma said by way of explanation. It was one of those rare moments when I was told the circumstances of a decision affecting my life.

Stevie was what Mamma called a 'fussy baby'. Aunty Daphne

couldn't breastfeed and Stevie couldn't digest cow's milk, so Uncle Jack bought Millie, a cantankerous goat. Millie didn't like the idea of being the wet nurse. She butted and kicked buckets over in protest, and had to have her legs tethered at milking time.

The entire universe seemed to revolve around this one tiny person. Everything was done to a strict time schedule, and Stevie was definitely in charge. Aunty Daphne worked herself to a frazzle, preparing and cooking special foods, making up formulas, sterilising bottles, changing nappies. The laundry tubs were always full of washing at various stages of the process. Aunty Daphne showed me how to hold and feed the baby, and bring up any wind. Stevie was big, and I had to sit in the armchair so I didn't drop him.

Aunty Daphne had always been thin, but now she was fading away to skin and bone. I never saw her sit down for a meal. She drank tea, smoked cigarettes and swallowed Vincent's APC powders by the dozen. There was a slogan on the box: 'For safety's sake take Vincent's.' They were promoted as being safer than their competitor, the popular Bex powders, the addictive panacea to domestic drudgery that came with an unwritten guarantee of renal failure.

Not long after Stevie was born, Aunty Daphne became pregnant again.

'That bastard! Another baby so soon will kill her,' Mamma cursed.

After another long labour that nearly did kill her, Aunty Daphne gave birth to a daughter, Trudy Louise Le Strange. Aunty Daphne explained to me that the 'Le Strange' part of Trudy's name was in the McCarthy family's genealogy going back generations. Her funny name aside, I had never seen anything more exquisite than Trudy. She resembled a tiny porcelain doll, perfect in every way. Silky platinum-blond curls framed her delicate little face. Her big, peek-a-boo blue eyes sparkled as she giggled with delight at the slightest attention. I'd have carried her around all day if I'd been allowed to. As it was, I didn't put her back in the bassinette until she was asleep. In my private, make-believe world, Stevie and Trudy were my little brother and sister.

The transformation of Aunty Daphne from a pirouetting Giselle to a bedraggled housewife and mother wasn't the only shock that came with the births of Stevie and Trudy. To my amazement, Mamma transformed into a caring, loving grandmother, a complete contrast to my experience of her. I always thought that she didn't like little kids. Now I realised it was just me she didn't like.

6

An unexpected visitor

Spike, our red cattle dog, was bailing up the postman. 'Get around the back!' I yelled. The parcel was addressed to me. It was from Mrs McCarthy, Uncle Jack's mother, or Mackie, as I called her.

'Happy birthday, Katie, with love from Mackie,' was written on the card in very nice handwriting from a proper ink pen.

Mackie had always been kind to me, but I had no idea that she liked me enough to remember my birthday and send a gift. I couldn't believe my eyes when I saw the beautiful mohair cardigan, with six green buttons in the shape of Granny Smith apples to match the apple green wool. I raced to Mamma's dressing-table mirror to try it on. A perfect fit. How could Mackie have known my size? I hadn't seen her for years. I stroked the front of the cardigan. It felt as soft as the baby bunny rabbit I'd petted at the Royal Easter Show.

'Look, Mamma, Mackie sent this to me,' I said, spinning around so she could see how beautiful it was.

Mamma looked like she'd seen a ghost. 'Get rid of that! I am not having anything green in this house.'

Uncle Stan took the cardigan to work and dyed it black. It came back looking like the pelt from a dead cat and the prickles next to my skin were unbearable.

'We're having an unexpected visitor,' Mamma said, chasing a fly the size of a small bird around the room with a rolled-up newspaper, trying to hunt it outside.

That afternoon when I arrived home, there was a strange car parked out the front. My first thought was that we had more blow-ins from the bush. We'd only just gotten rid of the last mob who'd stayed for weeks, straining tempers and causing endless queues for the toilet. As I approached the front door I could hear raucous laughter.

'Here she is now,' I heard Uncle Stan say, as I turned the key in the lock.

A vaguely familiar, dark-haired woman was sitting at the dining table. Next to her sat a tanned, blond-haired man who looked very bored.

'Hello, Katie, do you know who I am?'

'Yes,' I replied, smiling back. Although she looked older than in the photograph I had seen, there was no mistaking that this was Phyllis.

Then I noticed the toddler who was holding on to furniture to get around the room. Phyllis picked her up and sat the girl on her knee.

'This is your little sister, Janet.'

I stood staring at this girl who had the saddest eyes I had ever seen. Was this really my sister? I scanned her face for any features that might help me find a connection. The man with them was introduced as Janet's father, Leslie Stacey.

Meeting my mother for first time and discovering that I had a sister I never even knew existed was overwhelming. It was as if they had just dropped out of the sky. I didn't know how I should react. I felt there must be something wrong with me because I didn't feel anything, at least not enough to rush into Phyllis's arms and cry, 'Mummy dearest, why did you leave me?'

Mamma was very animated at seeing her eldest daughter after an eight-year absence. I was confused. If this was Phyllis, whom Mamma always cursed whenever her name was mentioned, why was she so happy to see her?

Uncle Stan was overcome with emotion.

'Oh, darlin', it's so lovely to see you.'

He wiped away his tears and lovingly held his sister's hand. This was so typical of Uncle Stan. He was never judgmental.

'That'll be them now,' Mamma said, going to look through the curtains.

I recognised the sound of the car. As they came through the door, Phyllis stood up and fiddled with her hair. Aunty Daphne was carrying Trudy and Uncle Jack had Stevie in one arm and a case of beer under the other. We were in for a long night. After the babies were settled, Phyllis threw her arms around Aunty Daphne. They hugged each other and cried.

'G'day, Phil, you're lookin' good,' Uncle Jack said with a beaming smile.

He and Phyllis seemed pleased to see each other but they didn't hug.

'Hello, Johnnie,' Phyllis said, grinning.

As they sat around talking, drinking and reminiscing about the good old days, I got a bit anxious. I always did around adults who were drinking. Aunty Lorna could put away a lot of grog without wanting to fight everything that moved, but not Mamma; she turned into a fang-toothed monster on a middy of beer. Thankfully we never had alcohol in the house unless it was Christmas or some other special occasion.

When I got a closer look at Janet, I decided that she was the most pathetic kid I had ever seen. I picked her up. She was so light and thin I could feel her rib cage. I had brought home stray kittens with more meat on their bones. Her snotty nose ran and she constantly scratched her head. I hoped it wasn't head lice. Her eyebrows knitted together with the worried expression of someone who had lost a pound and found a penny.

Mamma could whip up wonderful meals from the most basic ingredients. The return of the prodigal daughter was cause for celebration, and Mamma pulled out all stops. She even made puftaloons topped with 'cockie's joy', a sticky golden syrup.

After dinner we younger kids had to leave the table while the adults continued smoking, drinking, telling jokes and catching up on eight lost years. The boys were hogging the television, as usual, and my eyes were smarting from the smoke-filled room. I went to my room around seven o'clock to listen to the radio, and found Janet flat on her back on the floor. Her muffled whimpering was almost inaudible; as if she were afraid someone might hear her. She looked like a flipped tortoise, her arms and legs flailing around aimlessly. As I tried to pick her up, she let out a sharp yelp. Something was wrong.

'Mamma, help!' I called from the doorway.

'Oh my God!' she cried, realising that Janet had fallen from the bed. By this time Janet was screaming the place down and Mamma had to struggle to examine her. 'Now, now, darling,' she murmured comfortingly. 'Hold still and let Nanny look at you.'

A few minutes later the emergency became apparent. 'We'll have to take this baby to hospital,' Mamma shouted.

This alarmed me; no one in our family had ever gone to hospital, except for Dan, who was always breaking his arm. Mamma got a sheet from the hall cupboard and wrapped Janet snugly so she couldn't wiggle around. Uncle Stan carried her to the car and Janet's father drove them to Parramatta Hospital. They were gone for hours.

Meanwhile, Phyllis and Uncle Jack got pretty drunk. At one stage Aunty Daphne got a blanket and some pillows from the hall cupboard and curled up on the lounge with Trudy and Stevie. She knew better than to ask if they could go home. I couldn't sleep, so I lay in bed wondering how my mother could leave me and then have another baby. What was it about me that she hadn't wanted?

Mamma's face said it all when she came back carrying Janet, whose arm was in a white sling. 'She's broken her collarbone,' she announced.

This hardly registered with Phyllis.

'This baby's a bloody disgrace!' Mamma said, glaring at Phyllis who by this time was too drunk to care. 'I have never been so embarrassed in all my bloody life. Her little bum is red raw, she is covered in ringworms and her head is crawling with fucking lice.'

Mamma got the scissors and hacked Janet's hair off right down to the roots. Then Uncle Stan helped to hold her while Mamma washed her head, gently swabbing the weeping sores with cotton-wool that had been dipped in a solution of Dettol. It stung her and Janet's bottom lip curled. I had to fight back my own emotion seeing her little baby face all distorted and tiny tears running down her cheeks. I took her free hand and placed it to my mouth. 'Don't cry, baby, this will make you all better,' I said, planting soft kisses onto her fingers, hoping to comfort and distract her.

She responded to the touch and gave me a half smile. Mamma sponged her all over and gently patted her dry. Janet's little fanny was the colour of a red apple. She flinched when Mamma applied the tea-tree ointment, followed by a dusting of Johnson's baby powder and a clean nappy. Janet was put back onto Mamma's bed, but this time she had plenty of pillows around her.

'Katie, keep an eye on her while I make up a bottle,' Mamma instructed, before leaving the room.

Phyllis didn't have anything as mundane as a bottle or formula with her, so Mamma had to improvise. Luckily Aunty Daphne had some formula, and a spare teat was placed on the end of a cleaned tomato sauce bottle. It didn't look flash, but it would do the job.

'Here, you can give this to her,' Mamma said, handing me the bottle and returning to the lounge room to clean up after the party.

Uncle Stan had gone to bed by now and Janet's father had left, leaving Phyllis and Uncle Jack singing along to the country and western records and polishing off the last of the beer. Bright moonlight streamed through my bedroom window. Janet's eyelashes flickered as if she were fighting sleep. She sucked quietly on the bottle, sizing me up.

'I'm your big sister,' I whispered. She stopped sucking as if she wanted to think about that, and her little mouth curled up at the sides.

There were no painkillers on the market for children back then, so Janet whimpered all night. The next morning, even though her eyes were still closed, she was crying and rubbing her ears with her free hand. I told Mamma something was wrong.

'Let me have a look,' she said, propping Janet on her knee. 'Jesus Christ! This baby has abscessed ears,' Mamma screeched, setting Janet off screaming again. Mamma handed her back to me and I walked around, trying to calm her down.

'There, there, baby. Nanny will fix you up,' I said, stroking her soft cheek.

It felt very strange talking to my little sister like that. I never thought about Mamma as my grandmother. As far as I was concerned, that's what Granny was. And even after I discovered that she wasn't my mother, my relationship with Mamma was never redefined.

Mamma warmed some kind of liquid in a spoon held over the gas flame. She told me to hold Janet's head while she dealt with the streams of putrid yellow pus. 'Keep her still!' she snapped as Janet squirmed, trying to push Mamma's hand away as she poured the liquid into each ear.

Janet was sobbing and it took a while to calm her down before the next stage of the clean-up process. Mamma poured some purple liquid into a saucer and soaked a ball of cottonwool. She gently dabbed the solution onto each of the ringworms on Janet's head. Fortunately this didn't sting and I was able to distract her with my doll Mary.

'You poor little bugger,' Mamma kept repeating as she worked her way all over Janet's scalp.

If Janet didn't look like something the cat dragged in before, now she was definitely not going to be an entrant in the Grace Bros Baby of the Year Contest.

7

Sisters

A few days later, Phyllis had a big row with Janet's father and he left in a huff and never came back. Not long after, Mamma and Phyllis had a huge argument. They were screaming obscenities and digging up things from the past that went back decades, hurling insults and abuse at each other and finally coming to blows.

'What about you and that fucking Fred Carlton? Don't think I have forgotten that!' Phyllis screamed.

'Get out of my sight, you slut!' Mamma screamed back.

Phyllis did exactly that, leaving Janet with us.

A few weeks later I was sent to Mitchell Farm and was surprised to see Phyllis there. That night, loud noises woke me. I got out of bed and crept down the hallway. The kitchen door was slightly ajar. I put one eye to the crack and strained in the poor light to see what was going on. Phyllis and Uncle Jack were drinking beer. Aunty Daphne sat staring into a cup.

'Come on, Daffy, have a drink with us,' Uncle Jack slurred. Aunty Daphne never drank alcohol, so this seemed odd. 'Are you too good to have a drink with us, Daffy?' he sneered.

Aunty Daphne didn't move a muscle. Uncle Jack walked over to where she was sitting. Grabbing her hair, he pulled her head back sharply as he tried to force the bottle into her mouth. Aunty Daphne clamped her mouth shut and the beer went all over her, saturating the front of her dress. As he walked away, Uncle Jack slapped the back of her head.

'Johnnie, for fuck's sake! Don't do that,' Phyllis said, before falling face first onto the table, and knocking over a glass of beer.

'Go to bed, Daffy,' Uncle Jack said in the tone he used for his dogs.

Aunty Daphne got up from the table and started to mop up the spilled beer.

'Didn't I tell you to go to bed?'

I ran back to bed and pretended to be asleep. When Aunty Daphne came into the room she got into Stevie's bed. It shook me to my core listening to her quiet sobbing. In the other room Uncle Jack and Phyllis seemed to be having a good time. It sounded like they were jumping on the bed.

The next morning Uncle Jack was brooding and silent. He stared into space while Aunty Daphne prepared breakfast as usual.

'Good morning, Uncle Jack,' I said, hoping my voice didn't give me away.

He didn't reply. I tried to avoid looking at him. Uncle Jack could read minds. He'd know I'd figured out that something wrong was going on.

'Good morning, Aunty Daphne,' I said, trying not to make eye contact with her either.

'Hello, love,' she replied flatly. 'Your breakfast will be ready in a minute.'

Phyllis stumbled into the kitchen wearing one of Uncle Jack's dressing gowns. Her hair was a tangled mess and a sour odour followed her to the bathroom. I was so ashamed that this vulgar woman was my mother and wished I had never met her. How could two sisters be so opposite? Even with a face puffy and red from crying, Aunty Daphne was the epitome of grace and good manners.

The only sounds in the kitchen came from the radio and the ticking of the old clock on the sideboard. The atmosphere was tense. Like seeing how long you could hold a tuppenny bunger in your hand before it exploded. Uncle Jack finished eating and left the table without a word.

'Uncle Jack is taking you back to Mum's after breakfast, Katie,' Aunty Daphne said, lifting a poached egg from the pan and placing it on a slice of toast on my plate. 'The sauce is on the table.'

Somehow I had inherited Uncle Jack's liking of tomato sauce with eggs.

Uncle Jack drove me back to Mamma's in total silence. As we pulled up I saw Mamma draw back the curtains. I jumped out of the car without saying a word and ran up the front path. Uncle Jack did a wheel spin as he sped away.

I was barely through the door before Mamma started pressuring me for information.

'What's that fucking bitch up to now?'

'Nothing,' I said, shaking my head. There were no words to describe what I'd seen, and to tell Mamma would have only meant more trouble.

Phyllis stayed at Mitchell Farm, and when Janet's birthday came round in December she was still living with us. To my surprise,

Mamma baked, iced and decorated a double-layer jam and cream-filled sponge cake. Janet loved the attention. We all sang 'Happy Birthday' to her. 'Hip hip hooray!' we cheered. She giggled with glee.

That Christmas was the first time Uncle Jack and Aunty Daphne didn't come over with the kids. Mamma and Uncle Stan cooked a wonderful meal, but it was spoiled when Mamma drank too much alcohol. Uncle Stan left in a huff to go to his fiancée's place; he knew he couldn't win an argument with his mother.

But Uncle Stan had done it again with his gift, a beautiful cane table and chair setting. Now I had somewhere to do stuff without forever being told to 'clean up this bloody mess'.

On the morning of my ninth birthday, Uncle Stan gave me an envelope containing a ten-shilling note and a holy picture of St Francis of Assisi, the patron saint of animals, birds and the environment – his favourite saint, and mine.

'Happy birthday, darlin',' he said, and gave me a hug.

I was happy to be one year older, one year closer to growing up. Being a kid was a bit like being in limbo. You had to wait until you could do a certain thing, go a certain place, see a certain photograph, or be given a straight answer to a simple question, like 'Who is my father?'

Uncle Jack had contradicted Mamma. 'Ray Burgess isn't your father,' he'd said confidently, without offering an alternative.

There'd be no cake or candles for my birthday, so I went to the lake for a swim. I came back late and lunch was over. The house was quiet. Mamma was nowhere to be seen. Janet, Pop and Granny were all having an afternoon nap. The boys were still at the lake.

'Where's Mamma?' I asked Uncle Stan, who was nervously pacing the floor, lighting another cigarette before he had finished the last one.

'She's gone over to Gloria Hartley's place.' He rubbed his hands together, a sure sign that he was anxious. For Mamma to go to Gloria Hartley's place something had to be up. She wouldn't be sitting around in that filth having a cup of tea. Curiosity got the better of me.

'I'm going over to the Hartleys',' I announced.

'No, love, you stay here.'

I went to my room. When I heard Uncle Stan turn on the radio and tune in to some music, I saw my chance. I climbed out the bathroom window and, crouching low, snuck around the side of the house. The Hartleys' back door was never locked; I crept into their kitchen. I could hear someone groaning and people talking in hushed tones.

'Jesus fucking Christ. Help me!' That was Phyllis. I heard a loud thump and then a scream became an agonising groan. 'Jesus, Mary and Joseph!' she screamed again.

'Shut up, you stupid bitch! You'll have the coppers here.' That was Mamma.

I tiptoed down the hall, ducked into the bathroom and hid behind the door. Mamma came in. I held my breath and froze. Something plopped into the toilet bowl. The cistern flushed. A few seconds later it was flushed again.

'Now get her out of here!' Gloria Hartley shouted, with panic in her voice.

Later that afternoon Mamma and Ellie Laughton were chatting over a pot tea. I was pretending to watch *The Mickey Mouse Club*, straining to hear what they were saying.

'She was too far gone. In the end Gloria had to jump on her belly,' Mamma said, pouring more tea. 'It was a boy,' she added, passing Ellie her cup. 'We don't need any more of that bastard's bastards in this world.' Mamma turned her head in my direction. 'I hope you heard all of this. You better keep your bloody legs together. I am not looking after any bastards you bring home.'

I was too young to realise I'd overheard the backyard abortion of the only real brother I'd ever have. It was one birthday I'd never forget.

Phyllis left town without coming to say goodbye. Janet stayed with us.

8

Be careful what you wish for

'You'll go on the street and hawk your fork just like your mother,' Mamma hissed though clenched teeth.

At nine years of age I had no idea what she was talking about but, knowing Mamma, I figured it would have something to do with sex. She was always saying things like, 'All men care about is their belly and what hangs from it.' I had to be told about such things because I matured early, but in truth all I was told was, 'You better keep your legs together now that you've started.'

Most of my friends were boys, but even if I had been inclined towards promiscuity at such a tender age, none of them would have dared to try anything with me. My eldest brother, Kev, had a fearful reputation as a street fighter and was the self-appointed guardian of my virtue. Unfortunately, Kev's fists weren't confined to the street. He also had a very cruel streak.

One afternoon a stray kitten I had brought home was nowhere to be found. I combed the garden calling her name – 'Sugar,

Sugar'. She didn't come. I felt desperate and went inside for a torch to look under the house.

'Where are you going with that?' Kev asked.

'I can't find Sugar – I'm going to look under the house.'

'The cat's not under the house. I took the mangy moggie to the lake and tossed it over the weir.'

'I wish you were dead!' I screamed, running at him and hitting him as hard as I could in the stomach before bolting out the back door.

'You little bitch!' he said, coming after me.

He pushed me to the ground and sat on my chest. I could hardly breathe. When he finally got off me, he laughed as he walked back into the house. Even if he hadn't done such a despicable thing, he was cruel enough to tell me he had.

'I hate you, I hate you. I wish you were dead!' I cursed, smashing my fist onto the ground.

There was much excitement when Uncle Les announced he was marrying his long-time girlfriend, Shirley. The date was set for 29 June 1959.

The night before the wedding, Aunty Daphne came to spend the night at our place. I was going to look after Stevie and Trudy while she went to the wedding. Uncle Jack wasn't going; Uncle Les hated him and so did Kev.

A car horn tooted out the front. 'That'll be Barry,' Kev said, running for the door. Barry, Kev's best mate, had just bought his first car and was showing it off. It was a novelty for anyone in our neighbourhood to own a car, so everyone went out to take a stickybeak.

'Oh Jesus!' Mamma said, when she saw the colour of the duco, a pretty apple green not unlike that of the mohair cardigan I once owned.

'Kev, love, please don't go out in that car,' she begged, as he and Robbie jumped in.

Kev laughed. 'Mamma, don't worry, I'll be alright.'

'Well, don't be late. Remember, you're Les's best man tomorrow,' she called as the car drove away.

Sometime in the early hours of the morning loud screams woke me up. I went out to the lounge room. There were two policemen, one each side of Robbie, who was covered in blood. Mamma was screaming, but not the kind of scream when people get a fright. These screams came from deep inside. They were agonising howls, as if her entrails were being pulled out. It terrified me.

'Uncle Stan, what's happening?' I asked.

'Oh, darlin', it's Kev. He's been killed.' He put his arm around me.

The policeman continued reading from a notepad. 'The vehicle took a bend at Glenorie. A passenger, believed to be Kevin Carlton, was thrown from the vehicle, hitting his head on a post at the side of the road. He was killed instantly.'

The policeman tried to avoid looking at Mamma, who was still howling and pulling at her hair and clothes.

Suddenly, she stopped crying and looked at Robbie. 'Jesus, Mary and Joseph,' she said. 'Why didn't he take you and not Kevie?'

Robbie slumped forward as if someone had king-hit him in the guts. The two policemen struggled to hold him up. Aunty Daphne rushed to Robbie and wrapped her arms around him. She was sobbing. Robbie's face was completely expressionless. He wasn't even blinking. He collapsed and had to be carried to bed. Aunty Daphne got a basin of warm soapy water and washed Kev's blood from Robbie's body and dressed him in a pair of clean pyjamas.

When Uncle Stan came back from the morgue after the official

54

identification, his tear-stained face confirmed the worst. Mamma's agony continued as she screamed, 'No . . . not Kevie', into the night. I felt completely lost trying to take this all in. Kev was dead? We'd never see him again, he was gone forever. Suddenly, all the rotten things that he'd ever done to me were forgotten. I wanted to tell him that I was sorry, that I did not mean to say that I wished that he were dead. But you can't take things back.

The next day the wedding went ahead. Mamma and Aunty Daphne never forgave Uncle Les's wife for refusing to call it off.

'That fat bitch! She couldn't even wait for us to put Kevie into the ground.' Mamma cursed every time Shirl's name came up.

The only members of our immediate family to attend, apart from the groom, were Uncle Stan and Robbie. When Robbie got home he collapsed again and had to be carried to bed. He slept for four days and was never the same after Kev died. Mamma went into mourning and wore black for six months, and Dan and I had to wear black armbands to school.

We had barely buried Kev when Granny took a bad fall and broke her hip. After that she went downhill very quickly. She was shown some mercy when her mind went walkabout to a place where she was oblivious to the loss of her bodily functions and the gruesome pressure sores on her buttocks. Looking after Granny was just like taking care of a small baby. After her bath she was powdered and put into clean clothes. Mamma brushed Granny's dentures and popped them into her mouth before combing her hair. Granny could hardly move her legs, so after breakfast she had to be shuffled out into the backyard for some morning sun while her bedding was washed and aired.

The only photograph in existence of Granny and Mamma together was taken in the backyard at Jeffrey Avenue. Granny looks glamorous and seems to be aware of the camera. Mamma has just given her a haircut. Standing next to Granny, Mamma looks like a train wreck, but the photograph is a testimony to what a devoted and loving daughter Mamma was.

Increasingly Granny retreated into her own world. She talked to unseen companions in a language only she could understand. One morning in 1959, a few months after Kevie died, Mamma was reading aloud from the newspaper. Albert Namatjira, one of Australia's most celebrated landscape painters, had died a broken man. Granny's eyes were streaming with tears, but she never said a word. Albert Namatjira achieved international recognition, but because he was an Aboriginal person, he had been refused an application to build a house in Alice Springs. The ensuing publicity embarrassed the government, so Albert and his wife were made honorary Australian citizens. As a citizen he could legally buy alcohol, but he was arrested and jailed for two months for supplying alcohol to an Aboriginal person, when all he was doing was having a beer with a cousin.

Looking after Granny took its toll on Mamma. Her hands were split open to the bone with dermatitis. Every night I had to help her paint the ghastly wounds with a stinking green paste that looked and smelled like something that had been scraped from the bottom of a sewer outlet. 'Jeeesus!' Mamma hissed, as I applied the paste as gently as I could, before helping her into the white cotton gloves she had to sleep in, as the ointment stained the bed sheets.

It was a blessing when Granny passed away in her sleep, but her death was still felt hard by all the family, especially Uncle Stan and Aunty Daphne. To them Granny was a saint; no one could say a word against her. The only time I ever saw Aunty Daphne lash out at Uncle Jack was when he called Granny 'The Old Lubra', which he didn't mean as a compliment.

'You know, she used to walk from Lorna's place at Lansdowne Street to Granville Station to get the train into Martin Place for the Dawn Service every ANZAC day,' Uncle Stan said, wiping the tears from his eyes after the funeral. 'Granny's mother was born on the banks of the Hunter River,' he repeated often. He was clearly admiring of our heritage, and what Granny in particular had contributed, having come from such, seemingly, humble beginnings.

As a Salvation Army nurse Granny was at the front line of human and natural disasters during two world wars and the Great Depression. She drove a horse and buggy hundreds of miles in the bush to tend to wounded soldiers and pray with the dying at the various makeshift military hospitals. She gave aid to the poor and destitute, regardless of race or religion, and never turned away a swaggie who was in need of a feed. She died never having been recognised as a citizen in her own country. In fact it would be another seven years before the Australian government granted citizenship rights to all Aboriginal people.

Now that Granny had gone, Mamma said that Pop wouldn't be far behind her. He had cancer and it was taking him a long time to die.

'He's being made to suffer for being such a bastard to me when I was a kid,' Mamma said, pouring a glass of sherry to ease his discomfort when the morphine wasn't enough.

Pop was Mamma's stepfather, and she had told me of the floggings with the stock whip and being sent to sleep in the woodshed in the middle of winter, without adequate blankets. There were no signs of this cruel man in the Pop I knew. He was particularly loving and affectionate with Janet, whom he called 'our little piccaninny'. She called him 'Fa', which amused him. Pop sat on the front porch for hours watching Janet's antics as she rode her dinky.

Stark naked and brown as a berry, she'd launch herself down the incline of the front path, squealing with delight.

Mamma had made a cake for Pop, and we were having afternoon tea when a car pulled up out the front. Janet was sitting on Pop's lap and Mamma drew back the curtains to see who it was.

'What does this bitch want now?' she said.

There was a knock at the door. Phyllis was standing there, with a handsome fair-haired man.

Mamma blocked the doorway.

'I've come to get Janet,' Phyllis said, attempting to push past.

'Well you can't bloody have her, so piss off.'

'Get out of my way, Mum, or I'll drop you where you stand.'

Phyllis and Mamma went for each other, hissing and screaming like a couple of vicious cats. Decades of pent-up hatred burst like a dam.

'You fucking bitch! I'll fucking kill you!' Mamma screeched, slapping Phyllis and pulling her around by the hair.

'Heinz! Get Janet!' Phyllis shouted as she tried to fend off Mamma's blows.

He hesitated as if wondering which one was Janet.

'The baby!' Phyllis called out.

'I hate you!' Mamma launched another attack.

Janet was screaming and I was trying to stay out of the line of fire. The man grabbed Janet, who was still sitting on Pop's lap clutching a piece of cake, the cream and jam filling squishing through her little fingers. There was a brief tug of war, but the tall man managed to pull Janet from Pop's arms.

'Fa! Fa!' Janet screamed, her little arms outstretched.

'Leave my sister alone!' I yelled at the man, trying to stop him.

He shoved me to one side and carried Janet outside. She was kicking and screaming, 'Kat! Kat!'

Pop struggled to his feet and cornered Phyllis. He managed

to get in a few punches before she got out the door. But poor old Pop was no match for Phyllis. She punched him hard, sending him groaning in agony to the floor and clutching his stomach.

'You fucking slut!' Mamma screamed at Phyllis as she went to help Pop. 'He is a sick old man.'

It all happened so fast. They were gone. Mamma put her head on the table and sobbed. Pop went to bed to lie down. I was left wondering why my mother would only come back for Janet. I had been discarded again. I consoled myself with the realisation that I wouldn't have wanted to go with her anyway. But I had no idea when, or if, I would ever see my little sister again.

I blinked hard. I wasn't imagining it. There she was, next to the willow tree, as clear as day, Granny smiling back at me. Then she was gone.

'I just saw Granny,' I said, as Mamma came through the back door with a load of washing.

'Yes, she's waiting for Pop, he won't be long now,' she said, putting the basket down and carrying on as if seeing a ghost was no big deal.

After Janet was taken away, Pop rarely left his room unless it was to shuffle across the hallway to the bathroom and back. He looked repulsive. Saggy folds of skin hung from his bones like fleshy drapery. The pain must have been immense as the cancer ate his body alive. At night he moaned and groaned like a tormented animal and sometimes it became too much. 'Jesus Christ, take me!' he'd cry out. Even with a pillow over my head I could hear him.

Mamma wrote to Aunty Lorna and told her that if she wanted to see her father before he went, she didn't have much time.

When Aunty Lorna and Uncle Bill arrived, I was pleased that they didn't bring all of their mob with them. Since I'd last seen

Aunty Lorna she'd had another child, a boy they'd called Allan. He was a cute-enough kid, about three years old, but was spoiled rotten and swore like a trooper. It was quite shocking to hear four-letter words intermingled with baby talk. Aunty Lorna thought it was funny, and her laughter encouraged him. If Granny had still been with us, Allan would have swallowed a lot of Sunlight soap and water that day.

On the morning Pop died, I nearly cremated him before he took his last breath. I was coming out of the bathroom when he called to me from his bed. 'Katie, pack me a pipe, love,' he said in a raspy voice that was barely audible.

I tried to avoid having to go into Pop's room. Apart from the stench, which no amount of disinfectant could mask, his teeth sat magnified in a glass of water on the bedside table. Being careful not to knock the glass and its contents over, I took a small wad from the fresh tin of Old Log Cabin tobacco and rubbed it in the palm of my hand, as I'd done many times before. Although I hated cigarettes, I didn't mind handling the pipe tobacco; it had an earthy smell, and was not harsh on the nostrils like cigarettes. After I'd massaged the tobacco into fine threads I filled Pop's pipe and packed it down lightly with my thumb, before placing the stem into his slobbering mouth to see if he could draw air.

'Good, love,' he said, nodding.

Pop was too weak to raise his hand to hold the pipe, so I lit it for him and tried not to look or breathe while he took a few puffs. Suddenly he started making a terrible gurgling sound, like he was drowning in his own saliva. I jumped back, dropping the pipe and sending smouldering ash and tobacco all over him. The hairs on his chest caught fire. I called Mamma.

'Oh, for Christ's sake, look at the bloody mess you've made,' she said when she saw me patting out the cinders on Pop's upper torso.

Pop was oblivious to the fact that I'd set him alight. His head was leaning right back, like a force-fed goose gargling a mouthful of marbles.

'He's got the death rattles. Won't be long now,' Mamma said, matter-of-factly.

The noise stopped abruptly.

'He's gone.'

Pop was motionless, staring at the ceiling without blinking. It was as if his soul had been in such a hurry to leave, it couldn't wait for his eyes to close. I sat there for a few moments gawking at him. *He's dead?* I had only seen one other dead person, a man who was fished out of the lake after a drowning; he was all blue and bloated. Pop looked like a sleeping bag of skin and bone. It was the strangest thing. Even though Pop had died, I could still feel his presence.

'You go now, Katie, I have to lay him out,' Mamma said, with the same tone of indifference as when she bustled me out of the kitchen.

I knew what 'lay him out' meant. Mamma had found her boss dead on the floor and had spared us none of the details. I didn't need to be told twice to leave the room.

9

Ward of the state

I was in fifth class at Parramatta North Public School. Our teacher was away and our class had to join 5B. The teacher, Mr Hewson, was a sadistic mongrel who caned the boys with the slightest provocation, and if he'd been allowed I'm sure he would have caned the girls as well. But in public schools the teachers couldn't cane the girls. Not like at St Monica's, where Ellie Laughton's kids went to school. The nuns were brides of Christ and could indiscriminately cane anyone's arse, and no one would have dreamed of challenging them.

I was about to take an empty seat in the front row when Mr Hewson grabbed me by the front of my blouse, lifting me clear off the floor.

'Half-castes sit at the back of the room!' he barked, tossing me backwards. I fell, smashing my hip against the desk. He turned and walked back to the blackboard. I got to my feet and ran for the door. 'Get back here and sit down!' he bellowed.

When I got home I found Mamma in the backyard hanging out the washing. 'What are you doing home? What's up with you?'

she asked, when she saw my tear-stained face.

'Mr Hewson called me a half-caste and threw me to the back of the classroom,' I blubbered, not expecting any comfort.

Mamma's nostrils flared as she spat the clothes pegs from her mouth and stormed into the house. She tugged her apron off and tossed it on the back of a kitchen chair.

'Come on, Katie, show me where to find this cunt!' she said, storming out the door without stopping to comb her hair or put on some lipstick.

'Mamma, what's a half-caste?'

'Never you mind. That bastard's got my black blood up. I'll give him half-caste!'

In her youth, Mamma had been a champion runner, and I had trouble keeping up with her as she charged towards the school. When we reached Mr Hewson's classroom Mamma barged in without knocking, almost pulling the door from its hinges.

She walked straight up to Mr Hewson, shaking her fist at him. 'You spineless bastard! If you put your bloody hands on one of my kids again I'll have you,' she hissed through clenched teeth. Mr Hewson looked shocked as he wiped her spittle from his lips.

That was Mamma, a paradox of inconsistencies and contradictions.

Not long after Pop died I was just drifting off to sleep one night when I heard a noise in the hall. It sounded like Pop's leather-soled slippers shuffling across the linoleum. A few minutes later I heard three distinct knocking sounds, as if Pop was knocking his pipe against the glass ashtray to remove the spent tobacco.

'Mamma, can you hear that?' I whispered.

'Yes, it's only Pop. He won't hurt you.'

*

Aunty Lorna had told Mamma about a job for a housekeeper–cook that was vacant at Nudgawalla, a sheep station in the far west of New South Wales, where Aunty Lorna and Uncle Bill were now living and working.

'I could put in a good word for you, Sally,' Aunty Lorna said.

Mamma wrote a letter to the Harveys detailing her work experience. She read the letter to me to check that it was worded properly. I was surprised to learn about some of the jobs she'd had, working for rich families and catering in the boardrooms of important business people. Mamma watched for the postman every day, anxiously awaiting a reply.

A Salvation Army van pulled up one day, but instead of coming to collect some bags he was delivering some that contained shoes and clothing.

'Go through these, Katie, and see if any of them will fit you,' Mamma said, handing me the large bag.

At first I was excited; my wardrobe was getting a bit tattered. I tipped the clothes onto the bed and picked through them, looking for something that I could wear. But retro-fashion was still too far into the future for me to fully appreciate the contents of those Salvo rag-bags.

'Mamma,' I wailed, 'these clothes are awful. I can't wear these.' I held up a ghastly dress, hoping that she might understand.

'You ungrateful little bitch!' she snapped. 'Well, you'll have to find something to wear, I can't afford to dress you.'

I knew better than to push it, so I picked through the clothes again and found two dresses made from nice material. This was going to be a challenge, but Aunty Daphne had taught me to sew, and when Uncle Jack bought her a new foot-operated Singer sewing machine, she gave me the old knee-operated Singer. It weighed a ton and the boys complained that the noise drowned out the television, but I loved it with a passion. Having my own sewing machine was a small piece of independence, and even Mamma complimented me when she saw the stuff I had made. Mamma might have been good at knitting, but she couldn't sew to save her life.

The shoes were the real problem. None of them fit my small feet. I had to stuff the toes with newspaper to keep them on, and the rubbing against my heel gave me blisters. How bizarre I must have looked – a frock remodelled with all the skill of a ten-year-old, hobbling around like a crippled chook in ill-fitting shoes. But that was the least of my worries. With these bags of rags came some disturbing news.

'You better behave yourself now,' Mamma commanded. 'I have made you a ward of the state and I can have you declared uncontrollable and taken away.'

Weeks passed and Mamma had not heard back from the Harveys. She was beginning to think the job wasn't going to come to anything. Having to take care of Granny and Pop, Mamma had only ever worked a day here or a day there, although, after the butcher had cut off her account because she couldn't pay him, she got a job as a kitchenhand at the Parramatta Psychiatric Hospital. Cooking or cleaning was the only work Mamma could do, and putting her hands in water and harsh detergents, the dermatitis flared up again. The wounds were brutal; her hands were like slabs of raw meat. Her patience with me was non-existent and I tried to stay out of her way.

One morning a large white envelope came in the post. 'You little humdinger,' Mamma yelled, jumping around the room. She'd landed the job at Nudgawalla.

It was a live-in position, which meant that she would have to leave Jeffrey Avenue and Dan and I would have to go with her. The thought of leaving the lake filled me with dread. But this was going to be a great adventure, starting with a ride in a steam train over the Blue Mountains and across the Western Plains. In my childish imagination I hoped we'd see the landscapes that inspired the work of Albert Namatjira. To be 'going bush' excited me as much as the thought of seeing Aunty Lorna again.

The Lion's Club Chocolate Wheel operated every Saturday morning outside Woolworths on George Street, Parramatta. A scrawny man, wearing a Balmain football jersey with the sleeves cut off walked up and down the footpath, waving the tickets above his head and shouting, 'A pick o' the lot for sixpence. Ya gotta be in it to win it.' The roll-your-own fag seemed to be glued to his bottom lip.

I gave the prizes the once-over to see if there was anything I'd like to win. There was a very smart Antler suitcase. It was grey with three black racing stripes front and back, and two silver keys dangling from the handle on a piece of string.

'Lucky last, four tickets,' the man called.

'Uncle Stan, can we get some tickets?'

'Alright, here you go,' he said, handing me two shillings.

The wheel spun and I felt an adrenaline rush as the leather flap clicked against the metal pegs separating the numbers. *Come on*, I urged, closing my eyes. As the wheel slowed I counted twenty clicks before it stopped.

'Number fifty.'

'Yes!' I grinned, holding up the ticket.

'You tinny little bugger,' Uncle Stan said, laughing. 'You never miss.'

Anticipating my choice, the man picked up the bride doll.

'No, thank you, I'd like the suitcase, please.'

Having shared a bed, a wardrobe and a bath with some-one or other since birth, even a suitcase measuring thirty-six by twenty-four by twelve inches felt like a capacious amount of personal space. Everything I owned fitted into the suitcase – with room to spare – and unless some nosey parker broke the locks, it was private and I didn't have to share it with anyone.

Our train was departing Parramatta station at nine o'clock and Mamma was getting edgy. The taxi was running late.

'If that bastard doesn't get here soon, we'll miss the fucking train,' she said, looking through the venetian blinds.

It was the start of the school holidays and the Argyle Street entrance to Parramatta station was buzzing with activity. Hordes of kids in uniform, from the various private boarding schools in Parramatta, were catching the train back to their family properties in the west. The train, a big black steam engine, was already at the platform, hissing steam and raring to go.

Uncle Stan helped Mamma get our luggage on board. Mamma rattled around in her handbag for some small change.

'Here, you kids, go and get some lollies and a block of Old Jamaica.'

Dan and I ran to the kiosk, squabbling over whether we'd get Minties, Jaffas or Fantales.

'All aboard! For all stations to Katoomba . . . change trains at Lithgow for Bathurst, Orange, Dubbo and all stations to Bourke,' the stationmaster called as he walked down the platform. He blew his silver whistle and waved a yellow flag, signalling to the driver.

'Come on, you kids, you'll miss the bloody train,' Mamma yelled.

Uncle Stan held the door open. It wasn't until then that I realised I was leaving him behind. Except for the times I'd lived with Aunty Daphne and Aunty Lorna, Uncle Stan had always been a big part of my life. He was the buffer between me and Mamma, and had stopped her flogging me on several occasions. The few times I could say I'd felt joy or happiness had involved him in some way.

'Say Ten Hail Marys to St Anthony,' he'd suggest if I lost anything. St Anthony was the patron saint of lost things, and, of course, the Hail Mary was the most potent prayer of all.

'Goodbye, Uncle Stan!' I called, hanging out of the window, holding back the tears.

Uncle Stan waved back, but his voice was drowned out by the deep chug-chug-chugging of the engine as the train picked up speed.

I didn't know how long we'd be at Nudgawalla, but I was hoping it wouldn't include Christmas, because without Uncle Stan it wouldn't be Christmas.

10

The station

Cigarettes, a newspaper and a block of Old Jamaica – Mamma was all set. I was fidgeting like a puppy with worms and knew it would quickly get on her nerves.

'I think I'll go and explore the train,' I said.

'Don't get into any bloody mischief,' she muttered, without looking up from the newspaper.

As the train rumbled over the bridge on Church Street I darted from one side of the carriage to the other. From that height I had a bird's-eye view of St John's, the church of the infamous 'flogging parson', Samuel Marden, whom we'd learned about at school. Our class went on an excursion to the church once and I wasn't allowed to go inside because I was Catholic. It was tantamount to committing a mortal sin for a Catholic to enter an Anglican Church.

The coloured lights capping the Art Deco façade of the Rivoli Theatre flickered against the black sky. Jack Papworth and his Old Time Orchestra would have been tuning up for the first dance in the glittering ballroom. Uncle Stan and Mamma were both wonderful ballroom dancers and before Kev died we went to the Rivoli every Friday night. Dan was my partner and we learned all the steps. I didn't like the barn dance; every dirty old man in the room used to pull me so close to him I could feel his 'old fella' against my chest.

Passing the window displays of Grace Bros department store, I thought about my friend 'light-fingered Lorraine', who always dressed in the height of fashion in the clothes she nicked from the store. A pretty blue-eyed blond, she was never even suspected of being a shoplifter, and once walked brazenly from the store with a new-season swimming costume stuffed into her pants.

I looked north, beyond the city lights. *Goodbye friends, goodbye lake*, I said to myself as the train picked up speed.

The toilet was at the end of the carriage. A sign requested that passengers not use it until the train had left a station. When I lifted the lid I could see why. The toilet was just a chute with a wooden seat. The hole was easily big enough for me to fall through. It would require a prayer and a tight grip on the handrail to stop me from disappearing onto the tracks below. Busting to go, I had to brave it. Gripping the handrail, I wiggled to the edge of the rim. My teeth rattled as the blast of cold air whistled up, giving me goose bumps on my bare bum. Was this where the expression 'put the wind up you' came from?

There was a sudden drop in temperature as the train crawled up the mountains to Katoomba. We stopped at elegant old railway stations, with hand-painted signs on wooden posts and cosy waiting rooms with open fireplaces.

The moonless night cloaked everything in darkness and between the stations there was nothing to see, but not even the choking smoke from the train's engine could mask the invigorating fragrance of the eucalyptus forests as we travelled through the Grose Valley. At Katoomba, a conductor placed two chrome containers filled with hot sand onto the floor of our compartment. This was the only heating provided for the freezing conditions, but it was very effective.

As the train pulled into Lithgow there was a fine mist in the air. It looked like there had been a fire somewhere and it was raining ash.

'It's snowing,' Mamma said, like that was nothing to get excited about.

'Snow!'

I had never seen snow. I held my hand out to catch some of the soft, fluffy flakes, but they melted on contact with my warm skin. I stuck my tongue out and tried to catch a few. The trees planted in boxes along the platform were covered in a white sheet. It was picture postcard beautiful but too dark to take a photograph. We had to change trains at Lithgow, so there was plenty of time to have a cup of tea at the kiosk and use a proper toilet. More cylinders of hot sand were placed on the floor of our compartment and we got on our way for the last leg of the journey. It was getting late, and Mamma pulled our blankets down from the luggage racks.

'Okay, you kids, I'm going to get some shut-eye, we have a long day tomorrow,' she said, making a pillow for herself by covering one of the soft bags with a coat.

She lay down full-length on the seat, leaving just enough room for Dan and me to squash ourselves in. I leaned against the window, Dan lay up close to Mamma who soon started snoring like a bear. Even if I'd wanted to sleep it would have been impossible. The windows were all steamed up so I rubbed away the moisture with the sleeve of my cardigan, which was filthy anyway from the smoke and soot from the train. We travelled through towns that had only two or three houses. Occasionally a single light twinkled far away, as if a star had fallen from the sky.

*

71

'Good morning, Mamma,' I whispered, through the dim pre-dawn.

'Hello, love,' she groaned.

Mamma lived with constant back pain. There was an operation she could have had, but she was adamant: 'I'm not letting any bloody doctor cut me open.' Every morning I had to help her get into a heavy, boned surgical corset which laced up at the sides. It took all my strength to get the laces as tight as she needed them to be, and she often got exasperated. 'Tighter! Pull the fucking thing tighter!' In the evening after her bath I rubbed her back with Goanna Oil, trying to avoid touching the big brown wobbly mole at the base of her spine.

The train came to a halt in the middle of nowhere. I squinted against the sudden burst of light as the fiery orb crawled over the horizon.

'What's that?' I asked, pointing to what looked to be a golden ocean of undulating waves shimmering like millions of tiny seashells rolling in with the tide. The breeze hinted, strangely, of just-baked bread.

'A wheat field,' Mamma replied wistfully, as if this splendid sight had struck a chord somewhere in her memory.

The terrain between Dubbo and Nyngan was dead flat, not a bend in the railway tracks for one hundred miles. As we made our way further west we entered a dry unforgiving landscape, where it seemed only the fit and the resourceful could survive. Fat black crows feasted on the carcasses littering thirsty paddocks that hadn't tasted a drop of rain in years. Mamma struggled to sit up just as we were passing a town called Nevertire.

'How did Nevertire get its name?' I asked. I loved to hear the stories about how towns got their names, and Mamma was a talking book on the subject.

'Well,' Mamma started, 'a whitefella was hunting a bushranger and he took a black tracker named Jackie. The whitefella was on horseback and Jackie ran alongside. They had been travelling all day and the whitefella dismounted to give himself and his horse a spell. Jackie was standing beside the campfire as the whitefella boiled the billy. He told Jackie to sit and rest. Jackie said, "Me nebber tire boss." And that's how Nevertire got its name.'

It seemed like the longest she'd ever spoken to me without yelling.

'The next stop is Nyngan,' Mamma said, combing her hair and concentrating to apply lipstick without a mirror.

Mamma's sister Vera and her husband, Bill Burt, and their eight children still lived in Nyngan. Of all the places my mob lived, Nyngan was our country.

As the train pulled into the station Mamma was hanging out the window, craning her neck. 'There she is!' she cried, rubbing her hands together excitedly.

'Yoo hoo,' Aunty Vera called from the platform.

Nyngan was a pit stop. The catering crew had a change of shift, goods were unloaded from Sydney and other goods loaded on for Bourke. Mamma and Aunty Vera had time for several cups of tea and a long chat. They talked in detail about our mob, some of whose names were only vaguely familiar. They went on and on about who had died, married or brought scandal on the family. Mamma wanted to know the whereabouts of every bloody member of our extended family.

'All aboard for all stations to Byrock and Bourke!' called the stationmaster, and we scrambled back into our carriage.

Between Nyngan and Byrock were miles and miles of boring scrub country. We passed towns with name signs bigger than the main street. The brittle landscape grew sparser of vegetation as we pushed further westward. To keep myself occupied I recorded, in minute detail, every step of the trip in a school exercise book I used as a diary. There was the lady in the dining car who ate breakfast with the skin of a fox – head, feet, tail and all – draped around her neck. Its lifeless black eyes stared at me over her shoulder.

'Next stop, Byrock!' the conductor called as he walked down the corridor.

'Righto, you kids. Get ready, we're getting off here.'

Mamma pulled our bags down from the overhead luggage rack and checked her lippy and fussed with her hair. Aunty Lorna had told Mamma that Frank Hadlow, Nudgawalla's manager, was an eligible bachelor.

'G'day, Mrs Carlton. I'm Frank Hadlow,' he said, tipping his hat and reaching forward to pick up our suitcases.

'Hello, Frank. Please call me Sally,' Mamma replied, rather flirtatiously, I thought.

Frank smiled at me. 'G'day, you must be Katie.'

'Hello, Mr Hadlow.'

'Call me Frank,' he said, flashing a brilliant wide smile and offering his hand.

It would take some time before I was comfortable calling an adult by his first name. I found it hard to tell the age of adults, but I guessed Frank was older than Uncle Stan and younger than Mamma. He had a stocky build with a big barrel chest and powerful tanned forearms. I had never shaken a man's hand before. Frank's hand was firm and strong and became the yard-stick by which all subsequent handshakes were measured. He spoke in a drawl so slow milk could curdle in his mouth between sentences.

'It's a lovely car, Frank,' Mamma said as Frank opened the boot of his brand new EK Holden sedan. The duco was peppermint green with a cream roof and door trim. I could tell Mamma was very nervous, but she had no choice but to face her fear.

'Thank you, Sally,' he said, packing our bags neatly into the boot. 'You'll find it a bit more comfortable than the old Bedford would have been. If you need anything at the store, you better get it now. We have a bit of a drive to Nudgawalla.'

As we left Byrock we drove into the setting sun. Frank may have picked up on the fact that Mamma was a nervous traveller, or maybe it was normal for him to drive very slowly. Either way, I was grateful. I was in no hurry. There was a beauty to this country unlike anything I had ever seen. The road ahead cut a path through the spinifex that went for miles, gradually narrowing to a point swallowed by the distant horizon.

A cloud of sulphur-crested cockatoos descended, screeching and jostling to establish the pecking order.

'Wow!' I said, as dozens of red kangaroos thundered past, leaving us to eat their dust as I wound my window right down. The car swayed in the slipstream. The massive bucks leading the mob were easily six feet tall, jumping, wild and free in such close proximity that I could have reached out and touched them.

We drove for what seemed to be forever in a straight line before we made a sharp right-hand turn and rumbled over a cattle grid in the road.

'Jesus!' Mamma jumped, as a flock of emus came from behind. There must have been fifty of them and, unlike the kangaroos, they were in no hurry to overtake. They ran alongside the car, dozens of pairs of big brown curious eyes gawking at us. Frank tooted the horn. Startled, they turned sharply and galloped into the distance. The spindly legs of the stripe-backed chicks pumped like pistons as they tried to keep up with the adult birds.

'What's that, Frank?' I asked, tapping him on the shoulder and pointing to what looked like strange tufts of cottonwool scattered over the ground.

'That's what's left of a sheep after the wild pigs have finished with it,' he said. I shuddered at the thought.

Driving into the hot afternoon sun had been punishing and it was a relief when it finally surrendered over the western horizon. We stopped at the first gate.

'You might like to get the gate, Katie. Just make sure you close it behind us.'

We drove forever in another straight line until we reached the second gate. There were ten more to come. It was too dark to see far ahead and after a while we entered a more thickly wooded area. In the distance I could see flickering lights.

Nudgawalla was more like a small town; in fact, it was bigger than many we'd passed on the journey getting there. Dogs started barking as we pulled up outside one of the fibro cottages. Aunty Lorna, Uncle Bill and the kids came out to greet us.

'Hello, Katie darlin'. Jesus, you're gettin' more like your mother every day.' Coming from Aunty Lorna this was meant to be a compliment. Phyllis was always considered the 'glamour girl' in the family, although I couldn't see it.

Living in the bush agreed with Aunty Lorna's family. Elaine's stutter was less pronounced, even though she was still a sourpuss. Denise was getting very chubby. Jimmy was chattering like an excited monkey, so it was hard to tell if he was just revved up or had developed a stutter like his older sister. Allan had grown quite a bit since the last time I'd seen him, and so had his vocabulary of profanities.

'Dinner's ready,' Aunty Lorna called, and she led the way with the lantern.

'Is there a blackout?' I asked when I saw the flickering kerosene lanterns hanging from a wire strung across the kitchen.

Aunty Lorna roared with laughter. 'No, love, you're in the bush now. Only the gubba has power on out here.'

'Who's the gubba?'

'Jesus, we're gonna have to teach you plenty.' Her great bosom wobbled like jelly and she chuckled with delight at my naivety. 'The gubba's the boss, Colonel Harvey. But don't you call him that.'

After dinner Mamma and Aunty Lorna drained several pots of tea as they caught up on all the news from Aunty Vera in Nyngan. I'd had very little sleep in the past twenty-four hours so I was pleased when Frank spoke up.

'I better get Sally and Katie over to the house. That was a wonderful meal, thank you, Lorna.'

I liked it that Frank called me Katie.

Dan was to share a cottage with Frank and a farmhand called Leon, so we dropped him off first. The main homestead was about two hundred yards further on. It was hard to see in the dark but from the outside it didn't look like much. I was expecting a grand two-storey colonial mansion, like Tara in *Gone with the Wind*.

'I'll just crank up the generator so you have some lights,' Frank said, disappearing into the shed behind the house.

The bedroom I shared with Mamma was bigger than our lounge room at Jeffrey Avenue and separated from the main house by a covered breezeway. The twin beds were set wide apart, for which I was very grateful. We each had a set of drawers beside our bed, and a table lamp. A built-in wardrobe took up one whole wall. The quilted bedspreads with deep red roses matched the box-pleated pelmet and lavish curtains that went all the way to the floor. French doors opened onto a verandah that had insect screens on all sides. We had a flushing toilet, separate from the bathroom, and – best of all – there were locks on the doors.

'Mamma, may I take a bath?'

'Yes, but don't put too much water into the tub. There's a drought. And don't let the water out. I'll use it after you.'

For the first time in my whole life I lay in a bath, relishing the fact that no one could barge in and invade my privacy. I knew I was going to like living here.

11

Apartheid town

Mamma had been making lists for days for the supplies she needed to order from Brewarrina. 'Katie, get on the blower and order these from Bre, please,' she said.

The wall telephone in Mr Harvey's office looked like something out of a Wild West movie. I had to furiously crank a handle on the side to make a connection. 'Hello! Nudgawalla, here,' I shouted over the din of a dozen people talking at once.

'We'll talk about that later, Meryl,' someone said, sensing that I was too young to hear the gossip that was being passed down the line.

After I put through the order I walked in the direction of Frank's voice. 'The boss will be here on Tuesday, Sally,' Frank said, handing Mamma a letter he had received.

'Oh good, that'll give me time to get everything ready,' Mamma chirped enthusiastically.

Mamma became a tornado of activity to get the house open in time for the Harveys' arrival. 'Come and give me a hand, Katie,' she said, leading me through the butler's servery, which separated the kitchen from the main dining room.

As I stepped into the family's sitting room I felt like Alice in Wonderland. The highly polished timber floors cradled exquisite oriental carpets that looked too pretty to walk on. Floor-to-ceiling rosewood cabinets, with leadlight glass doors and tiny brass keys, displayed beautiful china and glassware. When we'd finished dusting and polishing we walked down the wide hallway to the bedrooms. I stood there, gaping in disbelief. I thought only kings and queens enjoyed this kind of luxury. It was almost impossible to imagine that while we were living in Herne Bay, catching rainwater in saucepans and plugging holes in the wall with Bandaids, other people lived like this.

'Come on, Katie, I haven't got all bloody day,' Mamma said, bringing me back from my fantasy world. 'Here, take your end and make hospital corners,' she said, showing me how to fold and tuck the sheet, making the ends as neat as a Christmas box. 'We'll air the room for a few hours,' Mamma said, motioning towards the French doors that opened onto a private verandah.

I spotted a treadle sewing machine against the wall and thought that maybe Mrs Harvey might let me use it sometime.

'When the Harveys arrive I'm going to be busy, so stay out of my way,' Mamma cautioned. She was a bag of nerves as she fussed with the pink-and-white striped maid's uniform, white starched apron, and the silly little hat she had to wear.

Colonel Harvey strode towards us, head erect as if preparing to inspect the troops. After he'd introduced himself to Mamma and exchanged some pleasant small talk, he turned to me and smiled.

'Hello, Kay,' he said warmly, stooping slightly and extending his hand.

'I am pleased to meet you, Mr Harvey,' I replied politely, remembering what Aunty Daphne had taught me about being formally introduced. He had a good firm handshake. I knew I'd like him.

'It's Colonel Harvey to you,' Mrs Harvey corrected curtly, walking towards the house. She stopped and, turning in my direction, glared at my bare feet. 'Don't you own any shoes?'

My face flushed with embarrassment. I did have a pair of shoes, but I only wore them when we were going to town. I liked to keep them for best.

With the Harveys in residence Mamma's feet never touched the floor. Dinner was always three courses and the washing up was endless. Frank had started having his meals with Mamma and me in the kitchen and stayed back to help with the washing up, which meant we got to bed before midnight. Frank was a very easy man to like and I could tell that Mamma liked him. She giggled like a schoolgirl whenever he was around.

And Frank had started teaching me to ride. 'I reckon we better take you to town and get you fitted for a pair of boots,' he said one day.

The salesman measured my feet, before handing me a pair of elastic-sided riding boots, with a two-inch heel.

'They're so comfortable,' I said, and smiled, wiggling my toes. I wouldn't have to stuff them with paper to keep them on my feet, or suffer the agony of weeping red blisters on my heels.

'Try this for size, Katie,' Frank said, handing me a wide-brimmed Akubra hat. I turned and admired myself in the mirror. 'Never leave home without your hat, Katie', he said, nodding approval.

Striding from the store I felt like all of my Christmases had come at once. I could have been ten feet tall.

'Now we'll have to find you a horse that fits,' Frank said, chuckling.

One morning he came into the kitchen grinning like a Cheshire cat. 'I've got a surprise for you, Katie,' he said, and led me around to the back of the homestead. 'She's all yours.' He smiled, handing me the reins.

'My own horse?' I stared in disbelief and stroked the nose of the white pony.

'You'll need to let her know who's the boss,' he said. 'She came from a circus. But you'll be alright. You'll need to give her a name.'

'I think she looks like a little Pixie,' I said, slipping my foot into the stirrups and pulling myself into the saddle.

Frank sent a letter away to enrol me into the Blackfriars Correspondence School. While I waited for the study pack to arrive I spent as much time tagging along with Frank as he would allow. He didn't think I'd enjoy watching the lambs being slaughtered. He got that right.

When the next mail truck arrived Frank came into the kitchen carrying a large brown paper parcel. 'Your school pack has arrived, Katie.'

There were four modules in the study pack, which had to be completed and sent back every month when a new study pack would arrive. I would work flat out for two weeks and finish everything. This left the rest of the month free to go riding or droving with Frank.

'We're docking and mulesing today, Katie. You may not like to watch that,' Frank said one morning, taking his breakfast plate to the sink.

'I can handle it,' I said, having no idea what either involved.

'Righto, get your horse.'

When we arrived a mob of ewes was milling around the shearing shed bleating frantically. The shrill screams from the lambs inside sounded like newborn babies, as the men sliced at their tiny bodies before dusting them with a powder and shoving them out the door. This was too much for me. I ran from the shed, mounted Pixie and headed back to the homestead.

A few yards from the main gate Pixie propped. 'Giddy-up!' I called, giving her a little dig in the ribs.

She reared up, tossing me arse over kettle into the dirt, before bolting in the direction of the shearing shed. Under a tree, no more than fifty yards from me, an enormous wild boar was scraping the ground. I got to my feet and ran for the gate. My legs were heavy and I could hear the hooves of the animal gaining on me. The boar hit the gate with full force just as I flung myself over the top, landing flat on my back. The wire gate was all that separated us. Its foul breath was right in my face as the boar grunted and charged the gate, enraged that it couldn't get to me. Frank rode towards us, whistling and shouting and firing a rifle in the air. The boar headed for the scrub.

Frank helped me to my feet. 'Are you okay, Katie?'

'Yes, that was a close call,' I said, shaking from the ordeal.

'Here, you better get back on,' he said, handing me Pixie's reins.

'I'm too sore,' I pleaded. In truth, I was more scared than sore, but not prepared to admit it.

'It's better if you get straight back on,' he insisted, giving me a hand to remount. 'You'll be alright from here,' he added, knocking the dust off my hat.

My whole body was stiff and sore for a week. I shuddered at how close I'd come to being a pig's lunch.

*

Frank thought I could use a break from jillarooing. He tossed me the keys to his car. 'Everyone out here needs to know how to drive.' He walked around to the passenger's side and I got into the driver's seat.

It only took me a few goes to get the hang of driving in straight lines. One day I was feeling a bit more confident and got the car up to forty miles per hour. The roo came out of nowhere. I hit the brakes and swerved, causing the car to fishtail in the dirt. Frank's hat went flying out the window. After we retrieved it and set off again, Frank gave me a valuable life lesson.

'Never swerve for a roo.' There was a long pause. 'Or a sheep,' he said, brushing the dirt from his hat. 'Or a man,' he added a good five minutes later, chuckling to himself.

The big outing of the month was going into Brewarrina for a bit of shopping and to catch the latest John Wayne Western at the open air flicks. I got to drive Frank's car all the way to the end of the dirt road. When we hit the outskirts of town, Frank took the wheel.

Brewarrina is situated on the banks of the Barwon River, 500 miles from Sydney and nearly a hundred miles from Bourke. In the 1960s it was a town bitterly divided. When Mamma and I went to the pictures with Frank we were ushered to the comfortable seats at the back of the theatre. The next time I went with Aunty Lorna, and we were directed to sit on canvas slings at the front. It wasn't immediately apparent to me that this was segregation based on skin colour. I just thought Aunty Lorna had bought cheaper seats.

After the movie Aunty Lorna needed to buy cigarettes before we left town. There was a white line painted on the floor of the shop. The whitefellas in front of the line got served first, which I thought was very rude, as some came into the shop after us. When the shopkeeper saw me, she told me to step forward to be served.

'I'm with my aunty,' I said, taking Aunty Lorna's hand and waiting behind the line.

'They can kiss my black arse,' Aunty Lorna said as we walked back to the car.

When the Harveys went back to Sydney, Mamma could relax a bit. Aunty Lorna used to come over to the homestead to use Mrs Harvey's sewing machine.

'You make sure you leave it as you found it or she'll know you have been there,' Mamma said, not happy one bit about Aunty Lorna touching Mrs Harvey's things.

One day Jimmy, one of Aunty Lorna's sons, was skylarking and riding bareback on a frisky horse. He forgot to duck while riding under a low-hanging branch and was knocked backwards off the horse. I was the first person to get to him. Jimmy was an epileptic and the shock had started a seizure. Foam was coming out of his mouth and I was afraid he would drown in his own saliva. I got down into the dirt and struggled to lift him up, holding him in a sitting position, as his body convulsed violently.

'Help! Help! Aunty Lorna, help!' I screamed, but the wind carried the words away. I put my fingers to my lips and whistled until I was finally heard.

It was seventy-five miles on the dirt to Brewarrina Hospital. Uncle Bill drove, and I sat in the back seat with Jimmy's head in my lap. He vomited almost the whole way.

Aunty Lorna was terrified. I had never seen her cry. Jimmy was in a coma for the next few weeks and we didn't know whether he had suffered any permanent damage.

At the hospital Aunty Lorna put her arms around me. 'Katie, you saved Jimmy's life,' she said, holding me tight in one of her Aunty Lorna hugs.

When Mr and Mrs Harvey came back to Nudgawalla, Mrs Harvey was more abrupt with me than ever.

'Mrs Harvey said you can't come out droving with us anymore, Katie,' Frank told me, offering no explanation. With only Aunty Lorna's kids for company, Nudgawalla was going to get very boring.

Aunty Lorna let me hang around the kitchen and was teaching me how to make cakes and scones in the wood-fired oven. One afternoon Denise was sitting at the table cutting pictures out of magazines that looked like those I had seen in Mrs Harvey's bedroom.

'Where did you get those?' I asked.

She looked sheepish and didn't answer. I knew she must have stolen them.

Mamma came storming into Aunty Lorna's kitchen screaming at me. 'What have you done, you little bitch? Mrs Harvey wants to see you now!'

'I haven't done anything,' I insisted.

'Well, you better not have. I need this job.'

As soon as we were out of earshot, Mamma hissed her usual litany of insults and predictions.

'Nothing but a little slut . . . just like your mother . . . You'll go onto the street, just like she did . . .'

We found Mrs Harvey on the enclosed verandah of the homestead, outside her bedroom, standing in front of the Singer sewing machine. She glared at me. 'Who gave you permission to use my sewing machine?'

'I haven't used your sewing machine, Mrs Harvey.'

'Don't you tell me lies. Look at the mess you've made.'

What had happened was obvious and to prove my innocence I removed the bobbin and, after clearing the tangled threads in the spool, returned the bobbin to its socket and rethreaded the machine properly. I stood back, defiant.

Mrs Harvey looked a little embarrassed, but was undeterred. 'Well, you may not have used the sewing machine but you have taken my magazines.'

'I didn't take your magazines, Mrs Harvey,' I said, looking to Mamma for some support. She said nothing.

'Pack your things. You are leaving,' Mrs Harvey said curtly, before turning and walking away.

When I got back to my room my suitcase was on the bed. The locks had been broken. I packed my few meagre possessions and went over to Aunty Lorna's to say goodbye and see if she had a piece of rope I could use to hold my case together. Aunty Lorna couldn't look at me. Denise was nowhere to be seen and Jimmy was dancing like a demented lunatic around a fire in the forty-four gallon drum in the backyard. Pieces of blackened paper floated into the air.

'There go Mrs Harvey's magazines,' I muttered under my breath.

Uncle Bill found me a piece of rope and told me he was driving me to Byrock station, because Frank was still out droving. He tried to make conversation on the long drive to Byrock, but I was far too shattered for any idle chit-chat.

12

Back at the lake

The bus to Lake Parramatta was waiting in Darcy Street. I was hoping I wouldn't see anyone I knew who might ask questions. I must have looked a mess. There'd been a creepy man on the train so I had locked myself in the toilet and cried all night.

'What happened? Why are you back?' Robbie asked, as I came through the door.

Unable to hold back the tears of anger and humiliation, I told him about Mrs Harvey saying that I had taken her things.

'Mamma and Aunty Lorna both knew I hadn't used the sewing machine or taken the magazines and they said nothing. They just let Mrs Harvey send me away,' I said, the tears welling up again.

When Uncle Stan came home from work I had to go over the whole crushing story again.

'I didn't do it, Uncle Stan. Mamma knew I didn't do it,' I said, looking him right in the eyes. He'd know I wasn't lying if I looked him in the eyes.

'Never mind, love,' he said, putting his arm around me. It meant a lot that Uncle Stan believed me.

'Mamma couldn't dob on Aunty Lorna – her and Bill might've got the sack,' Robbie said, trying to make excuses for Mamma.

That night as I lay in bed, still reeling at the injustice of it all, images of the rich red earth and wide blue skies flashed through my mind. Although it ended badly, I would have more good memories of my time at the station than bad. Frank Hadlow had been one of the few people in my life who had shown any interest in me. In the haste with which I'd been dispatched from Nudgawalla, I'd left my Akubra and riding boots behind. I imagined that Jimmy would get my hat. At least I still had the lake.

The bush track at the end of Jeffrey Avenue led to Lake Parramatta. As I walked through the green corridor, flashes of bright red bottle brush and fluffy golden wattle lifted my spirits. Even the angry-old-man faces of the banksia looked cheerful. The fragrance of the eucalypts was intoxicating. High in the canopy, hundreds of birds charmed my ears with their wild songs; screeching sulphur-crested cockatoos, laughing kookaburras and chortling currawongs all clamoured to be heard. They sounded like an undisciplined youth orchestra waiting for the conductor to appear. A rustle in the thick carpet of dried leaves startled me; I froze. Snakes came out at the first sign of warm weather.

As I got closer to the lake my pulse raced. I was coming home from a trip away and looked forward to greeting my old friend. Goose bumps of excitement covered my body as I peeled off my outer clothes and lay them on the towel. Standing still, with my face towards the sun, I breathed in deeply. The sky, the colour of sapphires, was reflected in the water. Wild ducks skimmed across the surface dragging their feet, causing ripples that rolled like tiny waves.

At the edge of the lake, in front of the ranger's house, was an old boat ramp. Starting at the end of the sandstone retaining wall, I ran flat out to get enough momentum to propel myself into the air. With arms outstretched and hands together my body sliced through the soft cool water. It gave no resistance and swallowed me whole. I stayed under as long as my breath held, drifting just below the surface, lingering in the weightless comfort of nature's womb.

'Hey, Katie!' Nicky called when he saw me.

Nicky Kosytzen, my best friend, was about three years older than me and already a teenager. He referred to himself as a League of Nations baby. 'I am a white Russian, born in a French hospital in China,' he'd say, if anyone asked where he was from.

'What are you going to do with that?' I asked when I saw the coil of rope he was carrying.

'You'll see,' he said with a cheeky grin.

Nicky loved to be mysterious, but whatever he was up to it was bound to be exciting – and definitely dangerous. We walked around to the point, where Carl Sloane was sitting on a rock having a cigarette. He had been waiting for Nicky.

'This looks like a good tree,' Carl said, throwing the end of the rope over a huge branch hanging across the water. Nicky stripped off to his swimming trucks and shimmied up the tree like a monkey.

'That looks about right,' Carl called from below.

After Nicky secured the rope, Carl took the end and walked back as far as possible. Then he ran flat out and leaped off the edge of the cliff, shouting, 'Geronimo!'

'Why do you shout Geronimo?' I asked after he'd resurfaced.

'That's what paratroopers call out before pulling their rip cord. It's to get perfect timing,' he said, grinning.

Perfect timing was going to be important for anyone jumping from this rope – if they hoped to clear the boulders hidden below the water's surface.

There had been another drowning incident recently, and the council was threatening to close the lake to swimming. This was disastrous news. Mr Prendergast, who lived on the edge of the lake, motivated we kids to do something about it. So in the summer of 1960 the Lake Parramatta Life Saving Club was formed. It became the largest freshwater Life Saving Club in Australia. I had to lie about my age to do the Royal Life Saving Bronze Medallion.

We had a swimming carnival and the Ramsgate Life Saving Club came to the lake. They looked down their noses at us and called us Westies. Most of the swimmers in our club were regional champions so we whipped them good at the carnival. One of the Ramsgate kids swung off Nicky's rope. He didn't know about Geronimo. He landed on the rocks and was taken to hospital in an ambulance.

At the start of the December school holidays that year Mamma came back to Sydney to work at the Harveys' Collaroy residence. She was home for Christmas and New Year and was due to go back to Nudgawalla at the end of the school holidays in February. Naturally I couldn't go with her, so I was sent to live with Ellie Laughton.

Ellie's husband, Arthur, was a baker at the Buttercup Bread factory in Parramatta. He went to the Rose and Crown pub every day after work and got blotto. Like clockwork, around five o'clock Arthur would come careering down the street, out of control on his bicycle. He'd hit his front gate, at speed, and go arse over head, flying through the air like he'd been shot from a cannon. There was a kind of survival choreography to this routine, and Arthur knew to roll into a ball and cover his head for protection as the bicycle came crashing down on top of him.

'You stupid old bastard!' Ellie would scream, running towards him and beating off the dogs that were going for the fresh bread scattered all over the lawn.

Every night Ellie's screams could be heard all over the neighbourhood, but no one interfered. On Sundays Arthur metamorphosed into an upstanding family man. He sat on the front step reading the paper as he waved his kids off to church.

I had been living with Ellie for eight months when Mamma came back to Sydney in October 1961. I liked Ellie, but I was glad to be going home. The constant fighting and screaming was starting to get on my nerves. Besides, I was about to start high school.

In spite of all the upheavals, my last year of primary school had been very productive, thanks to my teacher, Mrs MacGregor, who had nominated me for school captain. I missed out, but I was head prefect and captain of both the sports and debating teams.

'Katie, I am very proud of you,' Mrs MacGregor said, giving me a hug when she told me I had almost become dux of the school.

Mrs MacGregor pulled some strings to get me into Macarthur Girls' High School at Rosehill. By rights I should have gone to Northmead, a co-educational school that was closer to where I lived.

'I am a firm believer in schools for girls, especially bright girls like you, Katie,' she said, handing me the list of things I was going to need.

I knew there was no way Mamma could afford what was on the list, and my earnings from my job at the kiosk over the summer would still not be enough. So, lying about my age, I got a job in a printing factory in Rydalmere. I started at seven-thirty in the morning and worked until three, Monday to Friday. The people were very nice, but the work itself was unbelievably monotonous. After three weeks I was nearly going up the wall. The printing plant was just a tin shed and by mid-December the heat was unbearable. My mind often wandered: the fun I could have been having at the lake. But there was nothing like the smell of those small brown envelopes, each containing three crisp new one-pound notes. Every week I gave Mamma half my pay and banked the rest.

Uncle Stan outdid himself when he wheeled a red-and-white Speedwell bicycle into the lounge room a few days before Christmas in 1961. 'There's nowhere to hide this, so you may as well have it now,' he said.

This had to be a dream! I was afraid to move in case I woke up. A brand new bicycle with all the shiny chrome bells and whistles, even a basket on the front and a skirt guard, so my school tunic wouldn't get caught in the spokes. I never imagined that I would own such a thing.

'Don't you like it?' Uncle Stan said, looking crestfallen when I didn't speak.

'Like it? I love it!' I said, running my hand over the black vinyl seat.

Moving slowly, just in case it really was a dream, I checked out every inch of the bike. 'Gee! There's even a tool kit.' I'd found a heavy little black pouch swinging from the back of the seat.

'Don't take the Lord's name in vain,' Uncle Stan admonished.

'Can I ride it now?'

'Yes, go on. You may as well. But don't expect anything else.'

'Uncle Stan, this is the best present ever!' I said, hugging him.

My own bike! I had to find Nicky and show him. I wheeled the bike onto the front path and straddled the bar. Positioning the pedals for take-off, I was away.

'Yes!' I called out, throwing my head back as the bike picked up speed. I must have been doing twenty-five miles per hour, sailing down Jeffrey Avenue with the wind in my hair and my feet pumping the pedals flat-out. Ian Murphy's mongrel dog ran out but couldn't catch me. The freedom was unlike anything I had ever known.

A week before I was due to start high school, a parcel was delivered to the door. Mamma hadn't told me that being a ward of the state meant that I got my school uniforms supplied by the government. So with the money I'd saved from working through the holidays I bought a black leather briefcase, a Parker pen, a pair of purple one-way stretch slacks and an orange knitted top.

In February, the start of the school year, the mercury in Parramatta often hit a hundred degrees Fahrenheit before noon. Macarthur Girls' High was run with almost military precision. There were strict rules and a school motto that translated as 'life force'. Every morning the students gathered in the quadrangle in the sweltering heat to sing 'God Save the Queen'. Wearing smart uniforms, with hats, gloves, neck-ties and black stockings, attire better suited to the Scottish Highlands, girls dropped like flies and were left where they fell until the anthem was finished.

Starting high school was a turning point for me. I loved everything about Macarthur Girls' High, especially science and cooking classes. Even the uniform gave me a sense of belonging to something. Up to that point, my life had been chaotic, always jumping from one place to another on someone's whim. Macarthur Girls' High was solid; it felt permanent and orderly, and I was hoping that was how my life was going to be from then on.

At my first swimming carnival I placed second in a diving competition, behind a senior girl who was a state champion. I knew I'd done a good dive and could hear the girls from my school chanting as I floated to the surface. 'Macarthur! Macarthur!' they yelled, stamping their feet on the wooden grandstand.

The sports mistress, Mrs Howland, handed me a towel as I

came out of the pool after my last dive. 'Perfect dive, Howarth. You entered the water like a stick,' she said, smiling.

Although the pool at Parramatta didn't have a diving tower, now that I had a bike I could get to the pool easily after school to do laps to stay fit and dive from the blocks, which was better than nothing. I dreamed of going to the Olympics.

13

An innocent mistake

'Janice is up the duff,' Mamma announced.

Ellie's eldest daughter was only fifteen but she refused to marry the father of the baby because she said she didn't love him. When she gave birth to a beautiful baby girl Mamma went straight into her nurturing role. She couldn't do enough for Janice and her baby. Janice's father was very unhappy about Janice being an unmarried mother, the first in our neighbourhood, and Mamma chastised him.

'Smarten yourself up, Arthur, this is your first grandchild. What does it matter if she's married or not?'

Mamma's attitude in this regard didn't extend to me.

'Don't you even think about getting pregnant. I am not taking care of any of your bastards,' she said when we were out of earshot of Arthur.

Uncle Stan and his fiancée, Shirley, had been engaged for eleven years, which was long enough to expect anyone to wait. Robbie was working, Dan only had one year of school left before he'd get a job and Mamma was still working for the Harveys, so there was no reason for Uncle Stan to put his wedding off any longer.

The wedding mass, on 29 December 1962 at St Monica's Church and celebrated by Father Brian Charlton, was the second wedding in the new church. I was one of the bridesmaids and Robbie was best man. Uncle Stan gave me a lovely crystal brooch as a gift for being in the bridal party.

Anxious that the day was perfect for Shirley, Uncle Stan attended meticulously to every detail. None of the guests was aware of the catering drama happening in the background. We had more blow-ins from the bush than were originally catered for and we couldn't have anyone going without a feed. Mamma performed something akin to the 'loaves and the fishes' and saved the day with some help from a family friend, Brian Lisson, who had a Holden ute and ferried the food from our kitchen at Jeffrey Avenue to the Masonic Hall at Northmead, where the reception was being held.

'Drive carefully, Brian, those wine trifles haven't set yet,' Mamma said, packing rolled-up paper around the bowls to stop them falling over in the back tray. Brian drove like he had nitro-glycerine on board.

All the kids from the lake came to the church to see me in a fancy dress. Darryl Sloane and Bruce Pearson gave me hell over the headpiece. Even though I felt like the pink-iced sugarplum fairy, I got lots of compliments.

'She looks like Elizabeth Taylor,' I heard someone say as I walked down the aisle trying not to fall over in the four-inch high heels, the toes stuffed with wet paper. I had no idea who Elizabeth Taylor was, but it felt good having people say nice things about me.

Aunty Shirley looked a picture and Uncle Stan had tears in his eyes as they waltzed around the room with a white handkerchief between their hands. Uncle Stan would never have dreamed of his lovely bride's hands coming in contact with his sweaty palms.

Pride would have stopped Mamma from letting us kids know, but with Uncle Stan gone, money was getting very tight. She'd go through the ashtrays for bumpers to get the makings of a cigarette. Some nights for dinner we didn't have any meat, and she'd make dumplings with gravy. It distressed her that she couldn't put meat on the table.

I brought my friend Darryl home for lunch. He laughed when Mamma said there was nothing in the house to eat. I didn't speak to him for weeks because he'd embarrassed Mamma.

Thursday night was housie night at St Monica's hall. The jackpot, which was the last game of the night, paid twelve quid. Mamma looked at the clock in the kitchen on Thursday and turned to me. 'Come on, Katie! Be my lucky charm. If we get cracking, we'll make it in time for the last game.' She combed her hair and put on some lipstick.

Mamma only had enough money for two threepenny tickets. She sat on a crate at the door, as all the seats in the hall had been taken. She picked up a piece of chalk from the floor just as the man at the front of the hall called, 'Eyes down, for the first number.'

'Number six, clickety clicks, number six!'

Mamma's hand trembled as she marked the numbers on the cards. 'Come on, come on . . .' she muttered, with only one number left to mark. '*Yes!* Housie, housie!' she yelled, nearly knocking me over as she jumped to her feet, waving the cards in the air.

'Whacko the diddly-o!' she chuckled, pocketing the winnings.

On the way home we bought a block of chocolate at the new

milk bar, next door to the church. The next day the fridge and cupboards were full.

Nicky was excited when he came to see me. He'd hatched a plan to stop Ronnie, a friend of his from Boy Scouts, from running away and possibly ending up in Parramatta Boys' Home. Carl, the only one among us with a car, was taking a day off work. Bruce, Darryl, Nicky and I would have to wag school.

While I was discussing the plan with Nicky, Dan was sitting on the lounge eavesdropping.

'So where are we meeting him?' Dan asked, presuming that he was coming with us.

'You're not coming,' I said.

Dan looked hurt, but I didn't care. I still hadn't forgiven him for destroying all my photographs. He'd torn them to pieces in a spiteful fit of rage over something really petty. All the money I earned from my job at the kiosk I spent on developing photographs I took with my box brownie camera. The only photographs that survived were those I'd already given to Mamma and Aunty Daphne.

As planned, we all met at Nicky's place to get changed out of our school uniforms. It turned out to be a waste of time – Ronnie had only been bullshitting about running away. So we all went swimming instead.

We got back to Nicky's around three-thirty. I was in the laundry getting changed when I heard his mother shouting. Mrs Kosytzen had a thick Russian accent, but I could still make out some words.

'Grandmother . . . police . . . Mrs Simpson . . . trouble . . . thirteen years old . . .'

If she were talking about my grandmother, trouble would be an understatement. I was bent over, putting on my stockings when I sensed someone standing at the door.

'Quick, get going! Your grandmother is sending the police around.'

'The police?'

'She's going to have us charged with carnal knowledge,' Nicky said, with a panicked expression that was unfamiliar to me.

Not wanting to show my ignorance, I didn't ask what carnal knowledge was. I had to find a phone box and call Uncle Jack.

I didn't have two pennies to make the call, so I called reverse charges. 'I'm in some kind of trouble,' I babbled down the line. 'Can you come and get me?'

'Calm down, princess. Where are you?'

Uncle Jack and Aunty Daphne had left Mitchell Farm by now and this was the first time I'd been to their new place at Seven Hills. Stevie and Trudy were already seated at the dinner table when we arrived. Trudy still looked like a little doll; however, there was something different about her, she'd lost her sparkle, somehow. I sat down next to her.

Aunty Daphne was standing at the sink with her back to me. Her hair was cut short, like a man's, and she was wearing a daggy old dress that fell down to her ankles. As she turned around, nothing could have prepared me for the shock. Both her eyes were black and almost closed. Her top lip was split open and swollen.

'Hello, love,' she said, and I could see that talking was difficult. She walked towards me carrying a meal.

'Thank you, Aunty Daph,' I said as she placed a meal of mashed potatoes, peas, carrots and grilled lamb chops in front of me.

Uncle Jack ate his meal in total silence, his eyes darting around the table like a watch-dog, ready to pounce if anyone blinked the wrong way. After dinner he went to the pub.

'So what happened?' Aunty Daphne asked.

'I wagged school. We were trying to stop a friend running away from home,' I said.

'Is that all?'

'I was in a car with some boys,' I told her. 'But they're my friends. How could that get the police involved?'

'If you were playing up, you could all be in very serious trouble,' she said.

'Aunty Daph, I don't play up with boys,' I replied, feeling my face flush with embarrassment.

'Then you have nothing to worry about. Go and take your bath.'

The next morning Uncle Jack was up early and attending to his pigeons while Aunty Daphne prepared his breakfast. But something was different. Then it hit me. It was the total silence. No radio in the background, even the pendulum clock stood still. Stevie and Trudy ate their breakfast without uttering a word. Aunty Daphne didn't speak to the children at all. Uncle Jack had absolute power and control over everything and everyone in the house. No one dared to speak unless spoken too.

Uncle Jack locked the phone and left for work without saying goodbye to anyone. After we heard the car drive away, Aunty Daphne turned on the radio and became visibly more relaxed.

A little while later the loud ring of the old black bakelite telephone caused Aunty Daphne to drop her cup, sending tea all over the table.

'Who could this be?' She picked up the handset.

'Yes, she will be ready,' Aunty Daphne said gravely to whoever was on the other end.

'Get ready, Katie,' she said, turning to me. 'The Child Welfare is coming to get you.'

The very mention of the Child Welfare sent a cold shaft of fear right through me. The welfare was the worst nightmare of every kid I knew. They had the power to do anything, and could take you away and no one could stop them. Now they were coming to get me. I stood silent for several seconds trying to take this in.

'I beg your pardon?' I asked, hoping that I may have heard her wrongly.

'The Child Welfare will be here at nine o'clock, so please get ready.' She sounded irritated at being asked to repeat herself.

'How can they take me away?' I asked, unable to hold back the tears.

'Katie, you are a state ward, they can do anything they like with you until you're sixteen.'

When Mamma told me that she had made me a ward of the state, I thought it was because she needed some help to clothe me. To now realise that I was the property of the state, like a hospital or a school, was unbelievable. *I don't belong to a family – the government owns me*, I said to myself over and over, trying to get it to make sense. I felt like I'd just been hacked from the family tree.

A black car pulled up outside a little past nine, and a short, stout woman got out. Bonnie was barking and going berserk at the wire fence.

'Around the back,' Aunty Daphne ordered her.

The buttons on the jacket of the woman's grey two-piece suit strained against the fullness of her bosom. Her hair was pulled back in a tight bun at the nape of her neck, and the permanent scowl on her face suggested that she had been doing this unpleasant job long enough to have lost all sense of humour. Everything about her was drab and institutionalised. Aunty Daphne knew she was powerless to stop this woman taking me away, and that it was pointless to even try to reason with her. I could see that she felt very self-conscious about her battered appearance.

Bonnie stood at the fence with her nose pressed against the wire, whimpering. I stopped to give her a pat. 'It's alright, Bonnie girl, I'll be okay,' I said. There was no fooling her; she licked my cheek.

The lady didn't tell me where we were going, and I was relieved when we passed Parramatta Girls' Home. We turned into a driveway. There was a sign on the gate that I thought read 'General Practitioner'.

We entered a waiting room and a tall man, wearing wire-rimmed spectacles and a white coat over his three-piece pinstriped suit, approached us. 'Follow me,' he said with an expressionless face.

We entered a stark white room that smelled of Dettol. He motioned me towards a high bed covered with a blue sheet.

'Remove your pants and get onto the bed,' he said before going over to a cupboard in the corner. I froze.

'Remove your pants and get onto the bed,' he ordered in a way that made me think I better do as I was told. I sat on the bed.

'Lie down and part your knees.' He had no comprehension that what he was asking me to do just wasn't possible.

My mouth went dry. I wanted to jump down from the bed and run. He pushed his massive hand into a thin rubber glove and snapped it in place as he came towards me. I slammed my legs shut.

He placed a hand on my trembling knee. 'Open your legs!' he demanded.

At least he didn't lie by saying, 'This won't hurt.' I was paralysed with fear, so he forced my legs apart and slid the gloved hand down the inside of my thigh. Without any warning, he pushed his fingers inside me. The sudden sharpness of the pain caused me to suck in a deep breath and shoot backwards, like I'd been harpooned.

'Mamma!' I screamed.

'Get dressed and wait outside,' he said.

My legs felt weak as I stumbled to the reception area, where the welfare lady was waiting. The doctor handed her a piece of paper; she read it and half smiled.

'You'll be alright now, dear. I'll take you home.'

14

The children's home

When we got back to Mamma's she was sitting at the dining table reading the paper. Robbie was working night shift on the railway so he was at home too, eating something at the kitchen table.

'Well?' Mamma asked, looking right past me to the welfare lady.

She handed Mamma the doctor's report.

'She's a virgin?' Mamma asked, her eyes popping with disbelief. This was obviously not the result she had been expecting. Her mind seemed to be racing, as if looking for another angle.

Dan was on the lounge watching television. He only had to sneeze and he got a day off school. He was biting his lip and looked nervous. He must have realised that I would figure out who had told Mamma where I'd gone that day. He was the only person, other than Nicky and the boys in the car, who had known what we were doing.

Mamma glared at me. 'Lucky for you and those boys you run around with, or I'd have had the lot of you locked up.' She snarled like a dog whose bone had been taken.

Feeling a bit cocky that I had defeated her, I made a big mistake. 'So this proves you wrong, doesn't it?' I said.

She wouldn't hit me in front of the welfare lady, but copping the strap later would be worth the satisfaction of seeing her face right at that moment.

'Get the little bitch out of my sight. She is uncontrollable,' she snapped, waving her hand like she was ordering a dog out of the house.

At first I thought that this was Mamma just being herself, throwing her weight around and saying things she didn't really mean.

The welfare lady looked amazed. 'Mrs Carlton, wouldn't you like reconsider this? Kay has been through a terrible ordeal and I'm sure she's not a bad girl.'

But Mamma wouldn't be reasoned with. 'I said take her away.' Mamma turned her back on us and walked to the kitchen.

Robbie and Dan said nothing. They would never have dared to speak out against their mother.

'Kay, please go and pack your things,' the welfare lady said.

I stood there stunned, trying to grasp what was happening and hoping that if I hesitated for long enough, Mamma may come to her senses.

Everything I owned still fitted into my small suitcase with room to spare. Not knowing where I was going, I left my box brownie camera in the bottom of Mamma's wardrobe not wanting to risk having it lost or stolen.

The trip across the city was a blur. We eventually turned into a driveway that had a sign on the front gate that read 'Bidura Children's Home'. The welfare lady and I walked down a long hallway with wooden floorboards that had been polished to a high shine. She knocked on the door of the matron's office.

'Wait here please, Kay,' the welfare lady said. After about five minutes she put her head out of the door. 'Please come in, Kay.'

'Has she seen a doctor?' the matron asked.

'Yes!' I jumped in, afraid that I may have to take another virginity test.

'Speak when you are spoken to, child,' the matron scolded.

The welfare lady handed the matron a piece of paper, and after reading it she picked up a pen and started asking me questions.

'What's your mother's full name?'

'Phyllis Elizabeth,' I said, pleased to be able to answer the first question.

'And your father's name?'

'I don't know, Mrs.'

'Please call me matron.'

'I don't know, matron.'

'You don't know your father's name?'

'No, matron,' I replied, blushing. 'I have been told two names, but I don't know the real one.'

'Have you had your needles?'

'Yes, matron, I had them at school.'

The matron opened my suitcase and looked through my things. 'Good heavens, are these your clothes?'

This was too humiliating on top of everything else that had happened. The only decent clothes I possessed were the purple slacks and orange knitted top. The rest looked like cleaning rags.

'Yes, matron,' I replied, too ashamed to look at her.

'None of these are suitable to wear here.' She picked up a telephone receiver. 'Mrs Burton, please come to my office. We have a new girl being admitted.'

Mrs Burton was a rotund lady with a bosom that seemed to

start under her chin and cascade down to her waist. She led me back down the long hallway, her bottom wobbling like she had two kids fighting under her skirt.

'Here we go,' she said, putting a bundle of clothes on a table and marking them off on a clipboard.

I couldn't believe my eyes. Two of the ugliest dresses I'd ever seen, which came down to my ankles, three pairs of grey cotton pants, two pairs of grey ankle socks, a nightdress and a pair of black lace-up shoes. I could have auditioned for Little Orphan Annie and skipped the wardrobe department.

There was nothing homely about Bidura Children's Home. It was an institution where neglected, abused, abandoned and orphaned kids were sent to await foster parents or adoption. Although this was not a place for bad girls and didn't have iron bars on the windows, everything was conducted according to a very strict schedule and punishments for disobedience were harsh. The worst time was in the dormitory after lights out. Sometimes the weeping was barely audible sobs, muffled by a pillow or a blanket. At other times the distress and despair were profound. The stories I heard from some of the kids made me feel that, by comparison, I'd been born into a life of privilege.

One Sunday I got a visit from Uncle Jack. He looked very handsome in his tweed jacket, fawn trousers and open-necked white shirt.

'I've made an application to adopt you. What do you think about coming to live with me and Aunty Daph full-time?' he asked, flashing that killer smile.

'That'd be good, Uncle Jack,' I said, hoping my voice didn't betray the fact that I still felt completely shattered that Mamma didn't want me.

'Here, put these under your pillow and don't you worry, I'll get you out of here.' He handed me a bag of black jelly beans.

Being adopted by Uncle Jack and Aunty Daphne was certainly more appealing than being locked up for three years, or going to live with a stranger, who could virtually do whatever they liked with me and send me back if I didn't cooperate.

When Mamma visited a few weeks later, she looked a ball of style in a new dress and her hair dyed blue and permed into a tight frizz. The new dentures seemed too big for her mouth, though. Her top lip, stretched to max, didn't make contact with the bottom lip, leaving her with a fixed grin. I thought of the entrance to Luna Park.

'Hello, love,' she said, as calm and sweet as you like, as if nothing had happened and I was just at a summer camp.

'Hello, Mamma, you look nice,' I replied.

'I've just come back from Nudgawalla. I think Frank's going to ask me to marry him.'

Mamma seemed like a very old lady to me, and as much as I liked Frank Hadlow, the thought of them getting married appeared far-out, ridiculous, even.

'Uncle Jack's going to adopt me,' I said, feeling a bit smug.

She smirked. 'That bastard's not going to get you. I have too much on him.'

There was really nothing much to say to Mamma, and after some long silences, she left. That night I wrote everything in my diary, and read it over and over again. I wasn't very sophisticated, but I was smart enough to see through this. Was it possible that Mamma had pulled this whole stunt so that she could go back to Nudgawalla and not have to worry about what to do with me? That night I was one of the kids crying in the dark.

*

The weeks dragged into months and life at Bidura was anything but a summer camp. There was a lovely garden at the front, but it was nothing more than a façade for the misery to be found beyond the heavy timber doors. The yard behind the home was completely paved with grey concrete, not intended to provide any comfort or hope for the kids who languished there in a state of uncertainty and fear about what lay ahead. Escaping from Bidura would have been as easy as walking out the front gate, but with no money and nowhere to go, I had no choice but to make the best of it.

To break the intense boredom and keep my mind from pining for the lake, my friends and my freedom, which didn't look to be coming any day soon, I spent a lot of time in the nursery helping to feed and comfort the babies. Some of them were very young, only a few weeks old.

'Where do these babies came from?' I asked one of the nurses.

'The newborns come from homes for the unmarried mothers who don't want them,' she told me matter-of-factly.

How could a mother not want her own child? I wondered. Especially these adorable little babies. How could any one of them not melt the coldest heart? But the number of newborns passing through Bidura seemed to be huge. If they were healthy, they didn't stay long. Those with the slightest imperfections or obvious birth defects, however, were not adopted. They were sent somewhere else, but where exactly I never knew.

Just when I thought I was starting to lose my mind Mrs Burton came to see me in the nursery. 'Get your things packed, Kay, you're leaving today.'

Uncle Jack smiled when I walked into the office with my case. 'Hello, kiddo,' he said.

I was so relieved I wanted to throw my arms around him.

We didn't talk much as we drove across the city. Uncle Jack had spent some time in a boys' home as a child, so he didn't need to ask me what it was like. When we reached the junction of Pennant Hills Road and Church Street at North Parramatta, we turned right. This meant we were going to Jeffrey Avenue. I hoped it was to pick up my bike.

'Hello, Johnnie,' Mamma said cheerfully as we walked through the door.

I never came to understand the nature of their very strange relationship. One day he was all the mongrels under the sun, the next he was 'Johnnie'.

'Hello, love,' she said to me, looking a bit sheepish. Maybe she realised that I'd twigged to what she had done.

My bike wasn't where I'd left it under the eaves next to the verandah, so I went around to the backyard to look for it. I heard Uncle Jack's car leave.

'Where has Uncle Jack gone?' I asked, running back inside.

'He wasn't going to get you. I have too much on him,' Mamma said, repeating what she'd told me at Bidura.

'Where's my bike?'

'I gave it away. You weren't using it.'

I wasn't all that surprised. It wasn't unusual for Mamma to give our things away. Her attitude was that she owned everything and everyone under her roof. Over the years I'd seen every lovely gift from Uncle Stan disappear, but losing my bike was devastating. Unable to hold back my tears of frustration and disappointment, I turned and left the room.

15

A narrow escape

'Don't let anyone know I've gone back to Nudgawalla or the welfare will take you away,' Mamma said, before sweeping out the door for a waiting taxi.

Not having Mamma living with us anymore, I more or less came and went as I pleased, and spent a lot of time after school at Parramatta pool. As I no longer had my bike, I had to walk home. The road that ran between the cemetery at North Parramatta and Richie Benaud Oval was the quickest way back, but it was a spooky stretch of road, especially at dusk. Late one afternoon, about halfway along the road, I heard a car behind me and instinctively started to run.

'Get her!' I heard a male voice shout behind me.

Before I knew what was happening, someone had grabbed me by the hair and was dragging me to the car. Another boy got out to help him. They tossed me into the back seat and slammed the door. I was caught in between these two stinking animals with no way to escape. The car sped away. I recognised the boys;

they were the Monroe brothers, from Granville. I was in serious trouble.

'I'm going first,' one said, cackling like a hyena as they started to rip my clothes off. Arms, legs, fists and punches went in all directions, but my damp Speedo swimming costume slowed them down. Squirming like an eel, I managed to get a very hard punch into the groin of one of the boys.

'You fucking little slut! I'm going to fuck your arse off,' he screamed, pummelling my face and body with his fists.

Everything was going black. I couldn't see. I heard myself call out, 'Robbie, help me!'

The driver slammed on the brakes, throwing me into a heap on the back floor.

'Fuck me dead! That's Robbie Carlton's sister. Christ! Get her out of here.'

The next thing I knew I was falling from the vehicle onto the gravel. It was pitch all around me, but I knew where I was. I had walked along this back road many times. I staggered to my feet. I heard a car coming and jumped into the scrub, landing on some-thing sharp. The car stopped. It was them again. I was shaking all over, terrified I might rustle the dried leaves and give my position away.

'The bitch has gone,' a voice said, sounding disappointed. They drove away.

I pulled the chunk of glass out of my knee, and limped home. Robbie was in the lounge room watching television. He looked up and saw the state I was in. 'What happened to you?'

'It was the Monroes,' I said, and headed for the bathroom.

Larry Monroe and his brothers, Doug and Dave, were notori-ous. I'd heard that they had been charged with pack rape once, but got off because the court said the girl had had it coming on account of the way she'd dressed and that she'd got into their car.

They came from Granville, but were always hanging around the lake. They knew of Robbie's reputation; he was the most feared street fighter in a very tough district.

Throbbing from head to toes, it was a slow and painful process getting undressed and into the bath. I lingered until the water was cold. I could scrub my body clean, but the terror wouldn't wash away.

Later, there was a knock at my bedroom door. 'Katie, can I come in?' Robbie asked, his voice uncharacteristically tender.

'Yes,' I called from the bed, unable to get up.

'Did they get you?' Robbie asked, sitting down on the edge of my mattress.

I knew what he meant. 'No, they realised I was your sister and threw me out of their car.'

The tears were streaming down my face as I told Robbie what had happened.

'Those fucking bastards,' Robbie hissed through his clenched teeth, shaking his head with rage.

We sat in silence for several minutes, Robbie deep in thought.

'There's no point going to the coppers, Katie,' he said, finally. 'You weren't raped and those bastards will only get a slap on the wrist.'

I was relieved. 'We can't go to them anyway, Robbie. If they find out I'm living here with you and Dan, with Mamma away, I'll get sent to a home.'

'Okay,' he said. 'I'll deal with this. Just don't tell anyone what happened.'

Robbie made it his mission to hunt down the Monroes. He was intent on giving them what he called 'a very serious slap'. He had one of his mates make him a steel knuckleduster, which he carried around in his back pocket.

*

Some months later Robbie asked me to go with him to the Lennox Hotel in Parramatta. They had put a restriction on single males getting into the pub without a female accompanying them.

'Robbie, I hate pubs. Why can't you ask someone else?'

'Because I'm asking you,' he said, without any further explanation. 'You can leave after we get in.'

Reluctantly I got dressed up and went with him. I still had a dress and rope petticoat that I'd borrowed from my friend Pam for the rock'n'roll dance in Parramatta, and the high heels from Uncle Stan's wedding. I was only thirteen years old, but because I had 'started' early, at nine, I already had a size 34B bra. I didn't need to do much to look old enough to get into a pub. Besides, in those days pubs were pretty slack on policing underage drinking.

No one stopped us as we went in through the beer garden. We'd been there for about half an hour, and I was about to tell Robbie I was leaving, when one of his mates came to our table and whispered something in Robbie's ear.

Robbie's face darkened. He put down his beer and, casting his eyes around, nodded to several of his mates, who followed him into the car park.

One of Robbie's mates came over to me. 'Robbie wants you to come outside to make sure these are the blokes he's after.'

'Katie, are these the bastards?' Robbie asked, without shifting his attention from their faces.

'Yes, that's them,' I said, turning to walk away.

'Wait, Katie, I want you to watch this.' Robbie handed me his jacket. 'Which one of you cunts was going to take my sister first?'

'He was!' Dave Monroe was pointing to his brother Doug.

'Okay, then he can watch while you get yours. And yours is just going to be a warm up.' Robbie removed his shirt and handed it to me.

Dave seemed to have a death wish. 'We'll get you next time,' he sneered at me.

'So you think there's going to be a next time?' Robbie said, slipping his right hand into the knuckleduster. It was a brutal accessory, designed to remove teeth and break bones.

'Hold him!' Robbie said as Doug tried to run.

'So you were going to fuck my sister's arse off, were you?' Robbie said, and he back-handed Dave so hard his head snapped backwards.

Robbie's first punch folded Dave in the middle like a deckchair. Robbie grabbed him by the back of his shirt and pulled him to his feet. The shining chrome of the knuckleduster flashed in the streetlight as it struck Dave's face hard, and with lightning speed. Several more shattering blows followed in quick succession. It sounded like shells crunching underfoot. Dave fell to the ground.

'Get up, you cunt! I'm not ready to give you a kicking yet,' Robbie snarled.

Dave didn't move. Robbie drew back his leg and kicked Dave hard into the lower back.

'Robbie, stop!' I called out. I was afraid that if Robbie kept going he would actually kill him.

Robbie spat on Dave as he lay on the ground. 'You're only breathing because my sister is still a virgin,' Robbie said. He turned and walked towards Doug, who was being held by the arms. 'And you're going to get as much mercy as you showed my sister, you fucking toerag.'

Robbie could have rendered him unconscious with a single blow, but he was like a cat with a mouse, enjoying the game and in total control at all times. This brutal violence repulsed me and left me numb with horror. I couldn't stand to watch it anymore.

*

Larry Monroe, the eldest brother, made the mistake of thinking that the lapse of a year meant the matter had been forgotten. Robbie and I were sitting on the edge of the lake one day, sharing a peaceful moment of being 'brother and sister', when one of Robbie's mates came running over.

'Hey, Robbie, Monroe's around at the point,' he said, excitedly. The boys loved a fight.

Larry didn't even try to defend himself. He just went to water. Robbie danced around him, slapping his face with open hands and trying to provoke a reaction. When Robbie got bored after a while he hit Larry hard on the chin, knocking him to the ground. Robbie raised his foot and gave Larry two hard kicks to the body.

'If you even look sideways at my sister again, you cunt, I'll kill you,' Robbie said, and he turned to walk away. He stopped and went back, giving Larry another savage kick. 'And that one's for Pam.' He spat on Larry's head and finally walked away.

My friend Pam had not been so lucky in her encounter with the Monroe brothers. They had taken her to a house and tied her to a bed, where she was repeatedly raped and burned with cigarette butts. Pam had been in and out of Parramatta Girls' Home and knew it was pointless to report the assault when it could be proved that she had willingly got into their car. In those days it didn't take much for sexual offenders to discredit their victims and be acquitted.

16

Over the road

'Frank has asked me to marry him,' Mamma said, beaming with joy. She set her suitcase down.

This news meant she was going away for good. Dan and Robbie were both working by now, but I was set to enter my third year of high school and intended sitting the Intermediate Certificate exam later in the year.

'Where am I going to live?' I asked Mamma.

'Well, you're not coming with me. I'm not having you kids around cramping my style.' She cocked her nose in the air and struck a pose of exaggerated snobbery, as if becoming Mrs Hadlow was going to elevate her station in life. 'I've arranged for you to go and live with the Andersons.'

Rick and Lillian Anderson lived over the road in a house no bigger than ours. They had had six children, three boys and three girls. Mrs Anderson was a scrawny woman, with a deeply lined face you could strike a match on. Sandy, her eldest daughter, was my best friend. She was excited at the prospect of me living with them, and of all my possible options it was perhaps the best. It didn't take long for me to pack my things and move across the street. Sandy's little sisters, who had been sharing a bed in her room, were moved into Mr and Mrs Anderson's bedroom.

Although Mamma had arranged to send money to Mrs Anderson for my board, there was no provision for any pocket money and my job at the kiosk was only during the summer. Living with the Andersons made me feel like I was an absolute charity case. When I needed money for a bus fare, I had to ask for it. When I needed Modess pads for my period, I was too embarrassed to ask for money and had to use toilet paper. It didn't miss Mrs Anderson's sharp eyes that my addition to the household had a direct relationship to how often she had to change the toilet roll, and she rarely let an opportunity pass to embarrass me.

'How much paper do you use?' she asked me once, in front of her husband and sons.

I blushed scarlet. Talking about bodily functions, particularly in the presence of males, revolted me.

One afternoon I went over to see Dan. Mamma had not only taken all the furniture, curtains and blinds, but she had even taken up the linoleum. Dan was sitting on the bare floorboards, with a plate on his lap. *How could she do this?* I walked from room to empty room. Usually it is teenagers who leave home. But in our case, our home left us. I was barely fourteen and Dan had just turned sixteen. The only furniture in the house was the boys' beds and a wardrobe. Perhaps Mamma wanted to show Frank that she had something to bring to the marriage, even if it was only a few sticks of old furniture. She even took the lawnmower. The front yard looked like a jungle, and it was sad to see Uncle Stan's garden buried under weeds.

The next time I went across the road to our house, Robbie and Dan had gone. Laddie, our blue heeler, was sitting on the doorstep. The pads of his feet were bleeding and he looked half starved.

I thought he might have been taken away and dumped and then found his way back. He was really on the nose and badly needed a bath, but I couldn't push him away. He was all alone as well.

The following afternoon I went over to give Laddie something to eat and he was gone. I felt completely abandoned. I ran around to the back of the house and sat under the willow tree that Uncle Stan had grown from a cutting from Mitchell Farm. I thought about the years I'd lived at Jeffrey Avenue. Images of Granny and Pop, Kev and Janet, and the special Christmases with Uncle Stan ran through my mind.

The back door won't be locked, I suddenly remembered as I sat there staring at the house. We never did have a key for it, and never needed one with a cattle dog in the yard. As I walked through the empty rooms I could still smell my family. It was hard to grasp that all the people from the only place I'd called home were now gone. Robbie and Dan hadn't even said goodbye. I was left with nothing, not even a photograph.

In the summer of 1963 Sandy and I got our first two-piece swimming costumes. Sandy's was a proper bikini that showed some of her breasts, but I could never be that bold. Although my cossie was hardly revealing, it did expose four inches of midriff, and this caused a stir among the boys at the lake. Michael in particular used to stare at me in a way that felt like he was undressing me.

Michael was twenty-two. He was tall, very muscled and wore his hair in a 'bodgie' style. He was perpetually flicking it up at the sides and pulling it down over his forehead like his idol, Elvis Presley. Michael's most arresting feature was his smile. It stopped me dead in my tracks and left me fluttering like a trapped bird. I had a secret crush on Michael, although until I got my two-piece I was doubtful he even knew I existed.

Michael had nicknames for everyone. Dan was Mr Magoo, because of his thick glasses and huge head. Mine became Midnight. I thought it was silly. One afternoon as I was leaving the lake, Michael drove his car very slowly alongside me. 'Would you like a lift home, Midnight?' he asked, leaning out the window and smiling that killer smile.

I only lived a few hundred yards from the lake via the bush track, but I jumped at the chance of getting a lift home with Michael. As we pulled up in front of the Andersons', I saw Mrs Anderson looking through the curtains.

Michael got out of the car and came around to open my door for me. 'Would you like to come to the drive-in on Saturday night?' he asked.

'Yes, I would. Thank you, Michael,' I said, trying not to sound too anxious.

I felt so grown up to be asked on a date. This was the first time anyone had invited me out. All the boys I knew were still at school and had neither the money nor the motor cars to go on dates.

The week seemed to drag. Saturday couldn't come quickly enough. I spent all afternoon getting ready. Usually I only wore make-up when I was going to the pub with Robbie, and then it was only lipstick. This time I was wearing eyeliner and mascara. Even though Michael knew how old I was, I wanted to look and feel older.

When Michael came to the door to pick me up, he shook hands with Rick Anderson, who asked Michael where he was taking me.

'We're going to Dundas Drive-in,' Michael said.

'Don't get a spot on that dress,' Mrs Anderson called from the lounge.

'You look good enough to eat,' Michael said as we drove away. 'But you're too far away. Come over here.' Michael found a parking bay that wasn't too far back from the screen. 'Would you like a chocolate or something from the counter?' he asked.

'No, thank you,' I said. I didn't want to risk dropping anything on the dress I'd borrowed from Sandy. I'd never hear the end of it.

Michael came back to the car with a packet of cigarettes and a Coke. He offered me a cigarette.

'No, thank you, I don't smoke,' I told him, adding under my breath, 'and I wish you wouldn't either.'

'You really are a good girl, aren't you?

I watched the movie with Michael's arms around me. I have no idea what we saw or who the actors were. Michael was such a gentleman; he didn't even try to kiss me, which made me feel very secure and comfortable.

We had only been going out for three weeks when one night Michael drove to a quiet spot at the lake and turned the engine off.

'It's time I kissed you,' he said, pulling me to him.

He put his hand under my chin and lifted my face towards him. His mouth came down on mine. It felt like a million tiny needles, making me tingle from head to toe. I was trembling like a leaf.

'Was that nice?' Michael asked, sounding very pleased with himself.

'It was very nice,' I said, snuggling into him.

The next night Michael took me to the same spot and as he kissed me I felt his hand slowly slipping between my legs just above the knee.

I grabbed his hand and removed it, pulling away from him. 'Please don't, Michael, I am not ready to go that far.'

'Alright, we'll take our time,' he said, pulling me close to him again.

The following evening Michael called round to pick me up, and we went straight to the parking spot at the lake.

'Well, are you ready to go all the way?' he asked.

'Michael, I can't. I just can't do that. You do know that I'm a virgin?'

'Of course I know that. That's why it's so special. No one has had you before. You will be all mine . . . forever.'

How I longed to belong to someone. Michael was saying all the sweet things I needed to hear. He worked his hand slowly up my thigh. My mouth went dry when his fingers reached the leg of my panties.

I grabbed his hand. 'Stop! Michael, please stop!'

'Stop playing games!' he snapped.

I started to cry. 'I'm not playing games. I'm just very frightened.'

'I'm sorry, Kay,' he whispered, kissing me again tenderly. 'It's just that I love you and I want you so much.'

That was enough for one night. I asked him to take me home.

The next day was 29 February, a leap year, a day that would only come around every four years. Michael and I drove down to the lake and got out of the car. He had come prepared with a blanket and a towel. We lay down on the grass and he started kissing me. He moved his hand up under my blouse and cupped my breast. I started panting with fear. He made no attempt to put his hand inside my bra as he squeezed my breasts. It hurt.

Softly kissing my neck and whispering, 'I love you, Katie,' he slid my pants down to my ankles. As he moved on top of me he reached down to undo his fly. I clamped my eyes shut as he forced my legs apart with his knees. The shock of feeling skin to skin at my opening made me suck in a deep breath and pull away.

'No, Michael, please don't.'

'Shhh, shhh,' he cajoled, like he was trying to quieten a horse. He held my shoulders and pinned me to the ground. He pushed himself into me a little way. The pain was so intense I lost my breath.

'Oh my God! No, please stop!' I begged.

'I can't stop now.'

'Stop! Please stop!' I pleaded again.

I just lay there, trying to block out what was happening and praying that the burning sensation would end soon. Michael wasn't looking at me. He was staring straight ahead. It felt like a dry stick was being forced inside me. For the next few moments, minutes – I have no idea how much time passed – I repeatedly begged him to stop. He grunted and groaned and then roared like a wild animal. The pain was excruciating. Then he fell hard on top of me.

'Please, Michael. I can't breathe.' I winced as he pulled away. I felt so degraded.

'That's it!' He grinned victoriously. 'You really were a virgin.' He held the bloodied towel up for me to see. Then he uttered the truest words he ever spoke to me. They still ring in my ears. 'You may have a thousand lovers in your life, but you will always remember your first.'

The next night he wanted to do it again. I really wanted to please him but it was still too painful.

'It shouldn't be hurting now,' he said. 'You're hopeless.'

'Well it does!' I said, feeling angry that he thought I was lying.

'You're just a little prick teaser.'

Two weeks went by and Michael hadn't come around. It was clear that if I didn't have sex with him then he was no longer interested in me.

A few days later Sandy spent the whole afternoon washing and setting her hair and getting dolled up.

'Where are you going? I asked.

'Out,' she replied evasively, picking up her handbag and flouncing from the room.

I was lying on my bed reading when I heard Michael's car pull up in front of the house. My heart started to race. I hadn't been expecting him. Hurriedly, I brushed my hair and checked myself in the mirror to make sure I looked tidy. When I walked into the lounge room Michael was standing there, smiling at Sandy and holding her hand.

17

Shattered dreams

'Spring at last,' I wrote in my diary.

It had been a long miserable winter, but I was trapped at the Andersons' and had no choice but to make the best of it. I took some comfort in the thought that if sex was the only way I could keep Michael, Sandy was welcome to him. I never let on how hurt I was. Sandy and I still did stuff together but I would never think of her as my best friend again.

The weather was warm enough for sunbathing, so Sandy and I went to the lake. Robbie was standing on the patio at the kiosk. I hadn't seen him since he'd left Jeffrey Avenue. I waved, but he didn't wave back.

'Get home!' Robbie shouted at me.

'No!' I yelled back, no longer afraid of him and tired of being bullied.

He got that look on his face, trying to intimidate me. Slowly and deliberately, he walked down the steps and crossed the road. He stood over me. 'I said, get home!'

'You're not the boss of me.'

He reached down and pulled me to my feet. 'I won't tell you again,' he said in the threatening tone I'd heard a thousand times before.

'I'm not going home just because you say so.'

He slapped me across the face, not as hard as he could, but hard enough to turn my face.

I fixed my stare on him, brought my hand up and slapped him back as hard as I could. 'I'm sick of you hitting me, you bastard!'

He was stunned. I'd caught him completely by surprise, although I wished I'd had the power of a king-hit behind me. Robbie raised his hand and brought it down. He had never hit me this hard before.

'You bastard!' I screamed, my face stinging like a hot iron had been pressed against my cheek. Clenching my fist, I took a swing at him. He grabbed my arm before it connected. Then he slapped me again, this time harder. I stumbled and fell to the ground.

'You bastard! Leave her alone,' Sandy yelled.

Robbie had never attacked me like this and it made me wonder whether Michael had told everyone that he'd 'taken my cherry' and this was my punishment. Shaking with rage and humiliation, I looked at Robbie defiantly as Sandy helped me to my feet.

'I hate you!' I said, before hitting him with the only weapon I had. 'I wish it had been you instead of Kev.'

One day Mrs Anderson seemed more agitated than usual.

'Your grandmother has stopped sending the money for you and we can't afford to feed you,' she said, her trembling hands sending cigarette ash all over the floor. 'She's going to have to take you back.'

I felt like a television from HG Palmer's, about to be repossessed.

It couldn't have happened at a worse time. There was only a week before the examinations for the Intermediate Certificate; I didn't know what to do. I didn't even know Mamma's address or phone number. I needn't have worried. The problem was solved for me.

On the following Friday our class spent the whole afternoon with Mrs Stapleton, our year mistress. She briefed us on what to expect in the first exam and gave us tips for studying over the weekend. The final bell rang and everyone wished each other luck. As I was packing up my books, Mrs Stapleton came over to my desk.

'Kay, you need to go to Miss Llewellyn's office before you leave,' she said gravely.

I thought someone must have died. I walked down the corridor and knocked on the headmistress's door.

'Come in,' she called. 'Howarth,' she said as I stood before her desk, 'do you have any library books?'

'Yes, Miss.'

'Well, you'll need to hand them in. You are exempted from school from today.'

'I am sorry, Miss, I don't understand.'

'You're leaving school today. You have been given an exemption due to hardship.'

I stood there absolutely stunned. I was being taken out of school the week before the Intermediate Certificate. Any chance of getting a decent job or a cadetship as a journalist and one day becoming a writer had just flown out the window. With the single stroke of a pen all my hopes and dreams had been shattered. It was devastating.

'The library will be open until four. You need to hand the books in today,' Miss Llewellyn said, her expression softening when she saw the tears flooding my face.

That's that, now I'm really buggered, I thought as walked home wearing my uniform for the last time. I'd left school without being able to say goodbye to either my teachers or any of my friends.

'I bet she'll still get the money from the government,' Mrs Anderson said snidely at tea that night.

It hadn't occurred to me until then that being a ward of the state until I turned sixteen meant that Mamma was receiving some kind of financial assistance to support me. I had no idea how much this was, but I imagined it would have been enough for Mrs Anderson to feed me.

A week later I started working at Woolworth's at Ermington, which was very inconvenient to get to from North Parramatta. I paid Mrs Anderson one pound five shillings a week for my room and board and the rest was mine to keep. The monotony of stacking shelves in the toy section was broken only by the hordes of little kids that ran wild while their mothers did the grocery shopping. I had to stop them from pulling the heads off the dolls and breaking everything they picked up.

It was a job, and although I badly missed school, I did enjoy having a bit of money in my pocket again. So desperate was I to be loved and accepted, though, I began stealing the clothes from the damaged dolls and giving them to Sandy's little sisters. I lied, saying that we were allowed to take the clothes home.

Living with the Andersons always presented a problem for me when I had my period. Having a job meant that I could now afford to buy my own pads and didn't have to use toilet paper, which I used to flush down the toilet. At Mamma's we had a forty-four gallon drum in the corner of the backyard for burning paper waste and other combustible material, which helped to cut down on the garbage. At the Andersons' I had to wrap my soiled sanitary napkins in newspaper. I'd put them in my bottom drawer and wait until the boys had gone to bed before sneaking out of the house with the bundle for the bins at the park at the end of the street. One evening when I came through the door after work Mrs Anderson flew at me.

'You dirty, filthy little bitch!' she hissed, her face contorted with disgust. 'What's this?' She was pointing to a parcel on the table where we ate our meals.

Mr Anderson and his sons were sitting on the lounge and couldn't look at me. I was mortified with embarrassment.

'I am not having this filth in my house,' she screamed. 'Get out! You dirty, filthy little bitch!'

I picked up the parcel and ran out of the door. After I had dumped it in the bins at the park, I sat on the swings and bawled my eyes out. Michael's car went past. I could only imagine what Mrs Anderson would say about me.

I walked to the public phone box and called Uncle Jack reverse charges. I hadn't seen or spoken to either him or Aunty Daphne since he dropped me at Mamma's the day I came home from Bidura.

'Hello, McCarthy residence,' said a familiar voice on the end of the line.

'Hello, Uncle Jack.'

'What's happening, kiddo?'

'The Andersons are throwing me out. I have nowhere to go.'

'I'll come and get you tonight. Get your things ready.'

Uncle Jack knew where the Andersons lived, as he and Mr Anderson often had a beer together at the Old Northern Hotel, across the road from St Monica's.

Sandy didn't say a single word to me as I packed. I had no idea if Mrs Anderson had found the waste snooping around, or if Sandy had given the parcel to her mother, knowing what her reaction would be. It didn't take long to get my things together. My suitcase was a bit tattered by now, and I hoped the frayed rope would hold long enough to get me to Aunty Daphne's.

Mrs Anderson couldn't resist a parting shot. 'And you were stealing from Woolworths,' she said, sneering, looking well pleased that she had all the dirt on me to toss back into my face.

As I waited for Uncle Jack at the front gate, misty rain saturated my hair and clothes.

'Come inside, Kay,' Mr Anderson said

'No, thank you, Mr Anderson.'

Finally Uncle Jack's car pulled up. It was new, one of those odd little cars that old ladies wearing white hats drove to lawn bowls. It really didn't suit him.

Mr Anderson came outside to greet Uncle Jack. He looked very sheepish, even nervous. Uncle Jack got out of the car and they went inside. I would die from embarrassment if the Andersons told Uncle Jack what happened. When they came back outside they were laughing about something.

'Goodbye, Kay,' Mr Anderson said, trying to put his arm around me.

I backed away. I really didn't need anyone touching me. 'Goodbye, Mr Anderson.'

Before I got into the car I paused for a moment to look across the road at our old house. There were lights on. The new people had moved in. I never got to meet them and tell them not to worry about old Pop Higgins doing the nightly shuffle across the hallway, but I knew he wouldn't hurt them.

18

The doll's house

Uncle Jack went straight to the pigeon coop. As I walked down the path to the back door I could see that Aunty Daphne had given up on the idea of getting a garden going. She was in the kitchen, standing at the sink with her back towards the door. She had the same hideous haircut and drab appearance. As she turned to face me nothing could have prepared me for the shock of seeing her pregnant again.

'Hello, love,' she said. Her mouth was too swollen to smile and her eyes were dull.

Stevie and Trudy were at the table doing their homework. They both looked up and smiled but neither of them said a word.

I stuck my head in the lounge room and was surprised to see Robbie there. I hadn't seen him since the day he'd bashed me up at the lake.

'Hello, Katie,' he said, smiling as if nothing had happened.

Robbie was getting more and more like his mother every day. Mamma created turmoil one day and carried on as if nothing had happened the next. Well, I was sick to death of playing those games.

'Hello, Robbie,' I said coldly.

Robbie had moved in with Aunty Daphne. He was sleeping in the back room, so I'd have to share a room with Trudy and Stevie. They slept in bunk beds and I had a single bed up against the window. It was a bit cramped, but I was relieved to be away from the Andersons.

Since I no longer had my job at Woolies, I had to find work, and fast. The Bonds Spinning Mills at Pendle Hill had some vacancies. Aunty Daphne had worked at a spinning mill before she married Uncle Jack, and told me that I'd have to lie about my age to work machinery. I went for an interview and told them I was eighteen, knowing I'd get away with it. I got a job starting the next day at seven in the morning. It was intimidating to watch the nimble fingers of the women who raced up and down watching the lines.

A petite, dark-haired woman wearing a hair net approached me. 'Hello, my name's Nina,' she said with an accent.

'Hello, Nina, I'm Kay.'

'You never do this?' she asked.

'No, this is my first day.'

'Is easy. I show you,' she said, smiling.

One morning, as we were all lining up to get to the hot water urn to make our tea, an Australian girl pushed into the line. The woman she tried to shove out of the way was directly behind me. The woman protested in her own language and there was a bit of a jostle.

The Australian girl snarled. 'Get out of my way, you piece of wog shit.'

I turned around and put my arm around the lady, who was very distressed. She didn't need much English to know what 'wog shit' meant. 'Get to the end of the line and wait your turn, you bitch,' I snapped.

The girl glared at me like I was some kind of traitor, fraternising with the enemy. 'Who are you to tell me what to do?' she said, smirking like a toughie.

'You'll find out if you don't bugger off and leave this lady alone,' I said, stepping towards her.

Nina chuckled. 'You tough girl, Kay.'

'I hate bullies,' I told her.

The atmosphere at Aunty Daphne's was tense. Uncle Jack's moods had become more pronounced since the last time I'd stayed there. He barely spoke a word to anyone, just sat solemnly at the head of the table, eating his meals in silence. Everyone was too afraid to move a muscle.

One evening I came home from work and Robbie was gone. I didn't ask what had happened and I didn't really care, although I suspect it had something to with Aunty Daphne's battered face. She would never brook any interference, not even from her brother. It was chilling to realise that Aunty Daphne was taking those beatings at night yet never making a sound. Each morning she'd have a worsened black eye or another split lip, or she'd walk holding her ribs.

With Robbie gone I moved in to the back room. Having my own room again was bliss. I bought a transistor radio, with an ear plug, so I could listen to music and talk-back shows in bed. Every night I cried myself to sleep without really knowing why. Perhaps because I'd held so much in, pretending that nothing mattered, when I was alone the floodgates well and truly opened.

In the early hours of one morning Aunty Daphne gently shook

me awake and whispered in the darkness. 'I am going to the hospital, love. You will have to get the kids ready and off to school.'

The next morning I got Stevie and Trudy up and explained that their mum would be back in a few days with a new baby. We were having breakfast when Uncle Jack's car pulled up. He tended to his pigeons before coming inside.

'Well? Has the baby been born?' I asked.

'Yes, a beautiful little girl,' he said, smiling from ear to ear.

It was so nice to see Uncle Jack smile again. It had been a very long time since I'd seen him looking happy. Stevie and Trudy looked excited too, but didn't utter a word.

After Uncle Jack left for work we all jumped around the lounge room squealing with delight. Uncle Jack had told us they had decided to call the baby Roberta. I thought it was a lovely name.

That evening, after Stevie and Trudy had gone to bed, I was about to turn off the television and go to bed myself when I heard Uncle Jack arrive. I was hoping he'd have some news about Aunty Daphne and the baby, so I waited for him to come inside. Uncle Jack wasn't the kind of drunk who fell about slurring his words, but he was a drunk nevertheless.

'Hello, Uncle Jack, your dinner is in the oven. I'll get it for you,' I said, walking towards the kitchen.

'I'm not hungry right now, Katie. Come over here and talk to me.' He sat on the lounge and patted the seat next to him. 'You're just like your mother,' he said, with a soppy grin on his face.

He meant it as a compliment, but if there was something I was determined never to become it was like my mother. This was the first time Uncle Jack and I had been alone in a room, ever. Usually there were other people around. Mamma's words were ringing in my ears. 'He doesn't care about you. When you're old enough he'll take your cherry.' At the time I hadn't known what she'd meant.

'Uncle Jack, I'm very tired. Can we talk tomorrow?' I asked, dodging his outstretched hands as I walked past. He leaned so far forward he toppled onto the floor. I didn't wait for him to get up. 'Good night, Uncle Jack,' I said hurrying down the hall.

I stopped to check on the kids. Trudy was still awake, her angelic little face smiling at me in the dim light.

'Good night, Trudy,' I whispered, and kissed her.

'Good night, Katie,' she said, with a muted giggle.

Sometime during the night something woke me. I thought I'd heard some whimpering sounds coming from the bathroom. I listened. It sounded like Trudy.

I got up and went to the bathroom door, knocking gently. 'Are you alright Trudy?' I whispered.

'Yes,' she sniffled.

Trudy was nearly eight years old so I knew she would not be wanting help with her toilet. I went back to bed.

The next morning at breakfast Trudy was trembling like a frightened little bird. 'Are you feeling okay?' I asked, thinking she may be getting sick.

'Yes,' she said softly.

That afternoon the phone rang. 'Hello?' I answered. I couldn't imagine who would be calling. Aunty Daphne's phone never rang.

'G'day, Kay,' the familiar voice said.

'Carl, is that you?' I hadn't seen much of Carl since the day I wagged school to help Ronnie Simpson.

'Yes, Dan gave me your number. I was wondering if you'd like to go out with me next Saturday.'

Carl had never shown any interest in me beyond being a mate. It felt very odd for him to be asking me on a date. But I missed the lake so much and thought it would be nice to see an old friend again.

'What did you have in mind?'

'You live pretty close to Blacktown Drive-in. Would you like to see a movie?'

'Sure.'

'I'll pick you up about six-thirty,' he said, sounding quite excited.

When I told Uncle Jack that Carl was coming over to take me out, he wasn't too pleased. 'You're too young to be running around with men in cars,' he snapped.

I had no intention of letting him control my life the way he did everyone else's. 'I've known Carl forever,' I said defiantly. 'He's just a mate, taking me to see a movie.'

As we drove to the drive-in Carl tried to make light conversation. 'Dan's living at the Greys' boarding house in Factory Street.'

'I haven't seen Dan since he left Jeffrey Avenue,' I said. 'He didn't even come to say goodbye.'

'He lived in the cave at the lake for a while.'

Dan lived in a cave? I found that hard to believe.

'Sandy Anderson's pregnant,' Carl then told me. 'She's getting married to Michael next week.'

'Good luck to them,' was all I could manage to say.

When the movie started Carl slid across the seat and put his arm around me. It didn't feel right.

'What do you think you're doing?' I asked, removing his arm.

'What's the matter?'

'I said I'd come to a movie with you. That is not an invitation for anything else.'

'But you can turn it on for Mick,' he said, smirking.

I felt my face flush with anger. 'Carl, I am not a slut, so don't you ever treat me like one! Take me home.'

We pulled up in front of Uncle Jack's house. Carl was looking contrite. 'Will I see you again?'

'No, Carl. Goodbye.'

Uncle Jack was watching television when I came through the door. He looked up but didn't say anything.

The next day Aunty Daphne came home with the most adorable baby girl, a little cherub, just like her big sister. Uncle Jack was totally besotted with the new baby. He nursed her and sang to her, just like he had with Trudy when she was born. After dinner, when the kids had gone to bed, Aunty Daphne made Uncle Jack a pot of tea.

'So where did you go last night with that punk?' Uncle Jack asked, glaring at me over the rim of the teacup.

'To the drive-in, like I told you.'

'No you didn't,' he replied sarcastically.

I stared at him in silence. Mamma was always accusing me of telling lies about where I'd been.

'Uncle Jack, I am not a liar. We went to the drive-in.'

Aunty Daphne looked pale and frightened, like she was going to faint. No one ever spoke in her house unless spoken to, and to speak back to Uncle Jack was unheard of. He didn't tolerate insubordination of any kind. He had everyone exactly where he wanted them, submitting to his every whim.

'You are not going out with any boys again,' Uncle Jack said.

'You can't pick my friends for me,' I said, trying to remain calm.

'If you want to stay in my home, then you'll live by my rules,' he said abruptly, pushing his chair away from the table. He walked out of the house and a little while later we heard him drive away.

I could tell Aunty Daphne was very upset. 'Katie, don't talk back to him. He won't do anything to you, he'll take it out on Trudy.' She sounded scared.

'It's probably better if I leave, Aunty Daphne. I don't want to create any trouble for you or Trudy.'

Although I'd never seen Uncle Jack hit Trudy, I knew he did. I'd seen the red welts on her little legs. It seemed best for all concerned that I leave this madhouse.

'Yes, love, you're probably right. You won't change Uncle Jack's mind once it's made up.'

I looked back at her. 'Why do you put up with this?'

Suddenly she turned on me, her eyes wild. 'You mind your own business,' she snapped. 'You have no idea what's happening here. Mamma's always on my back. "Why don't you leave him?" she says. What does she know? He'll kill us all if I do that.' From what I'd seen, I knew she wasn't exaggerating.

Aunty Daphne took the tea cups to the kitchen and I went to the back room to pack my bag. I tied a new piece of rope around my case. I had no idea where I was going, and even wondered how bad it could be to live in a cave at Lake Parramatta.

As I was walking down the path to the front gate I stopped to get a better grip on the sewing machine Aunty Daphne had given me. I saw my doll Mary, a Christmas present from Uncle Stan, lying in the dirt. She had been stripped of her beautiful clothes, her hair was matted and both her legs were missing. Something made me turn around. Trudy was at the window. Her bottom lip was quivering.

19

Same old suitcase in another hall

It was a long walk, mostly uphill, from Parramatta Station to Factory Street. My arms felt like they were being pulled out of their sockets. I was carrying a suitcase in one hand and the heavy old sewing machine in the other.

It had occurred to me that I was actually homeless. If the Greys didn't have a vacancy I had no idea where I'd be sleeping that night. Some of the houses in Factory Street had boarded-up windows. I knocked on the door of a house that at least looked lived-in and was taken aback when an ugly old hag opened up and stuck her head out.

'Yes,' she said, without smiling.

'Excuse me, Mrs, could you please tell me where the Greys' boarding house is?'

'I'm Mrs Grey.'

'Is this where Dan Carlton lives?'

'Yes, he lives here.'

'I'm his sister, Kay. I was hoping you may have a room vacant.'

'I don't usually take girls,' she said, standing back from the door to let me in.

Mrs Grey told me how much board I had to pay each week and rattled off the house rules and meal times. Just in case I missed it the first time she sternly repeated, 'Under no circumstances are you to entertain men in your room.'

She showed me to my room and I was pleasantly surprised to find that it was nicely furnished. There was a lovely old rosewood dressing table and matching wardrobe. The bed had a pretty blue-and-white chenille cover. The window faced north-east, so I knew I'd get plenty of morning sunshine. I had to share a bathroom with Dan and two other male residents. There was a common dining room and a small lounge room with a television set.

I was relieved to have a roof over my head but too tired to unpack. I kicked off my shoes and fell onto the bed. Within minutes I was dead to the world. It was dark when someone knocked on my door and woke me up. 'Dinner's ready,' Mrs Grey croaked outside my door.

I tidied myself up and went to the bathroom to wash my hands before dinner. Everyone was already seated around the dining table.

Dan looked up from his plate. 'Hello, Kay,' he said and smiled, quickly returning his attention to his food.

'Hello, Dan,' I replied, taking a seat.

When Mr Grey introduced himself I was surprised that he was Mrs Grey's husband. She looked old enough to be his mother. Mr Grey was tall and quite good-looking. I couldn't understand what he possibly saw in Mrs Grey. She looked like a witch. She walked with a cane and was so stooped over she had to twist her neck to look at you when she spoke.

Dan was very chatty over dinner. He talked about his mother as if she were the epitome of motherhood. I had to bite my tongue.

The way I saw it, the moment Mamma was given the opportunity of having a better life she grabbed it with both hands, leaving Robbie, Dan and me without a thought as to how we would live. This trivial detail seemed to have escaped Dan's attention. I didn't want to sit and listen to his distorted version of reality, so I excused myself from the table.

Mr Grey worked at Reckitt and Coleman, and said they were looking for staff. The next morning I got a lift with him. I was given a test and the results showed I was too smart to work in the factory, but there was a job for a laboratory assistant. Once again I'd lied about my age, and I told them that I had the Intermediate Certificate. I knew this would become a problem because the job required that I enrol at Granville Technical College the following year. I figured I'd cross that bridge when I got there – it was eight months off, a very long time. I could never plan that far ahead. Anything could happen in the meantime.

The weather was warming up and Factory Street wasn't far from the lake. I got into my new bikini, shorts and a blouse. I could have taken the shortcut along Jeffrey Avenue, but decided to go the long way.

All the gang, including Sandy and Michael, were there. Sandy's stomach was already beginning to show. Nicky was pleased to see me. I took off my shorts and top and all the boys whistled. My new cossie was a proper bikini that showed some cleavage and my belly button. Michael looked at me and smiled. I just ignored him. Sandy got the huff and said she was going home. Michael followed her.

That day John McNorton was at the lake. He wasn't part of the lake gang, but I'd seen him around. He seemed a bit shy, but I could tell he liked me. He smiled whenever our eyes met and eventually plucked up the courage to come over and talk.

'Hello, Kay,' he said, holding his cigarette between his teeth.

'It's nice to see you,' I replied.

John wasn't easy to get a conversation going with, but we managed some basic small talk.

'Would you like a lift home?' he asked, when he saw me getting ready to leave.

John lived on O'Connell Street, close to Parramatta jail. It wasn't out of his way to drop me off at Factory Street.

'Would you like to go around with me?' he asked shyly, without looking at me, when we pulled up at the Greys'.

'Yes,' I said, 'that would nice.'

John was softly spoken and, unlike most of the other boys around the lake, he never used bad language. I liked that. He came around to pick me up every evening. After we'd been going around for about two weeks he took me to meet his family. Mrs McNorton asked me a lot of questions, but I just told her the first stupid thing that would come into my head. How could I explain my family and where I'd come from? I hadn't figured any of it out myself, and now it was all gone and didn't matter.

Mr McNorton, Harry, was a surly-looking man who didn't say much. John had two younger brothers. They were all very friendly, but there was a kind of aloofness between John and his father.

The Christmas I spent with John and his family that year was the most wonderful Christmas I'd had since Uncle Stan left home. We had roast turkey with cranberry sauce and I'd never tasted anything more delicious. Bon-bons were pulled and everyone blew the paper whistles that rolled out like goanna tongues with little feathers on the end. Even Mr Mack got into the spirit of things and put on a paper hat. Best of all, no one got drunk and ruined the day.

On my fifteenth birthday John was looking very nervous as he

143

handed me a little box wrapped in silver paper. 'Happy birthday, Kay,' he said, reaching across to kiss me.

'John!' I stared at him wide-eyed in disbelief. 'Is this an engagement ring?' It was a tiny diamond, but a diamond all the same.

'Yes, will you marry me, Kay?' he asked with a nervous smile.

I was so touched. He hadn't even tried to get into my pants, and now he was asking me to be his bride.

The McNortons gave us a little engagement party. Mrs Mack must have figured out that I had no family because she didn't ask if there was anyone I'd like to invite. John's Aunty Peggy, Mrs Mack's sister, gave us a set of 'His' and 'Hers' towels. I bought a Chinese camphor chest and started putting together my glory box.

'You are very young, Kay. I think you and John ought to wait a while before you get married,' Mrs Mack said to me that night.

A few nights after our engagement party, John became very aroused when we were kissing at the park. 'Let's get into the back seat,' he suggested.

For several months we had been leaning across the bucket seats in the front of the Volkswagon with the stick shift stuck between us preventing any real intimacy. I thought it would be nice to lie in his arms, so I agreed.

Neither of us were big people, so we had plenty of room in the back to lie down next to each other. I thought I would melt with the joy of being so close to someone who loved me but wasn't expecting anything from me.

'Now we're engaged, can we go all the way?' John asked shyly.

All the horrible memories with Michael came flooding back. I told John I was not ready. He looked hurt but said it was okay.

That night I thought about our relationship. John had been so good to me. He picked me up from Mrs Grey's drab boarding house every night and took me home to his family to have dinner. He'd given me a diamond ring and asked me to marry him before he'd even laid a hand on me. John was such a decent man, whereas Michael had just taken what he wanted without so much as a 'beg your pardon'.

The next night we went parking again. Being with John for the first time was nothing like the experience with Michael, but sex left me totally cold. I hated everything about it.

One Saturday morning while I was waiting for John to pick me up and take me to watch him play football, I polished all of the furniture in my room with liquid mahogany furniture polish, a new product from Reckitt and Coleman. Using an old torn pillowcase, I applied the polish. Everything looked and smelled wonderful. That afternoon Mrs Grey bailed me up as I came through the door.

'Pack your things and get out!' she screamed at me.

I was stunned. 'What have I done, Mrs Grey?' I said, hoping I hadn't stripped the varnish from the wardrobe.

'I told you that you were not to have men in your room.'

'I haven't had any men in my room,' I replied, indignant at the suggestion and that she'd used the plural.

'Well then, what's this?' She waved a piece of rag in my face.

I stepped back to see what she was talking about. It was the torn pillowcase. 'That's furniture polish.'

'I know male stuff when I see it. Now pack your things and get out!'

I left my things on the Greys' front verandah while I walked around the corner to the new shops at North Parramatta to phone John. A boarding house had recently opened on O'Connell Street, adjacent to the new Parramatta Leagues Club. It was like a hotel, so I thought they'd probably still have some vacancies. I asked John if he would pick me up and take me there. As we drove away from the Greys' I told him what had happened and, somewhat embarrassed by the question, asked what sperm looked like.

'What do you mean?'

'What colour is it?'

'It's white . . .'

'But the polish was pink.' I burst out laughing.

John waited while I checked if there were any rooms available at the new boarding house. There was only one share room left on the ground floor. At nine pounds a week full board it was more than half my pay, but I took it.

As I stumbled down the narrow hall at O'Connell House to find my room, I bumped into a man coming the other way.

'Sorry, whacka. Let me help you with that and all,' he said, taking the sewing machine. 'Bloody hell! This is heavy.'

'Try carrying it two miles uphill,' I said.

Peter had the most beautiful smile I had ever seen. He told me he'd come from Liverpool in England, that a 'whacka' was a mate and he was 'chuffed' to meet me. My roommate, Rita, came from London and spoke with a very strong accent too. She was fanatical about her grooming, and getting ready for bed was a real production. She brushed her hair a hundred times every night, smothered her body in oil and slept in the nude. With no flyscreens on the windows, Rita's warm sweet-smelling flesh was a magnet for the mosquitoes that feasted on her throughout the night. 'I hate this place! I want to go home,' she'd wail, slapping her body.

The next night when I came in for dinner, Peter motioned me with his hand, inviting me to join him and his friends at their table. 'This is my brother John,' he said, pointing across the table at a nice-looking man who seemed a few years older than him. Going around the table he introduced the other men. They all spoke with broad accents and while they might have known what each other was saying, I was completely lost.

Rita had told me not to leave my washing unattended on the clothesline. 'They'll steal anything around here, even your knickers!'

One Saturday afternoon I was wearing my new bikini, which was a daring two inches below my navel, and a top that pushed my cleavage together. I hadn't plucked up the courage to wear it in public yet, but it was quiet at the house so I was on the roof sunbathing and standing guard while my washing dried.

'Well, look at you, kid,' a voice said.

I looked up. Peter was licking his lips and rolling his eyes. I reached for my towel.

'Now, what did you want to do that for and all?'

Peter was only wearing shorts, no shirt. His muscles were defined and there wasn't an ounce of fat on his hairless brown body. His teeth were so white and perfect they didn't look real. His hair was jet black and he had the most amazing brown eyes. We talked for a long time. He told me about the voyage to Australia and the fun he'd had on the ship. He was really missing his mother and sister, who were still in England.

Every night I looked forward to dinnertime and the conversations around the table. The older men were engaged in an ongoing – and often heated – debate about the Vietnam conflict. They didn't call the conflict a war at that time, but it seemed to be escalating, and the general feeling was that Australia had no business being part of it.

Spending time with John McNorton became more and more tedious. All we did was go to his mother's for dinner, play Scrabble and have sex in the back of his car. It was coming up to the ANZAC Day holiday in April, and Peter had asked me if I would join him and a group from O'Connell House for a picnic in Parramatta Park.

'Thank you, Peter, but I don't think my fiancé would appreciate that,' I said.

'Then don't bring him,' Peter replied, with a cheeky grin.

Peter worked in a factory just one street away from Reckitt and Coleman. One afternoon as I was leaving work he was waiting at the gate.

'What are you doing here?' I asked.

'Waiting for you. The company I work for is having its annual ball and I was wondering if you'd like to come with me.'

My relationship with John was making me more miserable by the day. We never talked about anything, never went anywhere or did anything that might stimulate conversation. I felt like I was just a convenience for sex.

I told Peter I'd love to go with him but I'd have to break up with John first. Peter looked like he was going to burst with happiness. He reached across and gave me a kiss on the cheek. I nearly melted at his touch.

'The ball's on May the 8th,' he said, then cracked me a smile.

That only gave me a couple of weeks to break the bad news to John. I decided it was better to get it over with. When John came to see me that night I told him that I was breaking off our engagement.

'It's that Peter guy, isn't it?' he said, looking very hurt.

I tried to let him down gently. 'I haven't been happy with our relationship for some time, John. I don't love you enough to marry you.' I removed my engagement ring and gestured to hand it back to him.

'Keep it,' he said.

'No, I can't do that.'

'I don't want it,' he said, walking away.

At the ball, men lined up to dance with me.

'Where did you learn to dance like this?' Deanie, a mate of Peter's, asked as he took my hand for another go-around of the Gypsy Tap.

'My Uncle Stan taught me.'

As Peter and I danced the last slow dances together, he held me close to him. This was the first time I had danced like this with anyone, and it would be the last time I'd dance for more than a decade.

When Peter and I got back to O'Connell House I felt intoxicated even though alcohol had not passed my lips. He didn't need to do too much sweet talking to get me to his room.

20

Facing the music

'Oh my God, Katie. Are you sure?'

I'd just told Rita that I thought I might be pregnant. 'No, but I think I better make an appointment to see a doctor.'

'Yes, you better, love. I'll go with you, if you like.'

Rita tried to keep the conversation light as we walked down O'Connell Street towards Parramatta.

'Here it is,' she said, looking at the piece of paper I'd scribbled the address onto.

'Oh no! I've been here before,' I said, baulking at the door. It was the same place where I'd been given the virginity test only two years earlier. I had no idea what the doctor's name was, but I did recall he was an older man. The doctor I made this appointment with sounded quite young on the telephone.

After waiting for a few minutes, a friendly looking man with a stethoscope around his neck came out to the reception room. 'Miss Carlton?'

To save a lot of tedious explaining I continued to use Mamma's previous name rather than my own surname, which was only ever used at school. 'That's me,' I said with a grimace.

'Follow me, please,' he said and he led me down the short hallway.

'What seems to be the problem?' he asked, smiling while motioning me to take a seat next to his desk.

I felt myself blush as I told him.

'When did you have your last period?' He took a thick rubber strip and wrapped it around my upper arm before pressing several times on a little pump. I felt some pressure building up in my arm.

'Early April? Maybe . . .' I must have sounded like a complete dope.

After some other preliminary questions he asked me to sit on the bench and he pulled a screen around us. As he did the examination I closed my eyes and clenched my teeth.

'I have some bad news for you,' he announced a few minutes later. 'You are approximately eight weeks pregnant.'

News of a pregnancy ought to be a joyous occasion, but in 1965 for an unmarried fifteen-year-old girl, it was a tragedy of monumental proportions. Mamma was going to have a field day.

'If you're going to do something about this pregnancy, you need to make up your mind almost immediately.'

The doctor didn't actually say 'abortion' but I knew what he meant. He paused. A long silence fell between us.

'When is my baby due, doctor?'

'Around the 29th of January next year.'

'Thank you, doctor,' I said, getting up to leave.

'You are a brave girl, Miss Carlton.'

At least he didn't call me foolish.

'Oh my God, what are you going to do?' Rita asked when I told her. 'You're not going to have it, surely?'

'As far as I know the only way I'm not going to have a baby is if I have an abortion,' I said.

'Well, sometimes that is the only sensible thing to do.'

There was nothing about having an abortion that seemed sensible to me. For a start abortions were illegal, but even if they hadn't been I wouldn't have had one. I wasn't going to do what Phyllis had, either to myself or my unborn child. This was my baby and no one could take it away. This wasn't a bicycle or a doll. This was my child and I felt a fierce protectiveness towards it, even though it was still only a tiny embryo. Besides, it was the first time in my life I'd had some control.

'I will never have an abortion!' I said, almost shouting.

As we strolled slowly back to O'Connell House, Rita sensed that I wanted to be left alone with my thoughts. She squeezed my hand from time to time, letting me know she was there to talk if I needed to. *I'm pregnant, I'm having a baby*, I repeated over and over in my head, trying to get this fact to sink in so I could start to figure out what I was going to do.

Peter was beaming. 'I've got some great news!' he said.

'I have some news too. But you tell me yours first,' I said.

He'd been called up to start his basic army training and had to report to Woodside in South Australia on 4 August. He could hardly manage to contain his boyish excitement at going into the army.

'That's great, Peter,' I said, biting my lip.

Although this news wasn't unexpected, the confirmation of Peter being called up for National Service still left a hollow feeling in the pit of my stomach. He would possibly be shipped off to Vietnam, where the situation was getting worse, even if the propaganda machine in Australia was playing it down. Why he thought it was such great news to be going into the army and risking getting killed in a war we had no business being in was beyond me.

When I told him my news, Peter was aghast. 'It's not mine! It can't be mine. I had the mumps when I was a kid – I'm sterile.'

His reaction shocked me to my core and I didn't believe him for a moment. I just stood there dumbfounded, unable to speak. It felt like a cold stake had just been driven through my heart. *Where did all the 'I love you, Katie's go?* I thought to myself, words he had spoken only a day earlier. Did he think I would say I was having his baby if I knew it wasn't his? Did he imagine that I would try to entrap him?

'This baby isn't yours,' I reassured him. 'But I wish it was.'

'Are you going to get rid of it?'

'No,' I said angrily.

Peter stormed off to the pub, saying he was going to celebrate his army admission with his mates.

There was no point calling John to tell him that I was pregnant. I didn't want him to know that I was having his child. There was only one thing for me to do. I'd have to go back to Mamma's and face the music.

Dan had moved from the Greys' and was now living in the dump next to O'Connell House. We seldom saw each other, but occasionally I'd bump into him on the street. I told him I needed to get in touch with Mamma and asked for her address.

'She's at Merrinong Merino Stud in Dubbo,' he told me.

'So that's it?'

'Yes, a letter addressed to Mrs Hadlow at Merrinong Merino Stud, Dubbo, will find her.'

That night I wrote to Mamma and Frank asking whether I could come for a visit. Mamma replied saying that she and Frank would meet me at Dubbo station, and I should just let her know when I'd be arriving.

On the morning before I was due to leave, I'd just finished packing and was lying on my bed resting when the manager of O'Connell House knocked on my door. 'Kay, there's a lady at reception asking about you.'

'Asking about me?'

'Yes, and she's very attractive.'

I had no idea who would be calling to see me, but the fact that my visitor was an attractive woman meant at least it probably wasn't some drab welfare officer again.

'Hello, Katie,' Phyllis said, smiling. She did indeed look very smart in her figure-hugging, red-and-white polka dot dress. At that moment, I felt proud that she was my mother.

'What are you doing here?' I asked, surprised, wondering how on earth she'd managed to find me. I'd forgotten that Dan was a prolific letter writer and had probably told Uncle Stan where I'd been staying.

'Janet's in the car. Would like to see her?'

'Of course! I'd love to.'

The last time I'd seen my little sister she was covered in jam and cream and screaming my name as she was carried from our house in Jeffrey Avenue. That had been more than five years ago. When Janet saw me she started jumping around like an over-excited puppy. She had grown so much – and she was the image of Phyllis.

'Hello, Janet,' I said, giving her a big hug. She clung to me like a limpet.

'We're going back to Cooma. Would you like to come with us?' Phyllis asked.

'When are you leaving?'

'Right now, today.'

154

'Thank you, but I'm going back to Mamma's tomorrow.'

'Why would you want to go and see that old bitch?' she snapped angrily. 'She never did much for you.'

That was probably true, but from where she stood Phyllis was in no position to throw stones.

'Goodbye, Janet,' I said, giving my little sister another big hug.

'Goodbye, Katie,' she said, waving, tears streaming down her face.

Phyllis gave me a kiss and got into the car without giving me her address or letting me know how to contact her. That was the first and last time my mother kissed me. I never saw her again, and it would be more than thirty-five years before my sister and I were reunited.

21

Paperwork

It was cold and blustery the night in August when Peter and Deanie took me to Parramatta station to catch the train to Dubbo. The train was already waiting at the station, and Peter was getting very anxious. I don't think he wanted to cry in front of Deanie.

'Don't worry, Katie, I'll write to you every day and when I get out of the army we'll get married,' Peter said, and he kissed me one last time.

Deanie was crying. 'If he doesn't marry you, I will,' he said, hugging me.

I didn't sleep a wink all night, trying to think how I was going to break the news to Mamma. The train pulled into Dubbo station around eleven the next morning. Frank waved when he saw me.

'G'day, Katie,' he said, beaming.

'Hello, Frank,' I said, giving him a hug.

'The car's parked right out the front.' He stepped back to let me go ahead of him. 'There's something on the back seat that belongs to you.'

It was the Akubra hat I'd left behind after my unceremonious expulsion from Nudgawalla. I put it on my head. It was a bit snug. My head had grown since I'd last worn the hat, but I was really touched that Frank had held on to it for me.

'Where's Mamma?' I asked.

'She's doing some shopping. We'll pick her up on the way.'

We found Mamma standing out the front of Fosseys, loaded up with parcels. Frank leapt out of the car to put the parcels in the boot, and I got out too to give Mamma the front passenger seat.

'Hello, love, how have you been?' she asked casually, as if she'd only seen me last week. In fact, we hadn't seen, or spoken, to each other since she'd left Jeffrey Avenue two years earlier.

On the drive to Merrinong, Mamma prattled on with all kinds of town gossip, name-dropping all over the place about how important this or that person was, and if they were related to Frank. I was grateful for Frank's slow, careful driving, and the sealed road connecting Dubbo with Gilgandra.

'When you're ready, Katie,' he said when he stopped at the first gate.

As I lifted the chain I could feel Mamma's gaze go right through me. I was four months pregnant, and, although I hoped I wasn't showing, nothing much got past Mamma's probing eyes.

We pulled up in front of a neat, cream-painted fibro cottage. Mamma had the remnants of what would have been a nice garden before the drought worsened.

'Home, sweet home, I'll be so glad to get out of this corset,' she sighed. Three gorgeous lambs came up to greet us, bleating and demanding attention. 'Hello, my babies,' Mamma said tenderly as the little balls of wool on legs jumped over the top of each other. 'They're called Little Joe, Adam and Hoss,' she said, reaching down to pat each of them on the nose. She'd named them after the brothers in *Bonanza*, the television show about a family of ranch-ers, which Mamma never missed.

As we passed a large aviary Mamma started to whistle the tune 'It's a long way to Tipperary'. The birds joined in, matching her tune note for note. 'Oh, my clever boys,' she chirped as she passed the cage. I had just witnessed more tenderness from Mamma in the space of five minutes than I'd seen in my life. Being married to Frank clearly agreed with her.

Mamma's house was immaculate as usual, even if the furniture from Jeffrey Avenue looked completely out of place in this coun-try setting. This was especially true for the massive vases arranged with plastic gladioli, the crushed velvet curtains and the venetian blinds.

'You can sleep in the spare room at the back,' she said, carrying some of the parcels to her room.

It was a very pleasant room that looked onto what would have been a river before the drought. I was pleased to see flyscreens on the windows because the black horseflies in the bush had teeth. I opened the window wide to catch whatever breeze might drift by. I took a deep breath. I loved the smell of the Australian bush, that earthy mixture of rich red dirt and dried gum leaves that lifted my spirits every time I got a whiff of it.

'We haven't got much left in the tanks, so go easy on the water,' Mamma said.

We had just finished lunch when Mamma turned to me. 'How far gone are you?' she asked bluntly.

I had been hoping that she might give me at least a day to settle in before we had to deal with that issue. I did a quick calculation in my head from May to August. 'About four months,' I said, my eyes cast downwards, trying not to look at her.

'You're too far gone to get rid of it.'

'I don't want to get rid of it,' I replied, pulling my head up sharply.

'Well, don't think you're staying here to shame me with the townspeople,' she said, her face growing dark.

If I couldn't stay here, what did she have in mind for me? As I was pondering this she flew at me.

'You dirty little slut! You're just like your fucking mother,' she screamed, grabbing me by the hair and slapping me around the head.

After all the beatings I had taken in my life she couldn't hurt me, at least not with her hands. If I had tried to stop her, she would have exploded and picked up the first object to hand. So I just took it, until she had exhausted her self, screaming, slapping and cursing. She stormed into her bedroom and slammed the door shut.

'What have I ever done to deserve this?' she howled.

This pitiful wailing went on unabated for hours. I thought that after she cried herself out everything might be alright. Frank and I were having breakfast the next morning when she finally surfaced.

'You and your big belly! Like I said, you're not staying here. You'll have to go to the nuns.' Her eyes were glazed over and her nostrils flared. She flew at me again, slapping me around the face and head with a barrage of blows. 'You fucking little bitch! After all I've done for you. You go and do this to me?'

Frank looked horrified. 'Stop it, Sally, the girl's pregnant,' he said, standing between us.

'Pregnant, I'll give her fucking pregnant. What have I done to deserve this?' she shrieked, before retreating to her room where she resumed the sulking and wailing routine.

Frank looked more than bewildered. He had just seen a side to his sweet bride that he never knew existed. I went to my room and didn't come out for the rest of the day, although I badly wanted to ask her what she meant when she said I could go to the nuns.

A few days later Mamma told me that she had made arrangements for me to go to a place called St Margaret's to have the baby. There was no discussion as to what would happen to us after the birth, but, with nowhere else to go, I presumed we would go back to her place. It seemed that shaming her with my big belly was the issue; I reasoned that after the baby was born I would no longer have a big belly and things would settle down.

'If you know who the father is, you'll have to write to him for some money,' Mamma said. 'I haven't got any and I can't ask Frank to give you some.'

It was hard to write to John. I told him I was going to St Margaret's Hospital to have the baby and left it up to him to send me whatever he could. While we waited for a reply from John I stayed in my room, only coming out for meals. The very sight of me was like a red rag to a bull to Mamma, who shot me hateful looks and snarled through clenched teeth.

One morning when I collected the mail there was a letter from John's mother. The note was brief and it enclosed a money order for a hundred pounds. I was a bit annoyed that John had even told his mother that I was pregnant, and that he hadn't replied to me himself. Not a word. He didn't want this baby either.

Robbie had been conscripted into the army and came to say goodbye to Mamma before his basic training at Puckapunyal. The day he arrived he found me sitting beside the dried river bed reading some letters from Peter.

'Who's the father?' he asked, dispensing with any pleasantries.

'None of your business,' I replied, without shifting my attention from the letter.

'Who's the father?' he demanded.

I stood up to face him. 'What are you going to do, tough man? Knock me to the ground?'

He stormed off. I hadn't told Mamma who the father of the baby was. I couldn't trust either her or Robbie not to make trouble for John McNorton. The next morning Robbie left without saying goodbye to me.

The trip from Dubbo back to Sydney was a blur. I didn't sleep all night. Finally the train pulled into Central station and Mamma and I walked straight to Coles on Liverpool Street for maternity dresses. After going through the racks of pathetic-looking sacks, I found three that were reasonable. I paid for them with some of the money Mrs McNorton had sent me.

We caught a bus that let us off at the big iron gates of an impressive sandstone building. It looked like a prison. I was relieved when we crossed the road. We walked down a filthy windswept street, its gutters choked with waste papers, garbage and bottles. The pungent smell of cat piss lingered in the air as we picked our way through the maggoty garbage strewn all over the pavement.

An old blackfella was sitting on the footpath, propped up against the door of a pub. He had a bottle wrapped in brown paper between his legs. 'Got a smoke, sister?' he asked, holding out his hand as we approached. Mamma stopped, took a cigarette from her bag and handed it to him. 'Bless you, sister,' he said, taking the cigarette from her hand. He put it to his mouth and Mamma lit the match for him. 'Thank you, sister,' he said, smiling.

'Here we are,' Mamma said, turning to walk up some steps.

As she pushed open the frosted glass doors there was no

mistaking that this was a hospital. We waited in the reception area, where a huge portrait of a gentle-looking nun dressed in the traditional habit hung on the wall.

'That's Sister Mary MacKillop,' Mamma said, pointing at the portrait. 'She's the founder of the Sisters of St Joseph of the Sacred Heart, who run this hospital.'

Mamma's knowledge didn't surprise me; she'd spent time in a convent as a girl and never had anything nice to say about the nuns. She used to tell me horrific stories about babies' bones being dug up in the convent gardens.

About an hour passed before a nun dressed in a white habit came over to us. 'Sister Anne will see you now,' she announced, before leading us into an office.

Seated behind a large wooden desk was a tiny woman whose heavy brown habit seemed to engulf her. Her mouth smiled but her piercing grey eyes were cold. 'We have some paperwork to complete, Mrs Hadlow,' Sister Anne said, looking at us over her wire-rimmed glasses.

She asked a few questions about our family's health; of course, none of the questions on my father's side of the family could be answered. Then she placed a document in front of Mamma and handed her a pen. Mamma signed it. Sister Anne smiled.

'Please sign here,' she said, handing the pen to me and pointing to a pencil cross at the bottom of the page. The document was written in legal mumbo jumbo.

'What is this?' I asked.

'It is the consent form, dear. Just sign here.' She again pointed to the spot where I was to sign. Just above were the words 'I hereby relinquish all rights to the child.'

I put down the pen. 'This form is saying that I will give my baby away.'

'Yes, dear, this is the consent for adoption.'

I turned to Mamma. She was trying to look as if it were perfectly normal that someone would give me such a document to sign.

'I am not giving my baby away.'

'Now don't be silly, Katie. You know you can't keep the baby,' Mamma said in her best put-on voice.

This was too much for me to grasp. I sat in silence, trying to hold back my tears. We sat staring at each other, neither of us prepared to crack first.

Sister Anne finally broke the impasse. 'You have had a long journey. We will talk about this later.'

Mamma got up to leave. 'You'll be alright here, love. The nuns will take good care of you.' And then she was gone.

All my life Mamma had told me what cruel, evil bitches the nuns were and now they were going to look after me.

Sister Anne made a brief phone call and a young nun, not much older than me, came into her office.

'Sister Veronica, this is Kay. She will be with us until January next year. Please show her where the girls' home is and let her know the house rules.'

'Yes, Sister.' Sister Veronica smiled at me. 'Kay, please follow me.'

Sister Veronica looked to be about nineteen years old. She wore a white habit and the short veil of a novice nun. She was cheerful and chatty as she led the way down a path behind the main building. We approached a decrepit two-storey house that reminded me of Norman Bates's house in the horror thriller *Psycho*. I'd seen the movie with Dan and it scared the wits out of me. This place would be home for the next five months, until my baby was born. Where we would go after that was anyone's guess.

22

Unwed mothers

St Margaret's Home for Unwed Mothers was a former Victorian mansion. In its day it would have been the residence of an upper middle-class family. Important people would have left calling cards and received invitations to take tea in the parlour. By 1965 it resembled a tired old workhorse that was being flogged to keep it going. Everything about this place reeked of misery and sadness; any hint of hospitality and warmth had long been extinguished.

'This is the kitchen,' Sister Veronica said, showing no signs that the revolting mess was anything out of the norm. 'The girls cook their own meals from food supplied from the hospital.'

One glance told me all I needed to know about the girls I would be living with. 'How many are staying here?' I asked.

'We have about forty at the moment.'

'And this is the laundry,' she said, standing in the doorway of a room with no door.

I guessed the door had been removed to accommodate the rope that crisscrossed the room and sagged under the weight of all the wet washing. There was one beaten-up Hoover washing machine. Everything smelled dank and musty. The skirting boards were covered in a furry green mould.

'Are there any lines outside to dry our clothes?' I asked.

'The girls are not permitted to hang their clothes outside,' she said.

'Here is the recreation room,' Sister Veronica announced as we entered a dingy cavernous room. Positioned in front of a small television set was a cluster of filthy armchairs.

'We only use first names here, and if you want to change your name to protect your privacy, that's allowed. You are not permitted to leave the hospital grounds. And under no circumstances are you to have male visitors who are not related to you.'

I was hoping this induction wasn't going to take much longer. My bladder was full. I started jigging up and down.

'There is no smoking and, of course, there is no alcohol allowed in the house. The dormitory is upstairs. We don't allocate rooms – just find one that's unoccupied, move in and claim it.'

I squeezed my knees together, thinking, *Hurry up!*

'You can have the weekend to settle in and acquaint yourself with things before you report to work on Monday morning.'

'Sister, I need to go to the toilet.'

'Yes, yes, of course.'

Sister Veronica would have been aware that being pregnant makes the need 'to go' more frequent. She told me that she'd wait, as I needed to know the work schedules.

Now that I was comfortable, I could take in more. She talked so fast it was hard keeping up, but I got the gist of it. I was given a job, working eight hours a day for six and a half days a week. This represented a fifty-two hour week, and for the first time I hadn't needed to lie about my age or education at the job interview.

'Sister, I have one question. How much do we get paid for the work we do?'

'Paid? My goodness no, you don't get paid. The work you do is to keep you occupied and pay for your keep for the time you're here,' she said, eyebrows raised at my nerve.

The clock on the wall was at three, which explained why the house was deserted. The dormitory was a huge room with high ceilings. A corridor ran the length of the space with about twenty doors on each side; the flimsy plywood partitioning only reached slightly above the height of the doors and was painted a dull brown.

Gently, I knocked on the first door and, when I didn't get a reply, peeked inside. The room was obviously occupied. Some pretty underwear was drying on a makeshift clothesline strung from the end of the bed to a chair. The bed had been made and I could see that whoever occupied the room was very neat and tidy.

The rooms, more like cells, were about six feet by nine, with barely enough space for the single bed, small wardrobe and chair. The rooms on the left side of the corridor had windows. The rooms on the right were claustrophobic boxes, with the only light and air coming from above the partition. I was hoping that a room with a window would be vacant.

What a relief when I opened the last door and saw that the bed had been stripped and the wardrobe was empty. Every surface in the room was encrusted with years of caked dirt, and the floor looked like it hadn't seen hot water and a mop for decades. The ancient wardrobe had no locks and the chair was dangerously wobbly. I sat on the bed and there was no give; it was as hard as a park bench.

There was no way I could live with all this dirt and dust around, so I left my things on the bed and picked my way through the mess in the kitchen. I found a bottle of methylated spirits, a saucepan without a handle that would have to serve as a bucket, and a reasonably clean tea towel. For the next two hours I went into a cleaning frenzy, scrubbing my room from top to bottom. I couldn't find a mop, so I got down on my hands and knees and washed the filthy linoleum. While the floor was drying I found a cupboard that contained a pile of old sheets and pillowcases and a grey woollen blanket that felt like a steel-wool blend. After I'd made the bed and unpacked my things I was exhausted. For two days we had been travelling with very little rest. I lay down on the bed. The smell of the methylated spirits was overpowering. I coughed and the baby stirred.

'Yes, little one, we have had a big day,' I said, rubbing my hand over my tummy reassuringly.

Sister Veronica hadn't mentioned any rules about sending or receiving letters. I knew that if I couldn't get letters from Peter I would go insane. He'd made all kinds of promises about our future together when he got out of the army, and, even though that was too far off for me to even think about, I needed his tender words to help combat the loneliness and fear. Cut off from the outside world, just believing that someone out there cared about me, would keep me from completely unravelling and going bonkers. I took out a bundle of Peter's letters from my case and read them until I couldn't keep my eyes open.

I woke to the sound of a stampede coming up the stairs, followed by doors banging and girls screeching abuse at each other.

'That's mine, you bitch! You stole it,' someone screamed.

A very pregnant girl barged into my room without knocking. 'Get out of here! This is my room!' she shrieked.

'I'm sorry, I was told by the sister to take any room that was vacant,' I replied, without attempting to get up from the bed.

'Well you can just get your things and get out. This room's going to be mine.'

I had no intention of being stood over by anyone. I got up from the bed and faced her squarely. 'This room is mine and I'm not moving anywhere. So get out!'

Bidura had taught me how to deal with institutional bullies.

'You bitch!' she said, snarling, before turning and slamming the door behind her.

I hoped that the rest of the girls were going to be a little friendlier.

The bathroom was on the same floor as the dormitory, but there were only four shower cubicles for the forty or so girls. I hadn't packed a towel and none seemed to be supplied. After the water restrictions at Mamma's, it felt very extravagant to turn the taps for an instant shower. With hot water cascading all over my body, I cranked both taps to full and turned around and around, letting the hot water hit me with maximum force. It felt like thousands of little pin prickles massaging my back and neck and tingling all over my body. I groaned with pleasure after the long journey and hours of cleaning. There was no soap so I couldn't have a proper wash, but for now this was blissful. I squeezed as much water as I could from my hair and dried myself off with the dress I'd been wearing. I put on one of my new dresses and went downstairs to the kitchen to see if I could muster up something to eat.

It was a miracle that none of the girls got ptomaine poisoning. No one ever bothered to wash a dish or wipe a bench clean. Squashed cockroach carcasses littered the floor and mice droppings were over every surface. The white enamel on the stove top barely managed to peep through the rancid, baked-on overspills. Streams of grease ran down both sides of the stove, like trails of orange snot. The place should have been under quarantine, awaiting fumigation.

Having determined that there was nothing edible in the fridge, I checked the cupboards and found more cockroaches. I managed to find a carton of eggs and some thin white sliced bread. There was only one two-slice toaster and a kettle to boil water. I looked around to find something to boil my eggs in and discovered that the only saucepan in the place was the one I had used as a bucket. While the eggs were boiling I managed to find a plate that wasn't chipped, a glass and some cutlery. I washed the lot in very hot water.

Apart from the girl who had tried to bounce me out of my room, most of the other girls were friendly enough. But this wasn't a place where friendships would be forged. This was worse than an institution. In my experience institutions were orderly and hygienic, with rules and regulations that were supervised by staff. The only rules at St Margaret's were the ones I'd been told about – no smoking, drinking, entertaining male visitors or leaving the grounds without permission. Otherwise it was anarchy. The constant squabbles, even over somewhere to sit, were often violent. You had to watch everything you owned and stealing underwear from the clothesline was rife, which explained the makeshift clotheslines in the rooms. Since there were no locks on the doors, this didn't stop the really desperate girls. Leaving money in your room was as good as asking to lose it. We were reduced to living like outcasts and had to do the best we could to survive.

From what I could tell, all of the girls at St Margaret's were from Christian families, and they were all white. Some had come voluntarily, because they didn't want to bring the shame of a 'bastard' child onto the family. Being a bastard still carried a big stigma among white Christian families in the 1960s, and it was considered the norm to send unmarried pregnant daughters to homes like St Margaret's.

Conversations between the girls at St Margaret's were always guarded. No one really wanted anyone to know where they came from. There was never any discussion about the babies we were carrying but I gathered from the girls I spoke to that all of them had already signed the consent for adoption. The deal had been done and they had resigned themselves to the fact that the baby they were carrying wasn't theirs. The word 'mother' had been expunged from everyone's vocabulary. They were just the incubators. Whenever the nuns spoke about us collectively, it was always as 'the girls' – never 'the mothers'.

During the day many of the girls walked around like zombies, with vacant looks in their eyes. Never speaking, never smiling, some were only seen when they were working, choosing to spend the rest of their time in seclusion in their cramped cells. Being confined to St Margaret's was worse than serving a prison sentence. At least in prison we would have received three cooked meals a day and there would have been some kind of library, recreation, exercise or educational facilities available. This place was desolate. Night was the worst time, when the sound of heart-wrenching sobs filled the dormitory.

Karen, the girl with the tidy room and pretty underwear, shared a birthday with me, but she was a year older and would be seventeen the following year. From the way she dressed and spoke it was obvious that she came from a wealthy family. After her baby was born she was going back to school to finish her education at one of Sydney's exclusive girls' schools. Karen told me that her family was supportive and it had been agreed by both families that Karen and her boyfriend, Ian, were much too young to get married. As compensation for giving up her baby and a reward for not bringing shame on her family, Karen's parents had promised to buy her a car for her next birthday. To trade your own flesh and blood like that was way beyond my range of thinking.

Diana, the youngest girl in the home, was only about eleven

years old and blissfully unaware of her plight. The staff and nuns referred to Diana as the 'slow kiddie'. As her belly grew bigger, there was no more tragic sight than Diana sucking her thumb, and clutching a doll. Diana's father, who travelled with a circus, had dropped her off on his way north. By the time he was travelling south again, Diana would have had her baby with no one suspecting that Daddy had been a naughty boy.

Eileen was a married woman. Her husband was in the navy and spent a good deal of time at sea. When Eileen got pregnant and knew she couldn't pass the child off as her husband's, she came to St Margaret's. She was carrying the third baby she had given up through St Margaret's. Because she wasn't an unmarried mother, strictly speaking, the nuns treated her differently from the rest of us.

'Why don't you have an abortion?' I asked. It seemed like a reasonable question to put to a woman who didn't want to keep the child anyway.

'I'm a Catholic and abortion is a sin against the church,' she said, looking a little shocked at the suggestion.

Adultery was alright, I supposed. After all, a quick visit to the confessional booth and, voila, she'd be absolved.

Although the nuns didn't live up to the terrible stories of Mamma's childhood, they left we girls at the home in no doubt that they thought we were wicked, contemptible creatures. Some of the hard-faced old crones looked away to avoid acknowledging our presence whenever we passed them in the corridors.

'So how will I know when my baby is coming?' I asked Eileen, feeling embarrassed by my ignorance.

'You'll start to get some pain, which will get worse. Your waters may even break,' she explained.

'What happens then?' I asked, feeling anxious.

'You'll be taken to the labour ward. You'll be shown how to use the mask. This will lessen the pain and sedate you so you don't try to see the baby when you hear it cry. They won't tell you if it's a boy or a girl. It's better not to know.'

The thought of not seeing or holding your baby, or knowing if it was a boy or girl, was just too horrific to contemplate.

'Then what happens?' My anxiety was increasing.

'They bind your breasts to stop the milk production. Then you are taken over to the private ward. You'll get a room all to yourself to recover. They don't put you into the public ward with all the other mothers and their babies.'

I asked her how long they kept you in hospital after the baby was born.

'About ten days,' she replied. 'Unless you have a caesarean.'

Shivering with revulsion, recalling Aunty Daphne's scars, I asked, 'What happens to the baby?'

'There's a waiting list of parents wanting to adopt newborns. They'll have a couple waiting for your child to be born.' Eileen made it sound as blasé as someone requesting a popular library book.

'So people put their name down to get someone else's baby?' I asked, trying to get my head around the process.

'Lots of women can't have children, so they adopt.'

'Do they have to pay for the babies, or do they just give them away?' I asked.

'I'd imagine they pay something to someone, somewhere along the line. Perhaps they give a generous donation to the church.'

At night in my cubicle, while my baby danced around making his presence felt, I promised him that I would never, ever give him up for adoption. The bond I felt with my child could not be broken by anyone at any price, and my determination that no one would take him away from me was unshakeable.

My problem was working out how I would stop them.

23

Light duties

It was Sunday afternoon and the girls at the home were on free time. The queue to the laundry was as endless as the squabbling about where someone was in the line for the toilet. The weather was lovely, so I went outside and sat on the front step. A light breeze picked up the scent of the English lavender growing wild in front of the house – it reminded me of Aunty Daphne. A girl walked up from behind me.

'G'day, my name's Cheryl,' she said, offering me a cigarette from the packet she pulled out of her bra.

'Hello, I'm Kay. Thank you, but I don't smoke,' I replied.

'Neither did I until I came here,' she said, chuckling.

Cheryl's eyes darted in all directions and she listened intently before lighting the match. She sucked hard on the cigarette, drawing the smoke deep into her lungs and holding it. She started coughing and spluttering, reminding me of the first and last cigarette I ever put in my mouth.

Cheryl was about twenty, and by the look of her she was ready to have her baby any day. Like me, she had been in Bidura as a kid, and we swapped stories about our experiences. She gave me the run-down on the work duties and other tips for survival.

'Keep your head down and don't draw attention to yourself. Sister Anne will make your life a bloody misery if she doesn't like you,' she warned.

'Well I'm in for a rough time. She wasn't happy with me for not signing the adoption papers.'

Cheryl stopped puffing. She stared at me for a long time before speaking.

'What? You haven't signed the papers? You aren't thinking about keeping it, are you?'

'I am not going to give up my baby. I have a boyfriend but he isn't the father of the baby. He wants to marry me when he gets out of the army. He's a nasho.'

'You're off your rocker. I don't want the kid,' she said in a voice that wasn't convincing.

Even acknowledging their pregnancies was difficult for the girls at the home, and I could see that Cheryl was uncomfortable. She stubbed out the cigarette and put the butt into her pocket. The nuns often inspected the garden, looking for evidence that the girls had been smoking.

That night I lay in bed feeling my baby moving, fantasising about living with Peter in a cute little house with a white picket fence and a rose garden. The next morning I was up, showered, dressed and sitting on the front verandah catching the morning sun, as Sister Veronica arrived to ring the wake-up bell.

'Where will I be working, Sister?'

'You can start in the laundry. Cheryl will show you where to go.' She smiled, gripping the wooden handle of the brass bell with both hands. *No one will sleep through that!* I thought, cupping my ears. Sister Veronica seemed to enjoy this part of her duties.

We were not allowed to enter the laundry via the front entrance, so we had to walk around the hospital complex to the back door.

'You're gonna love Quasi,' Cheryl said, cackling as she waddled ahead like Mrs Puddle-duck.

Cheryl had nicknamed the laundry supervisor 'Quasimodo', or Quasi for short. She had nicknames for all the nuns. 'Mother Hubbard' certainly suited Sister Veronica.

'Come on, Quasi,' Cheryl called out, thumping her hand against the metal doors at the back entrance of the laundry room. 'We ain't got all day,' she added with a giggle.

As I stepped inside, the stench nearly bowled me over. Wire mesh trolleys parked against one wall were crammed with heavily soiled nappies and bed linen that looked like it had been used to mop up after the St Valentine's Day massacre. A swarm of blowflies dumped maggot eggs, wriggling with life, on a pile of soiled sanitary rags on the floor. I looked away. Nothing turned my stomach more quickly than maggots.

It was my job to transfer the dirty laundry from the floor to the tub of cold water to soak, then move on to another tub containing rags that had been soaking overnight. These had to be fished out with a long wooden pole and tossed into metal buckets, which were taken to the water extractor. The machine started off slowly before revving to a squeal that sounded like a cat was being mangled in the cogs. I then had to transfer the rags to another tub, which contained a solution of bleach so strong it sent me into a coughing spasm.

There were about ten commercial dryers along one wall. More wire trolleys were stacked with wet washing waiting to go into the dryers, and others held nappies and rags to be folded and counted into bundles of twelve and tied together with white tape.

By eight-thirty in the morning, after the washers and driers had been roaring at full capacity for two hours, the hot humid air had turned the laundry into a steam bath. The fumes from this foul-smelling cocktail of urine, blood, shit, bleach and ammonia was burning my nostrils and making my eyes water and my nose run. It was hard to imagine what this hellhole was going to be like come January, when temperatures would top a hundred degrees Fahrenheit and I'd be almost at full term.

The most strenuous and hazardous job in the laundry was working the rotating linen presser. This involved lifting heavy, soaking wet, starched sheets from a tub and carrying them to the bench in front of the linen press. Without plastic aprons we got soaked to the skin. It took four girls to work the press – two each side. Each sheet was pulled like in tug of war, stretched to remove any folds. Then the sheet was fed onto the hot metal roller, which dried and pressed it in one motion as the roller rotated.

'Ouch!' I cried out, dropping my end onto the filthy cement floor.

'You stupid girl!' Quasi yelled. 'Watch what you're doing. Now that sheet has to be washed again.'

It was difficult not to touch the scorching surface of the press when a sheet was being fed onto the rotating cylinder. It was virtually impossible not to touch it on the other side as the pressed sheet was being removed. Since no protective clothing, gloves or even a spatula were provided to lift the end of the sheet, our hands were covered with blisters and burns at the end of a shift.

One day, after a particularly hot and gruelling afternoon shift in the laundry, we returned to the house about six-thirty, totally exhausted. Some girls, too tired to cook, went straight to bed.

'What's that?' asked Diana, the kid from the circus, as she stopped at the kitchen door and pointed to the bench beside the sink.

'Oh God! It's alive.' I grabbed Diana by the back of her dress and pulled her away.

The main kitchen had sent some kind of leftover meat to the

home. It was a nice gesture except that it was swarming with maggots. My gut turned somersaults as I ran for the bathroom. With not much in my stomach to begin with I spent five minutes trying to stop the dry retching.

The only other food supplied by the hospital consisted of sausages, chops and occasionally bacon. There was never enough meat to go around, and tempers often flared over who should get the last sausage. The other basic staples were bread, cornflakes, eggs, butter and milk. I don't recall ever seeing anything resembling fruit or vegetables. In the evening the latecomers had to make do with cornflakes or eggs and bread for dinner. Some of the girls were so undomesticated they didn't even know how to boil eggs and lived on toast and cornflakes.

St Margaret's Hospital was the third-largest obstetric training hospital in Sydney. The main kitchen prepared hundreds of meals a day for the patients, nuns, nurses, medical staff and interns. Surely it would not have impacted on the hospital's bottom line, or destroyed Sister Anne's reputation for being able to run the hospital on a shoe-string, had the kitchen supplied another forty meals for the home girls, who worked in the kitchens and laundries without pay.

After a week of laundry duty I was rotated to the public hospital kitchen. This work was very unpleasant for the girls who suffered from morning sickness. It was our job to empty the breakfast trays from the public wards and scrape the uneaten food into the open garbage bins, before rinsing the plates and stacking them into racks ready for the dishwashers. Trying to get close enough to the sink to reach the tap was difficult for we shorter girls, and equally troublesome for others with advanced pregnancies.

There was never any attempt by the hospital staff to be civil. The only time anyone spoke to we unmarried mothers-to-be was to bark orders or hurl abuse for something or other. If a girl hesitated for a moment to let the steam rise from the dishwasher before attempting to handle the hot plates, one of the nuns would yell from across the room – 'Come on, girl! We don't have all day.'

The plates were very heavy and my back ached after carrying stacks of six at a time from the sink to the waiting trolleys, trying not to fall on the wet slippery floor. One morning a girl slipped and fell, smashing an armful of plates. Sister rushed to the girl, but seemed more concerned about the tableware than the wellbeing of someone who was seven months pregnant.

'You useless, clumsy girl!' she snapped.

The poor girl sat on the floor sobbing, unable to get up. She had bits of broken crockery all around her.

We pregnant girls from the home were considered by the nuns to hold no moral or social values. We were the 'children of the damned' and had to be not only shunned, but punished for our sins. Some girls with advanced pregnancies, good Catholics who went to mass every Sunday, got to work in the private hospital kitchen, where they could sit down and polish the silverware.

Unlike many of the girls at St Margaret's I had already worked in large factories where strong workers' unions made me acutely aware of my rights. I knew exploitation when I saw it and the exploitation at St Margaret's was patently obvious. This was a slave-labour camp, breaking all the rules and operating right under the noses of the Child Welfare Department, the Department of Labour and Industry, and the Department of Health and Safety, whose job it was to protect the rights of children and workers. The whole system seemed to let the girls at St Margaret's down. I wondered whether the outside agencies just assumed that the nuns would take good care of us, and there was therefore no need for the inspections that were carried out randomly on the homes of individual families and at workplaces across the country every day. Even if government authorities were not aware of what was happening at St Margaret's, it was implausible that the Sisters of St Joseph themselves didn't know they were flaunting the law and neglecting their duty of care, which made it inexcusable.

Cheryl was due to have her baby any day, and although her workload had been reduced, she still had to do the morning shift in the kitchen. One morning, Cheryl went into labour halfway through her shift.

'Oh God!' she cried, grabbing her stomach and leaning forward. 'Holy Christ!' She was unable to straighten up.

'Shhh, the nuns will hear you,' I whispered.

'Fuck the nuns!' she hissed.

I found Sister Veronica and told her that Cheryl had started labour.

'Goodbye, Kay,' Cheryl said, hugging me with tears in her eyes.

'Goodbye, Cheryl,' I said, hugging her back and holding her tight for a few seconds.

Cheryl had told me that after she had her baby, she wouldn't be coming back to the home as others did to say goodbye.

'I never want to see this fucking place again. I'm out of here as soon as I can,' she said.

Cheryl waved goodbye to the other girls and we all stood silent as she was led to the labour ward. There was no excitement or celebration. The mood in the kitchen was sombre. About twenty minutes later Cheryl returned to the kitchen.

'What's wrong? Why have they sent you back?' I asked, putting my arm around her.

'They said I'll be a while yet and should finish my shift. She clutched her stomach with the onset of another contraction. 'Those rotten bitches,' she groaned.

In thirty minutes Cheryl's contractions had become stronger and more frequent. Worried she might have the baby right there on the floor in front of us, I went for Sister Veronica again. This time Cheryl didn't come back, and I never saw her again. I heard she'd had a little girl, but it might have been a rumour.

The thought of never hearing my baby cry, or knowing if it was a boy or a girl, was terrifying.

Sister Veronica was flapping around with fabric in her hands, looking frantic.

'Is there any sewing to be done, Sister?' I offered. 'I can use an electric sewing machine.'

'You can?' she asked, looking surprised. 'I could use some help in the sewing room. Follow me,' she said, and led me to the sixth floor of the public wards.

We entered a large room with sweeping views over the city. In the centre of the room was a scrubbed wooden table. An electric Singer sewing machine had been placed at one end. Old biscuit tins held all kinds of haberdashery and two pairs of blunt scissors. One whole wall had floor-to-ceiling wooden shelving stuffed with bolts of fabric.

'We need something to go around the nursery cots to keep the wind from the babies. Do you think you could make something like that?'

'I think so, Sister,' I said, sounding full of confidence.

After a bit of thought, I designed and made a pleated wind guard that wrapped around the inside of the cot and tucked under the mattress. It was held in place with cotton tape. I was very pleased with the result.

'Here, Sister, I think this will do the job.' I smiled, handing her the finished sample.

'Kay, this is fantastic!' Sister Veronica said when she examined the piece. It felt good to get a bit of praise. 'Now, what I need you to do is make about three hundred of them.'

'I'll start today, Sister,' I said, hardly able to contain my excitement at the thought of seeing out my confinement sitting on my bum sewing. There was even a radio. Sister Veronica said I could listen to it, on the proviso that I did not tune it to 'rocker' music.

The view of the city was uninterrupted to the top of the Sydney Harbour Bridge. The AWA tower dominated the skyline. Knowing that there was a world outside, and that this time would pass, helped me to find the strength to make it through each day and not go barking mad. This was something I had learned when I was in Bidura. They could lock up my body up, but my dreams belonged to me.

'We need some matinee jackets for the newborn babies. When you run out of material I have some more,' Sister Veronica said cheerfully, and she handed me a whole bolt of pure white voile, a pile of lace trimmings and some baby patterns.

For every ten jackets I made for the hospital I made one for my own baby, which I smuggled back to my room hidden in my underwear. The nuns often searched our rooms, looking for cigarettes and other contraband. So I stuck a bag of the baby clothes to the back of my wardrobe using stickytape.

It didn't take long to realise that the sewing room was on the same floor as the nursery. The worst days were when the circumcisions were done. Sometimes men with beards and black hats came to the ward and chanted prayers – these babies cried but were comforted. It was always easy to tell the babies from the home; they were lined up along the corridor of the ward. A doctor, aided by a nurse, would unwrap a sleeping baby, do the business, rewrap the baby and move on to the next. These babies were not comforted. The frantic screams ripped my heart out. I wanted to run and cuddle all of them.

'It's just like lopping the tails off sheep. They don't even feel it,' a nurse told me when I suggested it was cruel.

'Have you ever seen a lamb having its tail docked?'

'No, I haven't,' she replied.

'Well, I have, and it hurts.'

24

The sweat shop

'Sister Anne would like to see you in her office,' Sister Veronica said one day when I bumped into her on my way to the sewing room.

I knocked on the office door. I hadn't seen Sister Anne since the day I'd arrived, and I had a pretty good idea about why I'd been summoned.

'Hello, dear. We have some paperwork to attend to,' she said, pushing the adoption consent document and a pen across the desk.

'Sister Anne, I am not going to put my baby up for adoption,' I said, stepping back from the desk.

'Don't be ridiculous, child. You can't possibly keep the baby. It is in your best interests and certainly those of the child that you give it up for adoption.' She pursed her lips at my impertinence.

I stood silent. We stared at each other. The telephone rang.

'Go back to work, we'll discuss this later,' she said, waving her hand to dismiss me as she picked up the receiver.

*

183

One Sunday afternoon Sister Veronica found me sitting in the grounds reading. 'Kay, you have some visitors,' she said, smiling.

I followed her to the waiting area, my heart pounding with the anticipation of seeing a familiar face.

'Hello, darlin',' Uncle Stan said, chuckling nervously and rubbing my hand as he did when he was anxious.

'Hello, Uncle Stan, Aunty Shirley,' I replied, feeling embarrassed for my condition. 'How did you know I was here?'

'Mamma wrote and told us you'd gone to the nuns,' he said, delicately avoiding words like 'pregnant' and 'baby'.

How she must have gloated that she had been right about me all along, that I was a slut, just like my mother. I wanted to tell Uncle Stan what a terrible place it was and beg him to get me out of there. But he revered the nuns; I knew he'd never believe me. Suddenly, my nose popped. Blood gushed like I'd punctured an artery, drenching the front of my dress, and splattering onto the floor.

Uncle Stan usually fainted at the sight of blood. 'Oh dear . . . should we call a nurse?' he asked, handing me his clean handkerchief.

'No, this happens all the time,' I said, holding my head back to try to stop the flow, as tears mixed with blood saturated the handkerchief and dripped from my fingers.

'Now, darlin', don't cry. You'll be alright,' he said, putting his arm around my shoulders.

After my nose stopped bleeding, we talked for about half an hour. When the bell rang they got up to leave.

'Will I see you again?' I asked.

'Yes, love. We'll be back in a couple of weeks. Is there anything you need?'

'The hospital doesn't supply toiletries and I also need a couple of towels.'

Although I'd found the hospital canteen and bought some soap, shampoo and toothpaste, it was very expensive. I didn't have much left of the money Mrs McNorton had sent me, and it was all the money I had in the world.

I walked down the path with Uncle Stan and Aunty Shirley, as far as the girls at the home were allowed to go.

They stopped and waved. 'Alright, love, we'll see you in a couple of weeks,' Uncle Stan called out before they turned and walked out the gate.

At Uncle Stan's next visit he handed me a bag containing a towel, a cake of Camay soap, some shampoo, a few pieces of fruit and a couple of little extras. It felt like Christmas. We never talked about the baby or what I would do after the birth. I guess he presumed, along with everyone else, that I would relinquish my baby for adoption.

There were people who called themselves Christians, and then there was Uncle Stan. He was consistent, and his code of ethics was biblical. 'Do unto others as you'd have them do unto to you,' he'd say. He never preached to anyone; his religion was a very private matter.

Uncle Stan and Aunty Shirley would have had to leave home before lunch, catch two buses and a train, and walk down a filthy street to visit me at St Margaret's, and they did it every second Sunday, rain, hail or shine, and they never came empty handed.

Peter kept his promise and wrote to me every day. Fortunately, he missed the short straw and wasn't sent to Vietnam. He said that he'd met Robbie, who had been transferred from Puckapunyal training camp and introduced himself. Someone had told Robbie that Peter was the father of my child and they nearly came to blows. I knew that someone had to be Dan. He lived next door to O'Connell House and would have seen me going around with

Peter and reached his own conclusions. Peter told me that Robbie was going to Vietnam.

When Uncle Stan came for his next visit, he confirmed that Robbie was due to leave for Vietnam, but asked me not to tell Mamma. Robbie didn't want her worrying. The secret was safe with me. Mamma hadn't even bothered to write since she'd left me at the hospital.

Apart from Peter's letters, the visits from Uncle Stan and Aunty Shirley were the only bright spots in a bleak reality. If it hadn't been for the odd *Daily Mirror* newspaper I picked from the rubbish in the kitchen, and the radio in the sewing room, I wouldn't have had a clue about what was happening in the world. It was a relief to see that the conflict in Vietnam only made page ten of the newspaper. I didn't want to even think about the possibility of Robbie being killed. I wished that I'd given him a hug the last time I saw him. I prayed to the Virgin Mary every night to keep him safe.

Sister Veronica told me to pack my things. I was being transferred. 'Sister Anne has selected you to go to Miss Sinclair's. You'll like it there,' she said, making it sound like a real treat. But I suspected it was going to be some kind of punishment, because I had refused to sign the consent for adoption.

Miss Sinclair was Sister Anne's spinster sister. She lived at Five Dock. *How will Uncle Stan and Aunty Shirley visit me?* I wondered. *Is there a train to Five Dock?*

Miss Sinclair had a smile that looked painted on and she didn't fool me one bit. Three other girls were staying at Five Dock and we took turns at cleaning, cooking, washing and ironing for Miss Sinclair. There was a vegetable garden that we had to take care of, even though bending and weeding was very difficult for girls in our condition. At seven months pregnant, I had to look sideways to see my feet; they had disappeared under my belly.

One of the bedrooms at Miss Sinclair's was used as a work-room. On top of a large table in the centre sat four electric sewing machines. There were four hard wooden chairs. Not long after I arrived, a man delivered several cardboard boxes, which he stacked against the wall. He handed Miss Sinclair a clipboard and she signed something.

'I'll be back this time next week,' he said. The man didn't even acknowledge our presence. It was as though we were invisible.

Miss Sinclair opened one of the boxes and took out something made from patterned plastic, which on closer inspection proved to be a shower cap with no elastic. Then she took a strip of nylon lace from the bundle in the box.

'Your job is to sew the lace onto the caps, like so,' Miss Sinclair said, before giving us a demonstration. 'They will be collected next week and you must have all of these boxes finished before the van gets here.' She walked out of the room.

The other girls and I looked at each other.

'I can't use a sewing machine,' one girl said.

'Neither can I,' said another.

The third girl just burst into tears.

'I'll show you,' I said. 'It's better than going back to the hospital and working in that stinking laundry.' I sat down to give them a crash course on how to sew in straight lines.

Each time a bobbin emptied or the cotton reel needed to be changed, I had to stop what I was doing and sort out the problem. When the van came back the following week we fell short by two boxes.

Miss Sinclair went ballistic. 'You wicked, lazy girls. It is a privi-lege for you to be here and you are expected to work!'

It was very enterprising of Sister Anne to use the girls from the home to set up a suburban sweat shop and provide domestic help for her elderly sister. The food was certainly a better quality and more plentiful than the hospital provided, but there was no privilege to be had working six days a week, for a snapping old crone, without pay.

One of the worst things at Miss Sinclair's was having nowhere to get away – to be on our own. We all needed to do that, from time to time. As decrepit as the home at the hospital was, we were able to release our emotion at night, without anyone tapping on the wall.

Sunday was our only day off and we were expected to accompany Miss Sinclair to nine o'clock mass at All Hallows' Church at Five Dock. Miss Sinclair would get all dolled up in her blue-and-white knitted acrylic suit, with a blue-and-white straw hat from David Jones, white gloves and a smart navy blue handbag on her arm.

'Come along, girls, we can't be late,' she'd say, leading the procession as we waddled behind her. She would walk about three paces ahead of us, nodding and waving to her neighbours, who gave her admiring looks.

At church children stared at us. Adults treated us like we didn't exist. No one even tried to make eye contact or smile. *So much for Christian compassion, and forgiveness*, I thought.

'Why does that girl have a big belly?' a little kid asked her mother, pointing at me.

'Because she has been wicked,' her mother said, leading the child away.

None of the other girls at Miss Sinclair's got visitors on Sunday afternoon, and as Uncle Stan and Aunty Shirley didn't come to visit me, I figured that Five Dock didn't have a railway station. Fortunately, our mail was redirected from the hospital. Miss

Sinclair would give me a disdainful look when she handed me the letters from Peter, which were always tied in a bundle.

One Sunday I refused to go to mass. I had no intention of being paraded like a circus curiosity so Miss Sinclair could impress the congregation with her act of Christian kindness.

'I'll report you to Sister Anne, you wilful girl,' she snapped.

But she must have thought better of it, or realised that without me the production in the sweat shop would come to a grinding halt every time a needle broke.

On Melbourne Cup Day Miss Sinclair got dolled up a bit more than usual, at least the hat was more elaborate than those she wore to church.

'I'm going out to lunch. Now you girls keep working. Just because I am not here, does not mean that you can slacken off,' she said, putting on her gloves.

Miss Sinclair drove a little cream Austin, a manual, which she never managed to fully control. You could have driven a Mack through her front gates, but reversing the car out always added more scrapes to the paintwork on the doors, as she careered into the fence post. It was very funny to watch her car 'kangarooing' its way down the road as she tried to get some synchronicity between the gears and the clutch.

The day was promising to be another scorcher. The sewing room was on the westerly side of the house and, with no awnings or blinds on the windows, the room was an oven by three. The plastic shower caps were like melted Kraft cheese slices to handle.

'Let's listen to the Melbourne Cup,' I suggested to the other girls.

'Do you think we can? What if Miss Sinclair comes back?' Suzanne asked. She was a sweet kid, about my age, and Miss

Sinclair's favourite because she massaged the old woman's gnarly feet every night.

'She's gone to a lunch. She won't be back 'til after the race. Besides, none of us has had a lunch break yet.'

There was a white cast-iron garden setting on the back patio. After I'd made up a jug of iced water, with some freshly squeezed lemons for a festive feel, I opened the kitchen window wide and turned up the radio so we could hear the race. We kicked off our shoes and sat back sipping our lemon water like we were holiday-ing – a million miles from reality. None of us knew which horses were actually running, so as the radio announcer called the names of the starters, I wrote each on a piece of paper. I chose Light Fingers. The jockey was Roy Higgins. That had been Granny's name, and it also reminded me of my shoplifting friend, Lorraine, from the lake. It felt lucky.

'And they're racing in the 1965 Melbourne Cup!' the caller announced.

Having heard the races on the radio in Mamma's kitchen for years, I could pretty well keep up with where the horses were in the field. As they rounded the turn to line up down the back straight, Light Fingers was well positioned. He could take the Cup if he didn't fall or die in the sprint to the winning post. I got to my feet as my horse moved up the field.

'Come on! Come on!' I urged, jumping up and down with excitement. Anyone would have thought I'd bet a million quid at long odds.

My enthusiasm was infectious and the other girls started cheer-ing their horses to the finish line.

'And the 1965 Melbourne Cup goes to Light Fingers. It's Light Fingers followed by . . .'

I was too excited to hear the other placegetters. 'You little rip-per!' I called out, hugging Suzanne.

We were all rolling around like Matryoshka dolls, nearly knocking one another over as our big bellies bumped together. We didn't hear Miss Sinclair's car come up the drive.

'What do you think you are doing?' she said, looking very wobbly and trying not to slur her words.

Since our day at the races had been my idea, I spoke first. 'We were listening to the Melbourne Cup, Miss Sinclair.'

'Well now you can go back to work. You are not here to be entertained and enjoy yourselves,' she said, hissing the 's' sounds as she struggled with poorly fitting dentures and the effects of a few glasses of bubbly.

It took all my control not to laugh as her cat toyed with her hat, which dragged on the ground behind her as she staggered into the house, nearly tripping on the back step. She must have passed out because we didn't see her for the rest of the day.

The next morning she called me to her room. 'Pack your things. You are going back to the hospital. You have shown no gratitude for the kindness you have been given.'

I had been at Miss Sinclair's for five weeks and it seemed like five months. Without the visits from Uncle Stan and Aunty Shirley, Peter's letters had become the glue holding me together. I never imagined that I would actually look forward to going back to the home. I hoped I'd get a room with a window.

25

Refusing to buckle

Many of the girls I had known before I was sent to Miss Sinclair's had already had their babies and left the home by the time I got back. That was the nature of the program. They came and went and there was never a shortage of replacements to take their place in the laundry and kitchens. Fortunately, I managed once more to get a room with a window. It was probably only vacant because it faced the pub across the road. For a feeling of more space and a glimpse of the moon I could put up with the night noises.

Miss Sinclair must have put in a good word for me because when I returned I was assigned permanently to laundry duty, the most dreaded job of all. Being in my last trimester wasn't a pass to get off working in the stifling heat. My shifts had been reduced but not by much; I got the weekends off.

There were no prenatal classes, so we had no idea how to deal with the changes our bodies were going through. My nipples were so dry and split I looked like a snake shedding its skin. It was agonising taking showers and wearing a bra. My nosebleeds were happening more frequently and my hair started falling out in clumps, probably a combination of stress and malnutrition. The lack of fibre in my diet kept me sick with constipation. The discomfort was immense. Added to that, I had chewed my fingernails to the cuticles and they bled. The only description that fitted was misery.

After each work shift I was utterly exhausted. It took all my strength to get back to the house and up the two flights of stairs to my cell. I was often too drained to think about food or couldn't deal with the filth of the kitchen, which didn't improve as girls came and went.

The constant anguish of how I could stop the nuns taking my baby increased as my due date drew closer. As exhausted as I was both mentally and physically, sleep didn't come easily. Lying in my bed, I prayed every night. Over and over I repeated the Hail Mary like some bizarre ritual hoping someone 'up there' would hear me. Having been conditioned to never ask for anything and be grateful for what I was given, it didn't feel right praying for me. My unborn child didn't have a voice, but I felt that he wouldn't want me to give him away to a stranger, so when I prayed I said, 'Please help us.'

One night, after I had finally passed out, I was suddenly awoken by a bright light shining into my face and swore I could hear Sister Anne's voice mingling with the sounds from the street. I struggled to sit up.

'Stop being difficult and sign these papers,' she hissed, shoving the document and a pen at me.

'I am not going to give up my baby,' I said, squinting against the glare and swiping the document off the bed onto the floor, nearly knocking the torch out of her hand in the process.

My defiance infuriated her. 'You evil girl, you will go to hell.' She bent down to pick up the document and pen and abruptly left my room.

Sister Anne's nightly raids at my bedside became a regular torment. With each visit her tone and manner grew more menacing. Every now and then she would change tack and try to convince me how much better off my child would be with wealthy parents who could give him all the things I couldn't. It was as if she already knew the couple she was talking about, who were waiting in the wings for my baby to be born.

By the second week in December, when I had still not signed the adoption papers, Sister Anne seemed to be personally supervising my punishment. I was sent to the general outpatients waiting room to see the doctor for my first and only check-up in the four months since my admission. The other women glanced at my ring finger and gave me disapproving, damning looks before burying their heads behind the covers of their magazines.

It was coming up to Christmas and I was looking forward to it so much. Peter would be on leave and he was coming to visit me. This was going to be very risky but we had to see each other, if only for a few minutes. There was a waiting room with frosted glass windows near the front entrance. I told Peter to meet me there and that under no circumstances was he to tell anyone that he was there to see me.

Christmas Day arrived and Peter was already there when I got to the waiting room. It took my breath away to see him in his smart uniform with shiny brass buttons, razor sharp creases in his trousers, and shoes that looked like he'd spent hours spit-polishing. He tried to kiss me, but he couldn't reach my lips over my enormous belly. We laughed.

'Look at you, kid,' he said, running a hand over my bulge. The baby kicked hard. 'Did you feel that?'

'Yes.' I laughed. 'I think he's broken one of my ribs.'

'So you know it's a boy?' Peter asked with some surprise.

'Not for sure. I just feel it is. He's so active – he'll certainly play football.'

I could feel the tiny hands and feet inside me pushing the front of my dress forward. To be talking about my baby as if it were a real person for the first time since conception filled me with emotion. I lay my head on Peter's shoulder and cried. He was silent for a long time. Eventually he spoke.

'Kay, you're not thinking about keeping the baby, are you?'

I pulled away and stared into those deep brown eyes looking for some compassion.

Peter looked uneasy as he took my hand. 'I want to be with you more than anything,' he said. 'But I don't want another man's child.'

For several moments I just stared at him, unable to speak. It seemed that everyone wanted me to give my baby away. What shocked me most was their blasé manner. As if it were something I could simply do.

'Peter, this is not another man's child. This is my child and I can't give him away. Please don't ask me to choose,' I begged, squeezing his hand. The pressure in my head was building. If I tried to hold back the tears, I knew my nose would explode. I buried my face in my hands and sobbed, the echo bouncing off the walls in the waiting room.

Sensing someone at the doorway I turned to see Sister Anne glaring back at me.

'Go back to the home immediately!' she snapped.

Peter kissed me goodbye and pressed a small gift into my hand. It was the pearl earrings I had admired in the window of Angus & Coote when Peter, Deanie and I had gone to Parramatta station in August.

Pearls are for tears, I thought, recalling one of Mamma's silly superstitions.

All afternoon I waited to be summoned. I had broken one of the big rules by having a male visitor who wasn't related to me. I expected the worst, without knowing what that would be. I was relieved when the rest of the day was peaceful. They even had a bit of a Christmas party, which was also a farewell to Karen, who'd had her baby and was now going home. She was very unhappy.

'I wish I hadn't given my baby away, but it's too late now,' she cried. 'I wish I'd had your courage not to sign the consent.'

Was my refusal to give consent for adoption courage or, as Sister Anne said, was it selfishness? I had no idea how I was going to raise my baby; we didn't even have anywhere to go after he was born. It was clear that Peter didn't want me and the baby, so that seemed to be my only hope gone. Uncle Stan and Aunty Shirley lived in a tiny garage on their block of land while they saved enough money to build a house. Mamma hadn't written to me, and neither had John McNorton, who knew where I was and that I was having his child. We were totally on our own.

On Boxing Day I was called to Sister Anne's office and was surprised to see Uncle Stan and Aunty Shirley huddled together, looking very distressed. *Robbie's been killed*, was my first thought.

Uncle Stan came over and took my hand. 'What have you done, darlin'?' he asked with tears in his eyes.

'I know Peter shouldn't have been here,' I said. 'But it's Christmas, and we just –'

'That is not why you are here,' Sister Anne said sharply, cutting me off mid-sentence. 'You were seen over at the hotel buying alcohol and cigarettes and that is strictly against the house rules.' She was smirking as she fixed her gaze on me.

What a relief! I almost laughed out loud. I looked at Uncle

Stan, expecting a reaction to this ridiculous accusation. He didn't respond.

'Uncle Stan, you know how ridiculous that is. Sister Anne has me confused with someone else.'

My aversion to alcohol and, particularly, smoking was well known in our family. But until he'd started visiting me at St Margaret's I hadn't seen Uncle Stan for three years. Perhaps he thought I'd changed. I stood there dumbfounded, waiting for him to say something,

'It was you,' Sister Anne insisted, breaking the silence in the room.

Turning to face her, I looked Sister Anne right in the eyes. 'It wasn't me, Sister. I don't smoke or drink alcohol.'

'I saw you myself coming back across the road smoking a cigarette,' she said adamantly.

'That's a lie!' I replied.

'Oh dear,' Uncle Stan gasped, bringing his hand to his mouth.

I knew that accusing a nun of lying would be close to sacrilege in Uncle Stan's mind. Or was he shocked, finally having realised that Sister Anne had accused me of something so outrageous?

In those days Darlinghurst was a skid row area. The pub on Bourke Street opposite St Margaret's Hospital was a slop-shop frequented by the lowest forms of life society could dredge up. Every night through my open window, I could hear the drunken brawls and sounds of women being gang-banged in the alley. For Sister Anne to say that she had seen me coming back from such a place was laughable at best, but at eight months pregnant, even she must have realised how ludicrous her accusation sounded.

'We can forget the whole incident if you sign these papers, child.' Her voice had become more conciliatory. 'But if you don't, you are going to be discharged immediately.' She pushed the now tattered documents across the desk towards me.

So that's what this is all about. Sister Anne clearly had no limits to the extent she was prepared to go to secure the consent to adopt my baby. Even if it meant lies and extortion. My mind was racing, trying to think ahead to where this was all going. *She can't take the baby without your signature.* I heard the words in my head as if someone, unseen, had spoken to me. It felt like I had been given some kind of strength injection. For the first time, ever, I had power over my own life. This gave me the confidence to speak back.

'I've worked like a slave in this hospital for four months and you are throwing me out because I won't give you my baby.'

'Worked? You haven't worked. Miss Sinclair sent you back here because you refused to work. You are a lazy girl.'

There was nothing more to say. I wasn't going to sign the consent for adoption, no matter what she threatened me with. I glared at her. *You'll go to hell!* I screamed inside my head. Her eyes widened, as if she'd read my mind.

Uncle Stan and Aunty Shirley were unable to speak or move. I left the room without saying another word and went back to the dormitory to pack my things. In my rage I nearly pulled the wardrobe over as I retrieved the baby clothes I'd stuck to the back. Several girls saw me leaving with my suitcase.

'Where are you going?' a girl I hardly knew asked me.

'I'm leaving because I will not sign the adoption papers.'

'I thought we had to sign the papers to be able to have the baby here,' she said, sounding surprised.

'You do. That's why I'm leaving. These bastards are not getting my baby.'

It was the season for peace on earth and goodwill to all and I was being tossed onto the street in one of Sydney's red light districts because I refused to relinquish my baby. I was eight months pregnant and two weeks away from my sixteenth birthday, so legally I was still a child. With twenty pounds to my name and everything I owned still fitting into one small suitcase, I left St Margaret's with Mamma's words ringing in my ears.

'You'll go onto the streets and hawk your fork just like your mother.'

If that's what it was going to take to look after my baby, then so be it. The only thing that mattered to me at that moment was that I had not signed away the rights to my unborn child. For the first time in my life I had something no one could take from me.

26

Nite'n'Day

Should I turn left or right? I wondered. This was a big decision. I didn't know where I was or where I was going. I heard a voice behind me.

'There you are, love.'

Uncle Stan and Aunty Shirley were both red-faced from crying. Uncle Stan put his arm around me.

'I was never at the pub buying cigarettes,' I said defiantly, trying to control my emotions and prevent a nosebleed exploding on the street.

'We don't need to talk about that,' he said, softly patting my hand. We walked up the street in silence until we came to a public phone box. 'I'll give Les a call and see if he can take you in. I'm sorry, love, but our place is too small.'

He fumbled in his fob pocket for some pennies. I couldn't hear what he was saying but he looked grave and was gesticulating with his hand as he spoke with Uncle Les.

'Les said we can take you over to his place,' he announced, stepping out of the phone box.

Aunty Shirley sighed. 'That's good, Stan,' she said, sounding as relieved as I felt.

As we waited at Central for the train to Cabramatta, people stared at me like I was a freak. In the 1960s not even married women with full bellies were seen in public.

An older woman eyed me up down with disdain. 'Have you no shame?' she muttered, before turning her back to me.

I hadn't seen Uncle Les since I was nine years old. If Mamma turned on anyone the whole family was expected to side with her, and she had definitely turned on Uncle Les's wife, Shirl, so we couldn't see them after they were married. I knew that he had two daughters, but I'd never met them. Sandra was five and Pauline was four.

'Why have you got such a big belly?' Pauline asked, with the ruthless candour of a child.

'I'm . . .'

'Katie eats too much ice cream,' Uncle Les cut in, giving me a wink.

Uncle Les was a career soldier and had served in every conflict involving Australian troops since 1941. His reward was a two-bedroom, fibro-and-tile war service house in Cabramatta. No frills, no extras, but it was a roof over my head and I was grateful.

The bedroom the girls shared was too small to take another bed, so I had to sleep on the fold-down Nite'n'Day lounge. This green monstrosity may have been comfortable had I not been pregnant or if there'd been some kind of underlay between the sheet and the hot sticky vinyl. My suitcase was stored under the lounge. One of my maternity dresses had been left behind at Miss Sinclair's and never returned, reducing me to wearing one dress while the other was in the wash, so I didn't need any hanging space.

After the long journey from St Margaret's my bladder was bursting. I started for the toilet outside.

'Where are you going?' Shirl asked when she saw me heading for the door.

'To the toilet.'

'It's daylight. You can't go out there, the neighbours will see you.'

'Shirl, I need to go.'

'You'll have to use this,' she said, handing me a plastic bucket.

For the next month I had to pee in a bucket in the laundry. This was quite a production every fifteen minutes or so – holding on to the edge of the laundry tubs to steady myself and trying not to miss the bucket. For anything else I had to wait until dark and scurry to the dunny like a sewer rat. This house arrest extended to collecting the mail from the front gate, and the one time we went out in the car, Shirl and the girls encircled me to try and conceal my 'condition' from nosey parkers.

That January, Sydney was in the grip of a heatwave. Shirl checked the thermometer on the kitchen wall every hour. The mercury never dipped below a hundred degrees Fahrenheit, night or day. Bushfires raged across the state as fierce winds blew smoke, heat and cinders in our direction. On the hottest days Shirl, who was an obese woman, worried me as she sprawled on the Nite'n'Day, fanning her skirt and gasping for air. I feared she would to cark it if we didn't get a break in the weather soon.

'May I use the sewing machine, Shirl?'

I'd seen the machine as I was putting the vacuum cleaner away. The sewing machine Aunty Daphne had given me had been left at Mamma's when I went to St Margaret's, and I badly missed the distraction that sewing always provided.

'Yes, but I can't show you how to use it. I don't have a clue,' she replied with a chuckle.

It was an electric sewing machine with a zigzag stitch and but-tonholer – and Shirl hadn't taken it out of its case. I gave her some money and asked if she'd pick me up some white linen to make a skirt. I'd been carrying some fabric for a top around in my suit-case; I hadn't had time to make it before I became pregnant.

'If I get some material, will you make some dresses for the girls?' Shirl asked.

'Sure, I'd like that.' I would have done anything to feel less confined in the stinking-hot house.

Every day after we got the housework done, I set up the sew-ing machine on the dining table and made sundresses for the girls and an outfit for myself to wear home from hospital. Shirl sat on the lounge with her feet up, watching television and proffering her opinions as the *Beauty and the Beast* panel responded to letters from bored or lonely housewives.

'Did you know that your family is Aboriginal?' Shirl asked, casu-ally, with no bearing on anything we'd been chatting about.

'Yes, of course I know that.'

This was like asking me whether I knew I was pregnant. It was a silly question. She seemed a little disappointed that I wasn't shocked.

There was no connection between Shirl and my family, and therefore no loyalty. She probably thought that because of my circumstances she'd found an ally, as she vented her anger and resentment towards Mamma, who had never forgiven her for not calling off the wedding when Kevie died.

I wasn't comfortable with it and I tried to divert the discussion. 'Did you know my father, Ray Burgess?'

'Ray Burgess isn't your father,' she said, but before I could take it further she launched into another story.

'Do you know why Phyllis and Mamma were always fighting?'

'Yes,' I replied, hoping to cut her off.

Uncle Jack had given me his version. It was a scandalous story, the events of which had caused Bill Gresham to leave Mamma, sending Phyllis and Daphne to live with Granny. I certainly didn't need to hear Shirl's version.

'Did you know that Bill Gresham never divorced Mamma?' She threw the comment into the room as she rummaged through the carton of Darrell Lea chocolates for a soft centre.

I took my foot off the pedal and looked up from the sewing. Shirl was grinning as she popped another chocolate into her mouth, a fitting reward for finally getting my attention. If Mamma didn't divorce Bill Gresham, then she could not have married Fred Carlton, which meant that Kev, Robbie and Dan were illegitimate. Suddenly I was seeing Mamma in a different light. To think she had once told me that she wouldn't raise any bastards I brought home. *What a hypocrite*, I thought.

'I never saw your wedding photographs, Shirl,' I said, hoping to end this conversation. 'May I see them?'

Mamma had never put a wedding photograph of Les and Shirl on her sideboard. As I looked through the album now and saw Uncle Stan and Robbie, I was reminded of that horrible night in June, the night before the wedding. They were the saddest wedding photographs I had ever seen. Uncle Stan and Robbie had tears streaming down their faces in every picture.

'Look at Stan and Robbie,' Shirl said in a tone of disgust. 'They weren't even wearing decent suits.'

Clearly she had forgotten that only hours before these photographs were taken, Kev had died in Robbie's arms and Uncle Stan had gone to the morgue to identify his dead brother's body.

*

'Happy birthday to me,' I said, struggling against the weight of my huge belly, as I pulled myself off Nite'n'Day.

Sixteen at last! I thought this day would never come. I didn't expect Uncle Les to remember my birthday; he wasn't around when I was born. But I did get a lovely birthday card from Uncle Stan in the mail and another one from Peter. Turning sixteen meant that I was no longer the property of the state. I felt like I was finally free of a terrible curse.

Shirl, meanwhile, had been pleased to discover that I could cook, and was happy to let me prepare most of the evening meals. Uncle Les was very complimentary, and presumed that Mamma had taught me. Mamma couldn't stand anyone around her when she was cooking; everything I learned came from watching Aunty Daphne or Aunty Lorna. After dinner we'd sit around the table having a cup of tea and making small talk. Uncle Les and Shirl never discussed anything concerning my baby and I didn't volunteer anything. I'd presumed that Uncle Stan had told them that I'd been discharged from St Margaret's because I'd refused to sign the adoption papers. But I couldn't be sure, because I knew Uncle Stan would have had trouble admitting that a nun had lied. I didn't want to risk any confrontation or being thrown out again. I had nowhere else to go. So I kept my mouth shut.

Uncle Les always brought home a newspaper and left it on the table for anyone to read. The news about Vietnam was disturbing and indicated that the fighting was intensifying. The propaganda from the government continued to downplay the slaughter by refusing to call it a war. Robbie was already in Vietnam, and there was no guarantee that Peter would not be sent.

Even though I knew it was all over between Peter and me, I hadn't been able to bring myself to tell him. He had been transferred to Woodside in South Australia and his letters kept coming – one a day as promised. He'd write pages and pages of meaningless words, making promises and dreaming dreams of us being together with never a mention of the baby. It was pointless, but I kept writing back, pouring my heart out and saying all the sweet things I knew he needed to hear. Peter's most recent letter was nothing more than a rambling of his sexual fantasies. I tossed it into my suitcase, and couldn't muster enough interest to reply.

Uncle Les was due to leave for Vietnam at the end of February on a tour of duty, and Shirl's anxiety was reaching fever pitch. I guess military wives don't want to dwell on the grim probabilities of war; they just hope their husbands return home safely. Shirl seemed more concerned about being alone and how she would cope with the girls on her own. As if Uncle Les needed to be worried about his family while he was dodging bullets.

'When you come out of the hospital you can come back and stay here, if you like,' Shirl said to me, with a smile.

Although this offer was very kind, I hadn't missed the subtlety of her not mentioning the baby.

27

Pain relief

On 28 January we watched the six o'clock news; the disappearance of the three Beaumont children from Glenelg Beach in South Australia had shaken the nation to its core. This was Australia, after all; this kind of thing never happened here.

'We're becoming more like America every day,' Uncle Les muttered scornfully.

'You look like you could be having twins,' Shirl commented, as I strained to pull myself up from a lounge chair.

My discomfort was immense. The dull ache in my back had started while we were watching the news. It wasn't severe so I said nothing, not realising that my labour had already begun. By nine-thirty I was exhausted, and needed to lie down, but had to wait until the movie that Shirl had been watching was over before I could fold down the lounge and go to sleep. When I finally got into bed, I heaved myself from one side to the other, unable to get comfortable. By one o'clock the ache in my back was getting stronger. Then it would stop, and I thought I might get some sleep. Only to have it start again, worse than the time before. I woke Uncle Les. He got dressed hurriedly.

'Pack a bag, Katie, I'll take you to hospital. How bad are the pains?' he said, handing me a small zip-up carry bag.

'The pain's bearable, but getting worse each time.' It didn't occur to me to ask which hospital. My mind was focused on the fact that my baby was coming. I packed my bag.

Uncle Les was by the front door jangling his car keys impatiently. I double-checked to make sure I had all the essentials.

'Come on, love. I don't want to put the bustle on you, but we'd better get going,' he said, taking my bag as we walked out the door.

It wasn't until we were on the road that I realised I'd left the letters from Peter in my suitcase. Shirl, I knew, would not be able to help herself from snooping through my belongings. Curiosity about the soldier who wrote to me from South Australia consumed her.

'Where are you taking me, Uncle Les?'

'To St Margaret's,' he said, keeping his eyes on the road.

'What if they don't take me back?' I had visions of my baby being born on the street. But my biggest fear was that they would drug me and take my baby and say it had died during the birth. All kinds of terrifying scenarios were racing through my mind.

'They'll take you back. I've spoken to Sister Anne.'

This did nothing to allay my fears.

As the pain got sharper I tried not to show any outward signs of discomfort. Uncle Les appeared shaken enough as it was.

'How frequent are your pains?' he'd ask every time we had to stop for a red light.

No one had told me that I ought to be keeping track of the time between each pain, and I didn't own a watch, so I took a guess. 'About ten minutes or so, I think.'

Uncle Les stepped on the accelerator.

We pulled up in front of St Margaret's. As I got out of the car the combination of fear and the weight of the baby on my bladder caused me to involuntarily pee my pants. I burst into tears with embarrassment.

'Bloody hell! We better get you inside,' he said, panicking.

Uncle Les took my bag and helped me up the stairs to the reception area. He went to the front desk and I sat down on a chair near the door, ready to bolt at the first sign of anyone with a hypodermic needle.

'They'll come and take you up to the labour ward now. Goodbye, love,' he said kindly, and he kissed me on the cheek. Before I knew it, he was gone.

A young nurse took my bag and asked me to follow her. Several other pregnant women, each accompanied by a family member, got into the lift. I felt conspicuously alone as the old lift rumbled up the shaft and came to a shuddering halt on the fourth floor. The heavy doors opened slowly, as if there was all the time in the world.

I stepped into the corridor. It was a hive of activity. Nurses were bustling around in all directions. Chalky-faced nuns wearing white habits and long, flowing veils floated up and down the corridor. They reminded me of stingrays skimming the sandy bottom of the aquarium at Manly.

'Follow me,' the nurse who had my bag said curtly.

We passed rooms with women groaning in agony, and others where the screams echoed off the walls as voices urged them to 'Push!'

The labour room was cold and cheerless and smelled of antiseptic. Harsh fluorescent lighting reflected from the glossy white tiles, assaulting my eyes. A narrow bed on wheels jutted out from the far wall. A metal cylinder with a black rubber hose and a small facemask was mounted to the wall at the head of the bed. There were several stainless steel trolleys, also on wheels, with some gruesome-looking steel instruments. I hoped they were not going to need those to deliver my baby. The nurse handed me a hospital robe.

'Remove all of your clothing including your underwear. Put this robe on and get onto the bed,' she said, before leaving the room.

The bed was too high above the floor, so I pulled a chair over and made a step to climb up. There was no pillow. I sat on the edge with my legs dangling over the side.

The nurse returned with a glass half filled with some kind of amber-coloured liquid. 'Drink this,' she said, handing me the glass.

I put the glass to my lips and as the nauseating smell of castor oil hit me, I gagged. 'I can't drink this,' I said, coughing and convulsing.

'Now don't you start giving us any trouble,' she said sternly.

'I'm sorry, but I just can't drink it.' I handed back the glass.

'I'll get some orange juice for the after-taste,' she said, and left the room again.

When she returned, I tilted the glass upwards and squeezed my nostrils together as the revolting liquid oozed slowly down the glass. It filled my mouth and I took a big gulp, pushing it down my throat in one go. Hurriedly, I reached for the orange juice and drank it as fast as I could. It was bitter. As the oil and orange juice collided, my body convulsed. It was a struggle to keep the repulsive mixture down.

The nurse dragged a trolley to the side of the bed. 'Lie down,' she instructed.

Although it was a warm night, her hands were freezing cold as she lifted the gown over my belly. Lying flat on my back, with a great protruding mound in the way, I couldn't see what she was going to do. I could hear her mixing something in a metal bowl.

As the cold wet sensation hit my pubic mound I shuddered and felt my face redden. It was acutely embarrassing to have someone touch me down there.

'Keep very still,' she said. I felt something pulling my pubic hair.

'What are you doing?' I asked, wincing at the discomfort.

'I'm removing your hair. It's more hygienic this way.'

It was agony lying flat on my back without a pillow to support my head or something under my knees to take the weight of the baby. The nurse hacked away at me with what felt like a very blunt razor blade. My skin was stinging and raw by the time she had finished.

'Now, roll onto your side.'

With some difficulty I managed to wobble over. I felt her part the cheeks of my buttocks with her hands. Then she stuck something inside me. I shivered with a combination of revulsion and fear. After a few seconds the warm bubbly liquid gurgled in my bowels. After months of a diet consisting of mostly eggs and bread, followed by four weeks of suppressed bowel movements while I waited each day for the sun to go down, I suffered from chronic constipation. The sudden extra volume inside an already constricted part of my anatomy resulted in an awful bloated sensation. I was distressed, worried about what would happen next.

'That'll take a few minutes. Use this when you're ready,' the nurse said abruptly, handing me a metal bedpan before leaving the room.

I felt ready to explode. The pain seemed to attack from every direction. It was hard to tell whether it was coming from my bowels, or whether it was labour pain, or both. I struggled to get onto the bedpan so I wouldn't soil the bed. Perched precariously, balancing on the rim, I couldn't reach the sides of the bed to steady myself. I fell backwards with my hands extended behind

211

me, arching my back. My arms felt like they were being pulled from their sockets. Suddenly there was an involuntary expulsion. What felt like jagged pellets ripped their way out of me, clanging against the metal sides of the pan. Dizzy and gasping for breath, another equally sharp pain gripped me and the whole agonising process was repeated.

'Help me! Please someone help me!' I called out. No one came.

Straining to keep my balance, I gritted my teeth against the searing pain. It took all of my concentration to hold on and not fall from the bed.

'Are you finished?' The nurse had walked back in carrying a metal wash basin.

I didn't think there could possibly be any more, and the urge to go had finally subsided. All I could do was nod my head.

She helped me off the bedpan, and, with the kind of indifference one might apply to a motor vehicle, she wiped between my legs and washed my whole lower torso with warm water before leaving me to it.

The pains were coming more frequently and getting stronger each time. A very tall nun with the sleeves of her habit rolled up to her elbows came into the room.

'I'm Sister Phillip. Let me have a look at you,' she said, lifting my robe and feeling my tummy. She parted my legs and pushed her fingers inside me, moving them around with a look of concentration. 'You'll be a while yet,' she said, and left the room.

I managed to raise my head up high enough to peek over my belly and look at the wall clock. It was 5.45 am. For the next four hours I was left alone to deal with the pain and terror as best I could. Wearing only a flimsy cotton robe, I shivered with the cold and fear. Goose bumps covered my entire body. I counted the minutes between each pain to get an idea of how much time I had to recover before the next one would start. They were still ten minutes apart, but each one was more intense than the one before. I didn't know how much more I could take before I'd lose consciousness.

I was still flat on my back when the next pain started. I gripped the sides of the bed until my knuckles were white, clenching my teeth together, growling like a dog with a bone. The pain wouldn't stop and I lost it.

'Help me. Please, dear God, help me!' I yelled in agony.

'Be quiet! There are other women on this ward,' an old nun, whom I'd never seen before, barked as she poked her head around the door.

As the pains continued I almost bit through my lip trying to hold back the screams. The pains were coming at shorter intervals now, and I only had a few minutes to regain my strength before the next onslaught. Just when I thought it could not get any worse, I felt like I was being torn in two, starting at my crotch. Unable to cope on my own any longer I screamed out again. 'Someone help me!'

Sister Phillip came back and examined me again. 'Give this poor girl some pain relief. She is almost fully dilated. She doesn't need to suffer like this.'

The nurse took the mask from the hook on the wall and placed it over my face. 'When your next contraction starts, take a deep breath,' she explained. 'Breathe easy, don't inhale too much at once.'

What's a contraction? I wanted to ask. I presumed she meant when the pain started. There wasn't much time to ponder this. As instructed I took a deep breath, then another and then another. As the ether took effect there was the most amazing relief. It didn't take the pain away altogether, but it made it more bearable. Afraid that I would become too heavily sedated, I only took a breath from the mask when I couldn't stand the pain anymore. I needed to stay alert.

I was just regrouping following a particularly strong contraction, when Sister Anne came into the room. She stood at the side of my bed staring at me.

'God is making you suffer for being such a selfish girl.'

The next pain started before I could respond. I took several gulping breaths into the mask; I wasn't going to give Sister Anne the satisfaction of seeing me in pain. Everything went blurry; when I came around she'd gone.

A bright overhead light shining directly into my face made me squint, and my legs were spread apart and hooked up into some kind of leather and steel contraption. There were several people standing around my bed. They were all wearing white jackets. *Who are all these people?* I wondered. *Why are they allowed to come in and look at me?*

Sister Phillip was positioned between my legs. 'On the next contraction, I want you to bear down,' she said.

I had no idea what she was talking about.

'Bear down,' Sister Phillip ordered as the next pain came. Instinctively I started to push.

'That's it,' she said.

The pain subsided and she told me to stop pushing. The process was repeated on the next contraction. I kept falling in and out of consciousness. My skin felt like it was being stretched to the limit. As the next contraction started so too did the urge to push.

'Don't push! Don't push!' Sister Phillip yelled anxiously. 'She's tearing,' she announced to the people standing around my bed. 'We'll have to do an episiotomy.' I felt like a laboratory rat.

I didn't know what an episiotomy was, but I was hoping it wouldn't involve any of the instruments I'd seen on the trolley.

On the next contraction I wasn't sure if they cut me or if I tore open. Either way, my flesh was on fire. A searing pain sent a flash of bright light across my eyes and my whole body shuddered.

'Oh my God!' I screamed.

I felt someone squeeze my hand.

'On the next contraction, I do not want you to push,' Sister Phillip said.

With no idea how to override the urge, I felt like I was being torn in half.

'Don't push! Don't push!' she yelled again.

Then I felt a whoosh. Everything fell silent. I was drifting and voices were moving further away. There were ghost-like shapes in the bright light but I couldn't distinguish faces. I heard a baby crying. It sounded a long way away, but I knew it was my baby.

'My baby!' I cried out. 'Give me my baby.'

I was ignored.

'Please, give me my baby,' I pleaded, feeling myself getting hysterical.

The people in the white coats were looking anxious. They talked over the top of me as if I wasn't there.

'Give me my baby!' I screamed, at the top of my voice, as I struggled to sit up.

I felt the warmth of someone holding my hand. When I looked up I saw a young man with tears in his eyes. 'I thought we had lost you,' he whispered, smiling.

They still hadn't brought my baby to me. Something was wrong. They are going to take him. I started to cry. 'Please show me my baby,' I begged.

A nurse carried a white bundle over to my bed. 'He's a fine big boy,' she said. 'He weighs 8.5 pounds.'

The measurement she added meant nothing to me. All I cared about was my baby. He was still covered in blood and amniotic fluid, but I had never seen anything more wondrous.

I was too weak to hold him so I took his tiny hand in mine. 'Hello, Adam,' I said, smiling and trembling with joy and relief.

Before I could say another word there was the sting of a needle and someone pulling on the thread as I was stitched back together. I felt something going into my arm, and then everything went black.

28

Turning up the heat

'When a girl gives up her baby for adoption she's put into a private ward,' Eileen had told me. So it was a relief to open my eyes and find myself in a ward with other women. I was stark naked except for the bindings around my breasts, which were so tight I could hardly breathe. It felt like a roll of barbed wire had been shoved between my legs, held in place with a thick wad of towelling. I was covered only with a cotton sheet and my feet were freezing cold.

The other mothers in the ward were all sitting up breastfeeding their babies. The lady opposite me was cuddling a baby wrapped in a pink blanket. She realised that I was awake and smiled at me. 'So you have decided to join us.'

'How long have I been asleep? What day is it?'

'February the 1st.'

I was frantic – I had been out to it for three days! What had they done with my baby? Who was looking after him? Why were my breasts bound? They did that when they took the baby. I started to panic but was too weak to even sit up.

Everything went black again. When I woke up I was wearing one of my nighties that opened at the front. I tried to sit up, but the stitches between my legs dug into my flesh. Lying flat on my back was the only position that was bearable.

The other mothers were nursing their babies, but no one had brought Adam to me. I knew where the nursery was, so, gritting my teeth, I rolled onto my side and tried to get out of bed to look for him. When I collapsed onto the floor in a pool of blood beside my bed, the lady in the opposite bed called for a nurse.

'What are you doing?' the nurse admonished, helping me back to bed. 'You've had twenty-eight stitches, you have to stay in bed for at least ten days,'

'Where is my baby?' I asked.

The nurse didn't answer but about thirty minutes later Sister Anne came to my bedside. She drew the curtain around us and forced a smile, but her eyes were as hard and cold as ever. I could predict exactly what she was going to say.

'Now, dear, you know that it is in your best interests, and that of the baby, if you sign the consent for adoption.' She offered me the documents and a pen.

'Please, bring me my baby,' I said, trying not to sound confrontational.

Sister Anne ignored me and proceeded to list all the reasons why adoption was the only option for an unmarried mother. It was true I had no husband, and no money. But at least I had a roof over my head, thanks to Uncle Les and Shirl. I knew I could help with the kids, the housework and the cooking to earn my keep until I could get a job. The most important thing was that if I didn't buckle and sign the consent form they could not take my baby.

And I wasn't going to buckle. 'Bring me my baby!'

Sister Anne scowled, before turning sharply and leaving the ward. She returned a few minutes later carrying a very distressed baby.

'Sit up!' she commanded.

It took all my strength to move into a sitting position and the pain shot right up my entire body. I felt like I was sitting on broken glass.

She thrust the screaming bundle into my arms.

'This isn't my baby,' I said, searching his features, hoping to find some resemblance to the chubby round-faced baby that had been handed to me after the birth.

'Of course this is your baby, now feed him!'

Sister Anne pulled at the bindings around my chest like she was trying to undo knotted rope. Adam's head thrashed about as he picked up the scent. Thinking I may have some milk to give him, I guided my nipple to his mouth and he latched on, sucking hard. The sharp pain caught me by surprise. I had never been given any instruction on how to soften my nipples in preparation for breast-feeding. Unmarried girls were not supposed to keep their babies, so what would have been the point?

After several agonising seconds he pulled away, letting out an even more intense scream. He drew his tiny legs up to his tummy and screamed until his face went purple and nothing more was coming out. He was in agony and there was nothing I could do to help him.

'See, you can't even feed this child,' Sister Anne sneered, before pulling Adam from my arms. I could hear him screaming all the way down the long corridor.

This was torture for both me and my baby, a cruel tactic to make my baby ravenous and inconsolable, with the intention of intimidating me into feeling incompetent. And it worked. I cried myself to sleep with Adam's pitiful wails ringing in my ears.

When I awoke, the lady in the bed opposite me was feeding her baby again. I watched with envy as the tiny bundle suckled contentedly. A nurse came into the room and I asked her to bring

Adam to me. She left without responding but a few minutes later she returned with Adam, who was still wailing with all his tiny might.

The nurse repeated the same charade of trying to put him to my breast, with the same result. Adam was hysterical. He set off every other baby in the ward. I started crying too as I rocked him in my arms. That was all I could do.

The lady in the bed opposite called the nurse over. 'What you are doing to this girl and her baby is a disgrace!'

The nurse went away and came back with a bottle of milk. I had no idea who this woman was but I will always be grateful for her compassion.

'Don't tell Sister Anne I gave this to you,' the nurse said, handing me a bottle containing a few ounces of warm milk, before scampering away.

'Can you manage that, dear?' the lady in the opposite bed asked.

'Yes, thank you,' I replied, putting the teat to Adam's mouth.

He was so hungry he started taking the milk too quickly and gulping down air. I had fed Stevie and Trudy many times, so I knew what to do. I held Adam in a sitting position until he sucked normally. As I watched my baby fill his belly with nourishment I was flooded with love for him. How grateful I was for having had the strength to get this far and not give in to the enormous pressures of the past few months. The future was still uncertain, but living my life one day at a time was not unusual. Hope and faith were all I had. I just didn't believe that God would put me through all of this and take my baby as well. I knew I had to stay strong.

'You are the most beautiful boy in the whole wide world,' I said, kissing the top of Adam's head.

He stopped suckling when he heard my voice. They say newborns don't smile, but don't believe it; he was smiling at me. Now that Adam wasn't suffering, nothing they did to me would make me consent to relinquish him for adoption. Suddenly I was as strong and protective as a lioness, ready to tear to pieces anyone who came near him.

About five days after he was born Adam was brought to me again. He was screaming, but it was different somehow, more high-pitched, like something was pinching him. I tried to feed him, but he wouldn't take the bottle. His nappy was wet. When I changed him I saw the telltale wad of cottonwool on the end of his penis.

'My poor baby,' I said, the tears rolling down my face. The circumcision had been performed without me even knowing about it.

That night, after Adam had had his last feed and been taken back to the nursery, I was just dozing off when Sister Anne came to my bed. She drew the curtain around us and leaned forward.

'Now, dear, you are being very selfish,' she started. 'We have a nice couple waiting to take your baby. They will be able to give him all the things you can't. You must think of the child.'

She placed the papers and a pen onto my bed.

'I am not going to put my baby up for adoption!' I said resolutely, pushing the papers away.

Sister Anne's contempt for me was palpable as she snatched the document from my bed.

None of my family had contacted me since the birth, not even Uncle Stan. I'd started to write to Peter a dozen times to tell him that I'd had the baby and had refused to relinquish him. Then I'd ponder the futility of it, and tear up what I'd written.

I was in the middle of another attempt at writing to Peter when I paused to look out the window, to contemplate the beautiful day and the world beyond. I could see the sky; it was a deep sapphire blue. *I bet the water at the lake is warm by now*, I thought.

'Hello, Katie.'

I looked round to see Uncle Les standing at the side of my bed. He didn't look comfortable.

'Hello, Uncle Les.'

'I just saw the baby. He's a lovely boy,'

'Yes, he is. I've called him Adam Jon.'

This seemed to exhaust our conversation. We sat looking at each other. Then the purpose of Uncle Les's visit became apparent.

'So, this Peter is the father of your baby.' He stated this as if he knew it for a fact.

'No, he isn't,' I replied, wondering how he knew Peter's name.

'Well, according to this, he is.' He handed me a letter.

It was from Dan, addressed to Uncle Les and mostly a bitter tirade, slamming Uncle Les for being a spineless bastard and letting Shirl bully him, and repeating all the usual invective Mamma had poisoned him with. He went on and on about Shirl not giving us time to bury Kev. This was nonsense I had heard a million times before. Dan didn't even know Shirl, he had only been eleven when Uncle Les got married and went out of his life.

Then I got to the next part. 'Peter Ashton is the father of Kay's baby,' Dan had written.

I shook my head and laughed out loud. Dan was such a bloody know-all, but this time he knew nothing. He had written this poison pen letter with no regard for the consequences. It was a spiteful, nasty letter that wasn't hindered by any intimate knowledge of the facts and why I even got a mention remains a mystery to me. It was easy to find an excuse for Dan's need to lash out. He was only sixteen and his mother had callously abandoned him only two years before. Mamma leaving the way she did hadn't affected me in the same way. She wasn't my mother, after all, but Danny was her baby. What really surprised me, though, was Uncle Les taking this irrelevant information on board as fact and making a big deal out of it.

'This is not a laughing matter, young lady,' Uncle Les said sternly.

'Dan has no idea who my baby's father is. Besides, what does it matter?'

'So there's more than one bloke who could have been the father?' Uncle Les asked with a look of disgust.

He tossed the rest of the letters from Peter onto my bed. Just as I'd suspected she would, Shirl had gone through my suitcase.

'It seems this Peter was more than just a friend,' Uncle Les said curtly.

'Did you enjoy reading my personal mail?' I asked, feeling my face blush at knowing they would have read all Peter's sexual fantasies.

Uncle Les looked embarrassed.

'Peter is not the father of my child,' I said bluntly.

'According to Dan he is.'

'Are the things Dan said about you and Shirl true?' I asked.

That seemed to bring Uncle Les around and he changed his approach. 'Katie, I'm going to Vietnam in a few weeks and Shirl would like you to come back and stay with her and the girls, but you can't bring the baby home.'

I stared at him for a long time before I could respond. 'So if the baby was Peter Ashton's I could bring him home?' I asked, trying to understand his flawed logic.

'Don't get smart with me, young lady.'

Uncle Les had been to the nursery and seen Adam, his great-nephew, and yet he imagined I could leave this hospital without this beautiful baby because there was some conflict in the minds of others as to who his father was.

'Uncle Les, could you give one of your children away?'

'This is different and you know it.'

'No, I don't know it,' I snapped.

It infuriated me that Uncle Les thought that because I wasn't married I could simply give my baby away, just like that, with as much regard as tossing old clothes into a rag-bag. That somehow being an unmarried mother made me different from other mothers. He was serious about expecting me to give up my son and go back to his place as the unpaid live-in domestic helper for his wife, while he went off to war. I wondered whether all my family were stark raving mad, or just Mamma and Uncle Les.

Uncle Les got up from the chair and walked away without saying another word. I would not see him again for more than twenty years.

I didn't know what I was going to do or where I was going to go. Even Uncle Stan seemed to have abandoned me.

29

If looks could kill

'You had better listen to what I have to say.'

It was two days before I was due to be discharged. I was drifting off to sleep when Sister Anne appeared once again at my bedside. Thinking at first that it was going to be more of the same, I turned my back on her. But her tone was more threatening than it had been. I sat up and faced her.

'I know that your uncle isn't going to let you go back to his place with the baby. I have contacted the Child Welfare Department and informed them that you are a homeless unmarried girl. If you have nowhere to go when you are due to be discharged, they will take your baby.'

She was looking very smug, like we'd been playing some kind of game of bluff, where she always held the power and enjoyed watching me fool myself.

'You have two choices, child. You can either watch the Child Welfare take your baby and put him in a home, or you can do the right thing and sign the consent for his adoption. We have a wonderful family already waiting to take him.'

She put the documents on my bed and handed me a pen. I smacked it out of her hand with such force it rolled across the floor. I picked up the documents and tore the pages in half. The hatred I felt for this woman was so intense I wanted to grab her by the throat and throttle the life out of her. This was not even about her winning anymore, because it was a lose–lose situation. She could not have cared about my son's wellbeing if she could gloat and threaten to have the Child Welfare take him away. At the very least, this was about punishment, although it did occur to me that she may have some other motive for wanting my son so desperately. I didn't imagine that wealthy childless couples could adopt a newborn baby without some payment involved. Perhaps even a payment in advance.

Sister Anne walked out and a paralysing despair engulfed me. I felt like I was on the edge of an abyss with nowhere to go but into the void. If they were going to take Adam it would have to be without my consent, and the thought of him in a home like Bidura was more than I could bear. I looked at the big window beside my bed and wondered if I'd be able to get out onto the ledge and jump from the building, taking Adam with me. If they took him away I would have nothing to live for, and he'd be better dead than living his life in an institution. I was starting to lose my mind.

The hopelessness of my predicament was overwhelming. After everyone in the ward was asleep I pulled the curtain around my bed and knelt down on the hard floor. Prayer was all I had left. I had to hope there was a Mother in heaven and that she would hear me. I started reciting the Hail Mary.

'Hail Mary, full of grace, the Lord is with thee. Blessed art thou among women, and blessed is the fruit of thy womb, Jesus. Holy Mary, mother of God, pray for us sinners now, and at the hour of our death. Amen.' Without stopping to take a breath, I started again from the beginning. 'Hail Mary, full of grace . . .'

It was a desperate chant, one I wasn't sure was being heard, but that night I prayed over and over until I collapsed with sheer exhaustion.

When I awoke I was curled up on the floor and shivering. The ward was quiet and it was still dark outside. I got back into bed. My eyes were closed but I sensed someone standing next to my bed. *It's her*, I thought. *What does she want now? She has won. They are taking my baby tomorrow.*

'There must be someone I can call who will help you.'

It sounded like Sister Veronica, but without opening my eyes I couldn't be sure whose voice it was. I knew that if I opened my eyes it might not be real. *My mind is playing tricks on me*, I thought, but I decided to play the game.

'YY 2525.' I recited the only telephone number I knew.

The next thing it was morning. A day I never wanted the sun to come up on. Would they let me see Adam one more time before they took him? Could I hold him and kiss him, or would they just come and tell me he was gone? Recalling the mournful sounds that came from Mamma the night Kev died, now I understood. Losing a child is a pain that defies description.

A while later Sister Veronica came to my bedside. She was carrying a telephone, which she plugged into the wall. 'You have a phone call,' she said, smiling.

'Hello, princess,' said the familiar voice.

The floodgates opened when I heard Uncle Jack's voice.

'What have you called your baby?' he asked. When I told him he chuckled. 'It'll grow on me,' he said.

Then Aunty Daphne came on the line. She sounded very excited. 'Hello, Katie. A little boy! How are you, love?' she asked tenderly. I burst into uncontrollable sobs. 'We've had a dreadful time,

Aunty Daphne. They're going to take my baby away and put him in a home.' I was gasping for breath.

'They're not going to do anything of the kind,' she said comfortingly. 'Now, who is the father of this child?'

'His name is John McNorton.'

'Well, he's just as responsible as you are. He'll have to help you. How do we contact him?'

'But, Aunty Daphne, I don't love Adam's father.'

'Love? What's love got to do with this? Katie, if you're serious about keeping this baby, the father has to help you. Now, how do we contact him?'

I couldn't remember their phone number, but I told her his mother's name and where they lived.

'Now, don't you worry, love. It will spoil your milk. We'll work something out.'

'Thank you, Aunty Daphne.' The relief was indescribable.

'What do you need for the baby?' she asked.

All I had were the few matinee jackets I had made. 'Just about everything.'

For the first time in months I cried tears of joy. I couldn't stop the torrent flowing. The lady in the bed opposite came over and gave me a hug. 'You are the bravest girl I have ever seen,' she said, stroking my hair.

That afternoon I got a phone call from Mrs McNorton.

'Adam is nice, but I prefer Anthony,' she said when I answered her question about the baby's name.

I didn't tell her that I had been going to call him Anthony, after St Anthony, the patron saint of lost things. As St Anthony was always portrayed carrying the baby Jesus, I thought he gave special protection to children. Given the circumstances, it seemed appropriate.

John came to the phone. 'Hello,' he said. His communication skills seemed not to have improved since the last time we had spoken. 'Can I come to see the baby?' he asked, sounding excited that he had a newborn son.

He arrived at the hospital that night carrying a bunch of flowers and grinning from ear to ear, having just seen Adam through the glass window in the nursery. It was both disappointing and surprising that his parents hadn't come to the hospital with him to see their first-born grandchild.

'He's unreal,' John said, shaking his head in disbelief.

'Oh, he is very real,' I said, and smiled.

Sister Anne didn't come back to see me again. Now that I had somewhere to go when I was discharged she couldn't take my baby. This was the sweetest victory I would ever know.

The next morning I was due to be discharged. A male doctor came to see me, asked a few questions, then left. A nurse came back and gave me a bottle of pills; she said they were iron tablets. Apparently I had lost a lot of blood and these pills were going to help me to rebuild my iron levels.

I showered and washed my hair for the first time since Adam's birth. I took out the outfit I had made, and, although it was creased and wrinkled, it fitted perfectly. After months of walking around with a huge belly it felt good to be wearing something with a waist.

The earliest time I could be discharged from the hospital was eight o'clock. I didn't want to spend a minute more in that godforsaken place than I had to, so I asked John to come and pick us up as early as possible.

None of the neonatal nurses came to see if I needed assistance giving Adam a bath. Never having bathed a newborn baby, I was scared that I might drop him, so I sponged Adam all over and popped him onto the scales. He weighed 8.1 pounds. His birth weight was 8.5 pounds, but I didn't know that it wasn't common practice then to discharge a newborn from hospital before they had regained their birth weight.

John carried Adam, who slept contentedly in a bassinette that John's mother had thoughtfully sent to me. I was very unsteady on my legs and my whole body felt extremely fragile.

The relief was overwhelming as we walked to the door. *Holy Mary, mother of God, thank you.* I repeated the phrase over and over in my mind.

'Goodbye, dear,' Sister Anne said cheerfully. She was smiling as she walked towards us in the corridor.

'Goodbye, Sister Anne,' I replied.

When Sister Anne recognised me she stopped suddenly. The smile vanished. If looks could kill I wouldn't have left the hospital that day.

30

A shotgun wedding

Adam squinted and rolled his little head from side to side, trying to avoid the glare coming through the back window of John's car. I reached over the front seat and struggled to pull the towel from my carry bag, to drape over his bassinette like a canopy.

Although it was stiflingly hot, I needed to pick up my suitcase from Uncle Les's and I asked John if we could make a detour.

The traffic was bumper-to-bumper along Parramatta Road. I turned on the car radio to find out what was happening in the world. The Beaumont children had not been found and I shivered at the thought of what may have happened to them. The heat-wave conditions were continuing for the rest of the week, with the mercury expected to reach one hundred degrees Fahrenheit by midday. Health authorities were warning people to take care, especially the elderly and those with very young babies.

Adam was restless. I was kneeling on the front seat and reaching over to gently stroke his little legs and arms, talking to him so he'd know I was near. Travelling backwards in a car was not a good idea, though, and the stop–start motion in the traffic was making me queasy. I asked John to stop at the next petrol station so I could damp down a towel and get into the back seat with the baby.

Frank Hadlow had shown me years before how to make a cooling device by spinning a wet rag. I unpinned Adam's thick towelling nappy, and he seemed to sigh with relief when I fanned him with the damp towel. He was beginning to stir as we pulled up at Shirl's house. I had no intention of hanging around longer than it would take to get my suitcase.

'We'd better take the baby inside while I get my things,' I said to John, going ahead to save time. 'It's too hot to leave him in the car.'

'Hello,' Shirl said in a standoffish voice, when she opened the door.

'I've come to pick up the rest of my things,' I said, equally coolly.

My suitcase wasn't under the lounge where I had left it.

'It's in my room. I'll get it. Can I have a look at the baby?' Shirl asked.

I put the case on the Nite'n'Day to transfer my things from the bag Uncle Les had loaned me to go to hospital. Being tidy, I always knew instantly if anyone had been through my things, and Shirl had had a good stickybeak. Even the baby clothes I'd secretly made had been taken out of the brown paper bag. I said nothing, but gave her a knowing look.

'This is the baby you were expecting me to give away to a stranger,' I said under my breath, as I walked to the bathroom to dampen the towel again.

'He is a lovely baby,' Shirl said, in a way that told me she had enough conscience to feel ashamed.

'Yes, he is.' We were standing at her front gate staring at each other. 'Goodbye, Shirl, and thank you for all you did for me.'

John said that if there were no traffic jams it would take about thirty minutes to get from Cabramatta to Seven Hills. We had been on the road ten minutes when Adam's dinner bell went off. Spinning a damp towel, fanning, stroking and talking in a soothing voice does nothing to ease the hunger pangs of a hungry baby, as I realised soon enough. Adam's high-pitched wail grew louder and his legs pumped like pistons.

Not knowing what else to do, I loosened my bra and tried to get Adam to take my breast. Although I couldn't give him any milk, I thought that having something to suck on might calm him down. But it made him worse when there was nothing for his effort.

By the time we pulled up at Aunty Daphne's house Adam's body lay limp in my arms. He was making a murmuring noise and it terrified me. It was what Pop Higgins had sounded like just before he had died. Aunty Daphne opened the front door and waved.

'Help me!' I yelled from the car.

Aunty Daphne came running down the steps. 'Oh my God!' she said, taking Adam into her arms before running back to the house. I could hardly walk, let alone run.

Either John didn't register what was happening, or he did and knew he'd better get out of the way. Either way, he carried my suitcase into the lounge room and said he had to get back to work. 'Can I come and see you after I knock off?'

'Of course,' I said.

'Quickly, Katie, we have to get this baby some fluids.' Aunty Daphne handed Adam back to me to put the kettle on and prepare a baby bath. Fortunately, she had bottles and teats around, as Roberta was still a toddler. 'Cool that water down while I get him into the bath,' she said.

Aunty Daphne always said please and thank you, but she didn't have time for those niceties this day. She cradled Adam in her arms and eased him into the bath, gently splashing water over his body. Adam looked limp, almost lifeless, as she held him in the water. He wasn't making a sound; it was as if all of his strength had been drained.

I was running the bottle under the cold tap, but it was such a hot day the water was still coming out warm. I got some ice from the freezer and put it into a saucepan around the bottle, jigging it about.

'What time was his last feed?'

'Seven o'clock.'

'He's way overdue. Why didn't you feed him?'

'I didn't have a bottle,' I said, unable to stop the tears.

'What about your milk?'

'They strapped my breasts up.'

'What?'

'I don't have any milk. They bound my breasts so I wouldn't get any,' I repeated.

'Didn't they give you a bottle with some formula to bring him home?' she asked in total astonishment.

'They didn't give me anything,' I said, feeling tears of humiliation and guilt at my stupidity for not asking.

'Did they tell you what formula they had been giving him?' By now Aunty Daphne was sounding very angry.

'They didn't tell me anything.'

I tested the boiled water on the inside of my wrist; it had cooled down enough.

Aunty Daphne lifted Adam out of the bath and held him in her arms with a towel draped loosely around him. 'Give me the bottle.'

Adam wouldn't take the teat and his little head flopped to the side.

No! I screamed in my head. *He's going to die! Please, God, don't take him.* I pleaded over and over. A tsunami of relief engulfed me when at last he started sucking, but the water only gave him enough strength to begin screaming again.

'You'll have to go to the chemist and ask for some formula for a newborn baby,' Aunty Daphne said, pacing the floor, trying to calm Adam down.

The chemist shop wasn't far but in the heat of the day, with twenty-eight stitches of hard catgut between my legs, it felt like a million miles. When I got back Adam had found more strength and continued his protest until we could make up a bottle of formula and cool it down.

'Let me do this, please, Aunty Daphne,' I said, reaching out to take Adam from her.

As I fed Adam, Aunty Daphne went very quiet; she seemed to be mulling things over.

'Those rotten bastards!' she said finally. 'They didn't get him, so they didn't give a bugger if he lived or died.'

Unlike Uncle Stan, Aunty Daphne had no love lost for the Catholic Church. She had gone to a Catholic school in Nyngan, and had heard all the stories from Mamma and Phyllis about the cruelty of the nuns. It was only for the fact that Aunty Daphne's phone was locked that Sister Anne didn't get a scathing earful from her that day. I didn't dare tell Aunty Daphne about the horrors of St Margaret's, or the treatment I was subjected to when I refused to sign the adoption papers. I didn't think she'd believe me; it was worse than any of the stories either Mamma or Phyllis had told.

'That's good, he's feeding nicely,' she said, hovering over me and supervising the feed. 'Don't let him gulp it down too quickly.'

When Adam fell asleep in my arms, I started crying with relief that he was out of immediate danger. But I couldn't entirely relax. In the extreme heat, Aunty Daphne's house was like an oven. I spun the wet towel and fanned Adam constantly to prevent him cooking.

'If I'd lost Adam after all we've been through, I would have thrown myself under a bus,' I said.

'Don't talk like that,' Aunty Daphne scolded.

More than twenty-four hours had passed since Sister Anne had stood at my bedside with her final threats. Since then I'd hardly slept. If I didn't lie down soon, I was going to fall down.

Aunty Daphne had made up my bed in the back room. She carried the bassinette out there as it was cooler than the west-facing lounge room. I put my head onto the pillow and the lights went out.

When I woke up Aunty Daphne was standing next to the bassinette, smiling. 'He's a beautiful baby, Katie. He looks like you.'

'How do you see that? I look at him and see his grandfather.'

'I've spoken to the McNortons and they're going to organise the wedding,' Aunty Daphne said.

This was the first I knew of it! I didn't love John but I would have married the devil if it meant not losing my son, and John was far from being the devil.

When Stevie and Trudy came home from school they couldn't comprehend that I was now a mother. It was hard enough for me to fully comprehend.

'Go to your room, Trudy,' Aunty Daphne said, sounding tense as we heard Uncle Jack's car drive into the carport. Trudy scuttled off like a scared little mouse.

Checking his pigeons was usually a higher priority for Uncle Jack than coming into the house to greet his family, but this day he came straight from the car. He didn't speak to Aunty Daphne, who was at the sink peeling potatoes for dinner.

'Hello, Uncle Jack,' I said.

'Hello, Katie,' he replied, grinning from ear to ear.

'The baby's asleep in the back room.'

Uncle Jack went down the hall and came back beaming. 'You've done well, kiddo,' he said approvingly.

Later, John came over and watched me feed Adam. 'Would you like to hold him?' I asked. 'Sit down, I'll show you how to hold him.' I chuckled at his nervousness.

'He's unreal,' John said, staring down at his son.

For reasons best known to Uncle Jack, he didn't like John right from the start. I guess he wouldn't have liked any man who had got me pregnant. The next evening when I heard Uncle Jack's car pull up, I suggested to John that perhaps he ought to leave before Uncle Jack came inside. As John was walking down the hall they collided. There was a heated exchange, which surprised me. Ordinarily John was a quiet, placid person. But he didn't let Uncle Jack push him around, and I was proud of the way he stood up to him.

'Get out of my house and don't come back,' Uncle Jack said.

After John had left, I decided to let things settle down. It was no use trying to talk to Uncle Jack when he was riled.

The next morning Adam woke me early for his first feed. Stevie and Trudy were still in bed, and Aunty Daphne was giving Roberta her breakfast, so I thought it might be a good time to speak to Uncle Jack. He was sitting silently at the end of the kitchen table, solemnly sipping his tea, just as he did every morning.

'Why have you told John that he can't come to see me?' I asked.

'I don't need to give you a reason,' he said, his blue eyes driving into me over the rim of the cup, trying to intimidate me.

I stared back, holding my ground.

'Do you want to marry that punk?'

This was only the second time in my life anyone had bothered to ask me what I wanted.

'Don't marry someone you don't love, Katie. You'll both be miserable,' he said, in a tone that convinced me that he was speaking from personal experience.

'Love? Uncle Jack, I don't know what love is.'

'You can stay here, you don't have to marry him.'

At this stage I hadn't figured out the more sinister undercurrent at Uncle Jack's, but I knew that I couldn't live in a place where everyone was afraid to speak without his approval.

'Uncle Jack, I appreciate your offer, but I'm going to marry John McNorton.'

'They don't care about you, Katie. That punk is only marrying you to keep his arse out of jail. The old girl went to see them and threatened to charge him with carnal knowledge.'

I was speechless. Mamma was up to her old tricks again and I didn't doubt that she was capable of having John sent to prison. Nor did I doubt Uncle Jack's capacity for wanting to make Mamma look bad.

'I am going to marry John McNorton,' I said firmly.

'Then don't be here when I get home.'

My face was burning with anger. Uncle Jack knew I had nowhere to go. He thought he could get me to bend to his will. I was sick of people giving me ultimatums. 'Alright, I'll leave today.'

Uncle Jack shoved Aunty Daphne to one side as he headed for the back door. He and I would never speak to each other again.

31

A girl, a suitcase and a bassinette

Uncle Jack left before I could ask him to unlock the phone, so I had no way to call John to pick me up. I was packed and ready to walk to the station just before Adam's next feed. I gave him a few more ounces of milk, which I hoped would hold him for at least four hours.

'Goodbye, Aunty Daphne, and thank you for everything,' I said, giving her a hug.

'I'm sorry, love,' she said, wiping the tears with her apron.

'It's alright, I know you can't do anything. But I'd have lost Adam if you hadn't helped me.'

My insides felt like they were going to fall out all over the floor when I picked up Adam's bassinette in one hand, and my beaten-up old suitcase in the other. As I was going out the gate I turned to wave to Aunty Daphne, but she had already gone inside and closed the door.

So soon after the birth I had no strength in my back or abdominal muscles, and carrying a heavy load in both hands was agony.

The sun on my face was vicious and I kept checking to make sure the shade canopy over Adam hadn't shifted.

The walk from Aunty Daphne's house to Seven Hills station was up and down dale for about two miles. Sheer determination, fuelled by rage, got me from one bus shelter to the next, where I sat in the shade to catch my breath. Each public phone box I came to had been vandalised.

'I'd rather sleep in the park than spend one more night under that bloody bully's roof,' I muttered to myself.

'What was that, dear?'

I snapped out of my stupor and looked around. A woman was sitting beside me. She must have thought I was a lunatic babbling to myself.

Finally, we reached Seven Hills station and I found a public phone that was working. John had to break for lunch before he could collect us. As I sat waiting, tears of anger and grief poured out of me. My nose started bleeding again and all I had was a nappy to catch the flow. Intermingled with my sobs were questions. What if Uncle Jack was telling the truth about why John was marrying me? Not that it mattered. I was all out of options.

How pathetic we must have looked. A distressed young girl, barely sixteen years old, with no wedding ring, a two-week-old baby in a bassinette in one hand and a beaten-up old suitcase in the other, sitting at a bus stop, with a nose bleed, as all the buses went by. Not a single person asked if I needed help. Some even gave a little 'tut-tut', as if to say, 'You should have kept your legs together.'

Adam was still sleeping soundly when John pulled up, but I was ready to drop. The strain on my body had caused a haemorrhage, and I was afraid the blood would seep through my clothes.

We drove a short distance and found a park with a public toilet, and I cleaned myself up as best I could.

*

'What's happened?' Mrs Mack asked, looking surprised when she saw my suitcase.

John hadn't been able to call his mother to tell her we were coming.

'Uncle Jack told me John wasn't welcome and if I didn't like it I could leave,' I told her, giving part of the story.

'Your grandmother told me about your Uncle Jack,' she said casually.

'When did you speak to my grandmother?'

'She came here to see me when you were in the hospital. She's a strange person, your grandmother,' she said, with a slight giggle.

This puzzled me. I had not told Mamma that John McNorton was Adam's father. *Dan, of course. He just had to meddle.* I could only imagine what Mamma would have told Mrs Mack, but it still annoyed me that she was inferring that my grandmother was a crazy person.

Mrs Mack showed me to John's room, which, although I'd been to their house many times before, I'd never seen. It was immaculate. John was either the neatest, cleanest male I had ever known, or his mother cleaned his room every day. There wasn't a speck of dust anywhere. The sun, filtering through the lace curtains, shone onto a collection of model locomotives lined up along the top of a book-case under the window. John hadn't told me that he was interested in model trains. There was photographic equipment lying around, and boxes of slides on top of his chest of drawers. Piles of glossy racing car magazines were neatly stacked on another bookcase next to his bed. John's room smelled nice, with just a hint of Old Spice aftershave. I lay down on the bed and closed my eyes. My body ached from head to toe. When I woke up the room was dark.

My God! Adam! I've missed his feed.

'I'm so sorry, Mrs Mack. I went out like a light, and I didn't even hear Adam cry.' I felt very embarrassed.

241

'I'll make you a cup of tea, dear,' she said.

Adam had been fed and changed and I could see some nappies flapping on the line outside. 'I'm sorry, Mrs Mack, I should have done that.'

'He didn't cry much,' she reassured me, 'just a little bit to say hurry up with my food. He's a very good baby, just like his father was.'

'I'll set the table, Mrs Mack,' I offered, going to the cutlery drawer. I had eaten at the McNortons' so often I knew my way around the kitchen.

That night after dinner Mrs Mack made up a bed for me on the fold-down lounge. John told me it was very hard for him sleeping in his room alone, knowing I was sleeping on the lounge, but I was grateful. I was in no hurry to have sex again anytime soon.

The McNortons were arranging for John and me to be married on 11 March. Until then I could relax. Apart from helping Mrs Mack with housework, my whole focus was on Adam and he was thriving.

A friend of Mrs Mack's gave Adam a magnificent vintage cane pram. Mrs Mack was a bit embarrassed that the pram was the old-fashioned kind with large pump-up tyres and spoked wheels, but I loved it. There wasn't one chip in the enamel paint. The studded satin lining under the hood and around the sides of the pram had no wear and tear, and it was spotlessly clean. It looked like it had just come off a showroom floor, a baby carriage fit for my little prince.

One afternoon I was in the Macks' garden watching Adam as he slept in his pram. He opened his eyes and gave me the biggest smile. My heart swelled in my chest, I'd never felt anything like it.

242

'Mummy loves you so much,' I said, stroking his soft cheek. Just then, two uniformed policemen walked down the side path and knocked on the back door. Knowing that policemen usually come to the front door, I figured they must have been mates of John's father, Harry. He was a guard at Parramatta jail, so he would have known a lot of coppers. They went inside and a few minutes later Harry Mack came out looking grim-faced. My first thought was that someone in my family had died.

'These policemen need to ask you a few questions, Katie,' Harry said nervously. I followed him inside.

They'd come to question me concerning the charge of carnal knowledge that Mamma had issued against John. I was floored that she'd done this, and wouldn't have blamed the McNortons one bit if they had tossed me out. Did Mamma really want to see me and my baby on the street, just to fulfil her prophecy? I was so ashamed I couldn't look at Harry. The policemen asked me some embarrassing questions and after they established that John and I were getting married, they left.

'Sorry to have bothered you, Harry,' one of them said, as they were going out the door.

This was too much. I buried my face in my hands and cried.

'Now don't you worry. We'll get all this sorted out,' Harry said, putting his arm around me.

That night I had trouble sleeping. I was searching for answers. *What does Mamma want from me?* The questions were spinning in my head. *Is she angry because I didn't give my baby away? Is she afraid that I might go back to her place, with a 'bastard', and shame her in front of the townspeople? Or is she such a controlling person that she simply can't stand to think that her days of controlling me are over?*

Harry must have had some pull because we didn't hear any more from the cops.

'We'll have to get you on the pill,' Mrs Mack announced one

evening, completely insensitive about discussing such things in front of males.

As I was still under eighteen I needed written parental consent to get a doctor's prescription to purchase the pill. Mrs Mack wrote to the doctor, but I couldn't comprehend how popping a tiny pill into my mouth every day could prevent me from becoming pregnant.

Living with the McNortons for those few weeks before I married John was the most peaceful period in my life up to that point. It was like a dream, and I expected to wake up to find Mamma hissing abuse at me through clenched teeth. Or to find Sister Anne shining a torch in my face, growling, 'You selfish girl. Sign these papers!'

Mrs Mack had a wonderful life. She didn't work outside the home. Looking after her family was her job, and, unless she had a private stash somewhere, Harry Mack must have been very generous because Mrs Mack changed her clothes twice a day, always smartening up and applying make-up before dinner.

Every year Mrs Mack and her sisters, Aunty Peggy and Aunty Betty, took a holiday to Manly Beach without their children or husbands. Mrs Mack had lots of hobbies and interests, and belonged to historical societies and art groups. She was a member of a card group of eight ladies, who once a week took turns in hosting afternoons of gin rummy and gossip.

'What are you going to wear to the wedding?' Mrs Mack asked me less than a week before the big day.

This had been worrying me since the date had been set, and I found it hard to believe that she hadn't figured out that I had nothing suitable, and no money. None of my clothes from before I was pregnant were formal enough, and, apart from my maternity dresses and the white linen skirt I'd run up, they were all I had.

'I don't have anything to wear,' I said, feeling crushed to admit it.

Mrs Mack handed me a brand new ten-dollar note, one of the first to go into circulation after decimal currency had been introduced.

I walked to town but couldn't find anything I liked for the money, so I bought some pink linen, enough for a two-piece suit, and a contrasting camisole to wear under the jacket. I still had the white shoes I wore to Uncle Stan's wedding, and they fitted me better now. This left me with enough to buy a piece of pink satin and a bit of lace to cover a pillbox hat, and a spray of artificial flowers to attach to the clutch purse I'd taken to the ball with Peter. I still had the crystal brooch Uncle Stan had given me for being a bridesmaid at his wedding. Talk about something old, something new.

Mrs Mack looked alarmed when I came home without a dress. 'Are you serious? You are going to make your dress? The wedding is in three days.' She looked worried.

'May I use your sewing machine please, Mrs Mack?'

I set it up on the table in the formal dining room that was never used, and worked furiously. I had no margin for error, but finished my wedding outfit with one day to spare. The ensemble was plain, as I didn't have time get too fancy. The straight skirt covered my knees and was rather matronly for my age. Mini-skirts were in fashion, but I didn't think it would be appropriate to get married in one.

'My goodness, Kay!' Mrs Mack exclaimed. 'Where did you learn to sew like this?'

'My Aunty Daphne taught me a bit and I have a book with sewing instructions,' I said, feeling very pleased with the result, especially the sleeves, which did look professional, if I had to say so myself.

245

'You are such a clever girl. It looks like you bought it in a shop,' Aunty Peggy said. I was bursting with pride. 'I have an old sewing machine I don't use. You can have it, although it doesn't have a buttonholer,' she told me apologetically.

John McNorton and I were married at St Mary Margaret's Catholic Church, Merrylands, on Aunty Daphne's birthday, 11 March 1966. Being a sinful unmarried mother, I wasn't allowed to walk down the aisle or get married in front of the altar. I had to enter by the side door and take my vows to the left of the tabernacle. John gave me a plain band of gold. I had not seen it before he put it on my finger, but it teamed beautifully with the engagement ring he had given me more than a year earlier.

The only family members to attend our wedding were Uncle Stan and Aunty Shirley on my side, and on John's, just his parents and brothers. Aunty Peggy took care of Adam for the day. After the ceremony the Macks paid for a dinner at the Parramatta Leagues Club. Mrs Mack had made a cake with the words 'Health, Wealth and Happiness' piped onto the top. John's middle brother, Brian, took a photograph of John and me, the only one we ever had taken together. But John's parents didn't have a photograph taken with their son on his wedding day, which I thought was very strange.

'Katie, this baby is a credit to you,' Aunty Peggy said, beaming, when I picked up Adam to take him back to Mrs Mack's.

John and I spent our first night together as man and wife in a squeaky bed across the hall from his parents. Mrs Mack suggested that Adam sleep in their room so John and I could be by ourselves. Our wedding night was the first time John and I had been together since Adam was conceived and it was the first time we had ever actually slept in a bed together. I made him turn out the light while I got changed. How bizarre! Here I was, married with a baby, and my husband had never so much as seen my breasts. John was disappointed when I told him that we couldn't make love.

'I'm not ready yet,' I said, hoping he'd understand without needing me to go into details.

John and I left the next day for The Entrance on the Central Coast, for a little honeymoon. It had all been arranged. How anyone expected that a girl with a six-week-old baby, who was still bleeding and walked funny with the stitches between her legs, could enjoy a honeymoon was beyond me. Adam stayed with the Macks, and being separated from him terrified me. On our first night away John tried again to make love, and was annoyed when I refused.

'I had twenty-eight stitches,' I said, hoping he'd realise it wasn't a head wound.

The lack of desire to have sex with John was not only because my body wasn't ready. My heart and thoughts were still very attached to Peter. Although he didn't want my baby, I couldn't just turn off my feelings for him. I felt like a coward, not writing and letting him know it was over, and that I wasn't going to give up my son. Still, I missed him terribly, and trying to imagine my life without him was hard.

We were supposed to be away a week, but I was fretting for Adam so much we came back after two days.

32

Change of address

There had to be something in the wind for John to show any outward sign of emotion.

'Are you going to let me in on the secret?' I asked.

'Mum and Dad have bought us a house.' He grinned excitedly. 'It's at Harris Park. Wait until you see the walls.'

John showed me the street on the Gregory's map. It was a tiny blip on the page, with a railway line running parallel. It was more than pretentious to call where we were going to live Harris Park; it was on the outskirts of Granville, closer to Clyde and just a stone's throw from the Shell Oil refinery that spewed black smoke and toxic fumes day and night. Granville had a very bad reputation, which may or may not have been deserved. All I knew was that the Monroe brothers lived there, and the prospect of having them for neighbours was a horror I didn't want to contemplate. The street didn't look close to any schools, shops or transport. Not that being close to public transport mattered; Adam's cane pram didn't fold down for boarding a bus or fitting into the boot of a taxi.

I couldn't believe that the Macks would buy us a house without even telling me, or at least taking me to see it. But I would have felt so ungrateful to not show my appreciation.

Mrs Mack took us to a second-hand furniture auction in Parramatta, and we bought an old lounge and a dining room suite. Her friends gave us bits and pieces for Adam's room. From the classifieds in the newspaper that John's company printed, we bought a Hoover washer and a second-hand fridge with a door that wouldn't stay closed. The whole house was furnished with change out of thirty dollars.

Although I was apprehensive about the location, I was excited to be moving into our new home. The Macks drove us down Harris Street and turned left. After a series of left and right turns, I was dizzy; I would never remember how to find this place. We came to a railway crossing and made another left-hand turn. Parker Street was a dusty dirt road, with no footpaths and potholes the size of moon craters. There were only four houses on one side of the street, and on the other side was the railway line that transported freight between Clyde and the factories at Rhodes.

My heart sank when we got to the house. If the inside was as bad as the outside, I didn't want to get out of the car. The front gate would definitely need to be repaired before Adam was walking; the missing palings left a hole big enough for a child to climb through.

It took a few moments for my eyes to adjust to the gloom in the narrow hallway. I had to place my hand over my mouth and nose against the acrid smell of animals. The lounge room walls and ceiling were coated with a light-brown film of nicotine. The venetian blinds were caked with fly shit. The filth and grime was repeated in every room, and although it was a warm autumn day the house felt like an ice box. I dreaded to think what it would be like in the dead of winter.

Just when I thought it couldn't get worse, we stepped down into the laundry. The floor was a layer of old bricks; cigarette butts and matches were stuck in the cracks. The back door had several wooden slats missing and daylight shone through the holes in the rusted corrugated iron roof. The toilet was a fibro add-on to the back of the laundry. Dozens of red-back spiders scurried for cover. *It'll be a challenge toilet-training a toddler in there*, I thought.

'The furniture truck has arrived,' Mrs Mack said excitedly, as if the junk we had bought was going to miraculously transform the place into something liveable.

As I walked back through the house taking it all in for a second time, it was impossible not to feel offended that I didn't get a chance to clean the place before we moved in. I never owned much growing up, but what I did have was spotlessly clean.

'What do you think?' John asked.

'Do you think we could take the smelly carpet up and polish the floorboards?' I asked, hoping not to sound ungrateful.

'It's not that bad,' Mrs Mack snapped, sounding cross. Both John and his mother were heavy smokers and their sense of smell was not as acute as mine.

'They must've been hippies,' Harry said, rolling his eyes at the orange, purple and black walls.

'Well, we'll leave you to settle in,' Mrs Mack said, heading for the door.

Harry gave Adam a kiss on the forehead, and kissed me on the cheek. There was never any show of affection between John and his parents.

Adam was due for a feed so I made up a bottle and sat on the lounge, trying not to breathe too deeply. 'Mummy will make this place beautiful for you, my darling,' I said, as I watched him fall asleep in my arms.

That night John wanted to christen the house by making love in our new bed. We had been married five weeks and we'd had sex twice. After the tear had healed, I had been too inhibited for fear that his parents would hear us. Not that we made much noise, with me lying as rigid as a corpse and John being no more physical than was necessary to please himself. I could barely stand to be touched, and just wanted to get it over with. Sex had always bordered on the traumatic for me. Even with Peter, it had been about the closeness and affection rather than the act itself.

'John, I am totally exhausted,' I said, hoping that he wouldn't get that hangdog expression. He did, but I was too disgusted by the filth and foul smells around me to care.

Every day for weeks I scrubbed until my skin was red raw. At last the house started to look and feel clean. I saturated the carpet, trying to get rid of the animal smells. Now it stank like a wet dog had pissed everywhere.

John painted the inside of the house himself, but didn't bother with anything as fiddly as masking tape. And who had ever heard of painting windows in the open position? He cleaned his brushes by wiping them against the back fence, which only enhanced the feeling of living in a junkyard. After the painting, John seemed to feel his work had been done. The rest was up to me. He went to work, came home, had dinner, then watched television or planned the next photo shoot.

John never asked me about my childhood or my family, and I never volunteered any information. It was as if I needed to shut the door on my past and never go back. I had no idea where Aunty Lorna, Robbie or Dan were living. The door had been well and truly closed at Aunty Daphne's. Uncle Stan lived too far away for me to walk to his place, and they didn't have a car. When I tried to write a letter, my emotions overflowed. I tore up what I had written, and cried.

John never discussed money with me or made plans for the future. I didn't know how much he earned each week or how much money he had in the bank. I presumed that he knew I was flat broke.

We went shopping on Saturday mornings and John gave me money for the groceries. I didn't think it was my place to ask for any allowance for myself, and he never offered, although I could keep the small change from the grocery shopping, if there was any.

Getting married was merely a change of address for John. Whatever this house was to him, it wasn't home. He didn't even bring his dog with him, and left all his books and other personal possessions at his mother's. She stored them in the garage.

John was clueless about domestic chores and had to be reminded every week to take out the garbage. I knew the shed was going to be a death trap for Adam if it wasn't cleaned up. And if it hadn't been for Harry, our yard would have looked like a jungle. Every second Tuesday, as regular as clockwork, he would arrive with his lawnmower and cut the grass. I'm sure his visits were more about seeing Adam, because sometimes the grass didn't need cutting. Harry would nurse Adam on his lap while I made him a cup of tea. He never asked how things were for me, and not feeling any family connection, I never said anything that might make me seem ungrateful for what they had done for me.

Mrs Mack never came with Harry on these visits. In fact she hadn't been to visit us since the day we moved in. Every Saturday night, though, we went to the Macks' for dinner and the usual game of cards or Scrabble. Apart from that, John and I never went anywhere. Not to a movie or a picnic, not for a swim, a walk, or even a drive. On one occasion we went to visit a friend of John who was also into photography. He showed us pictures he'd taken of his wife semi-naked. I was shocked. When we got home John wanted me to pose for him, but wrapping myself in a sheet and trying to look sexy was as far as I'd go.

One Saturday as we were strolling along Church Street, Parramatta, after doing the shopping, John ran into a mate he used to play Rugby against, whom he hadn't seen for a while.

'G'day, John, this is your son? He's cool,' Ian said, shaking John's hand and looking uncomfortable. 'This is my fiancée, Karen,' he added, introducing the girl he was with.

Karen and I didn't let on that we knew each other. I could feel her pain as she looked at Adam. When we'd met at St Margaret's, Karen had told me the father of her baby was called Ian. *How sad,* I thought. *They have a son they will never see.* I wondered if she got the new car her parents had promised when she gave up her baby.

That first winter was colder than anything I had ever known, and generally I didn't feel the cold. We only had one small electric heater, which was useless. After John had gone to work and the sun was on the front porch, I'd take Adam outside and sit him on my lap. When it rained and we couldn't go outside, I pulled the blankets off my bed and we'd sit huddled together on the lounge to keep warm.

At seven months Adam was rolling around the floor, trying to crawl, so that put an end to trying to make the carpets smell better. It also meant that I couldn't sew when he was awake as he was fascinated with the electric foot control on the sewing machine. So while John smoked his head off in the lounge room every evening, I busied myself sewing in the dining room. I kept the door shut to keep the putrid smell out.

We didn't even have a radio or a record player. Not having music around felt very strange; it had always been in my life in some form or other. If it hadn't been for Brian McNorton, I wouldn't have even known an Australian group called the Easy Beats was taking England by storm.

Every afternoon around two o'clock I made Adam a bottle and sang Dusty Springfield songs to him as he drank his milk and fell asleep in my arms. Then I carried him to my bed and stayed with him while he had his afternoon nap. Sometimes I slept, but mostly I just mused, trying to imagine what Peter was doing. *Had he been sent to Vietnam? If so, had he come home? Did he ever think about me?* When I punished myself like this I broke into uncontrollable sobs of self-pity.

Life was one big, mind-numbing cycle of poverty and isolation. We didn't even have a phone for me to call 000 in an emergency. Even Aunty Daphne had that much. I was totally ignorant of how unmet physical and emotional needs can lead to postnatal stress disorder or other forms of depression. The only time I felt love was when I looked at Adam or when he looked at me. Otherwise I felt totally worthless, incapable of giving or receiving any affection.

It was well into October before the weather warmed and my spirits lifted. After John went to work I'd get all the housework done, bathe and dress Adam, and we'd take a walk into Granville shopping centre. I never had more than a few cents in my purse, but it was good to get out of the house. Adam loved the outing, and chuckled with delight at every dog he saw.

On the way to Granville we had to pass a creepy house. Four very scruffy males lived there, ranging in ages from about eighteen to much older men. They reminded me of the Monroe brothers. As early as ten o'clock in the morning they'd be sitting on their front verandah smoking and drinking beer. They stopped talking as I approached, but I could feel their eyes all over me as I hurried past, pushing Adam's pram.

'Where's your husband? I'd like to give it to you, love,' one of them called out one morning, grabbing his crotch.

Rather than go past this house, I would walk three blocks out of my way to and from the shops. I was scared they would follow me home and find out where I lived.

Once a month Adam and I would go to the Parramatta baby health clinic, which was a six-mile round trip on foot. As we passed my old school, I recognised some of the girls sitting on the front lawn. They stared in disbelief when they saw me pushing a pram. I didn't stop to speak with anyone.

'Your baby is thriving,' the nurse at the clinic said, as she checked Adam's weight.

My whole miserable existence was made tolerable by these fifteen-minute visits and the compliments that told me I was a good mother. Adam grew more gorgeous every day and he was never sick, not even with a cold.

'He's obviously taking solids well.' The nurse smiled at Adam's chubby cheeks and bright eyes.

'He loves mashed potato, carrots and sausage – I push them through a strainer with a little gravy,' I told her.

'So you're not giving him canned baby food?'

'No, should I?' I asked, hoping that I wasn't doing anything wrong.

'No dear, it's just that you are so young I didn't expect that you would cook the baby's food yourself.'

My wardrobe was starting to look pretty grim, down to one skirt, an orange top, and a pair of orange shoes I wore when we went shopping and visited John's parents every Saturday. I was getting around the house in two threadbare house dresses that had been remodelled from my maternity clothes. When they were in the wash I was reduced to wearing John's old clothes around the house.

One Monday I had just hung out the washing when I heard Harry Mack's car. He had come a day early. As he got the mower and rake out of the boot, I raced to the clothesline. I would have died of shame if he had seen my shabby underwear hanging out to dry. It was bad enough that I was wearing John's clothes with nothing on my feet.

'What are you wearing those for?' he asked, giving me a queer look.

'I was just going to do some painting and didn't want to get paint on my dress,' I lied.

Adam's situation wasn't much better than mine. He was growing out of the baby clothes Aunty Daphne had given him. When I could no longer squeeze him into the all-in-one leggings suits, I cut off the bottoms, making them into t-shirts. John had stacks of clothes, some he never wore, and didn't mind my cutting them up to make clothes for Adam. But however well made, an infant's clothes made from adult fabric just looked odd.

'That's unusual material for a baby,' Mrs Mack commented one day. I wished I could have been forthright enough to tell her the truth about her tight-fisted son. But my indebtedness always left me feeling powerless to respond.

That night I told John how embarrassed I was that his father had caught me wearing his clothes, and asked him for some money. The next day I bought dress material for myself and some corduroy, appropriate to Adam's age, with some cute buttons and sew-on teddy bear appliqués.

Although I hadn't gone to church for a long time, I became worried about Adam not being baptised. Harry was a Catholic, and so was John, but I knew Mrs Mack wasn't. Neither John nor his parents gave me any money to buy Adam an outfit to be christened in. So, on a stinking hot day in November 1966, Adam had the original sin washed from his soul wearing an original ensemble made by his mother. Fortunately he was such a beautiful baby he'd have looked adorable in a hessian bag.

Uncle Stan and Aunty Shirley stood as Adam's godparents and gave Adam a lovely silver egg cup and spoon. Uncle Stan was so besotted with Adam that Harry Mack had to get in line to hold him. A photograph with Uncle Stan and Aunty Shirley in the front yard was the only one taken of Adam on his christening day.

33

No use screaming

Adam was walking before his first birthday, and the Macks had bought him a wooden playpen, which I set up in the backyard each morning so I could get the washing done. Adam hated being confined and complained bitterly, rattling the sides of the playpen vigorously. There was no way this contraption would hold him for long. I continued to nag John about fixing the fences.

One morning I put Adam into his playpen while I put on another load of washing. I was only gone for a few minutes but when I came back outside, he was gone. He had rocked the play-pen so hard it had tipped over onto its side and he'd made his getaway. He was nowhere to be seen.

'Adam!' I called out frantically.

A terrifying scream came from the shed in the backyard, where John and his friend Graham were always tinkering with something or other. 'Mum! Mum!'

I found Adam rubbing his eyes and running around bumping into things. The smell of petrol was overpowering. John had left

258

an open bucket of petrol on the floor, and Adam had managed to douse himself in it. I picked him up and ran back to the house. With no phone I couldn't call for help. Adam was gasping for breath as I stripped him of his petrol-soaked clothes. I turned the taps on full bore, kicked off my shoes, and got into the bath with him fully clothed. Adam fought me, grabbing at my hands as I poured warm water over his head, trying to flush the petrol from his eyes. I shampooed his hair and poured more water over his head. Now he had petrol *and* soap in his eyes, and his screaming went to a higher pitch.

'Bubby, please let Mummy do this,' I begged, as he kicked and squirmed.

I pulled the plug and ran more water, repeating the process. I wiped Adam's face with a soft washer and he calmed down. We stayed in the bath and I cuddled him until he stopped crying. When we were both in clean dry clothes, I made him a bottle and took him to bed. The drama had exhausted both of us.

As he lay in my arms, he stroked my face. 'Mum, Mum,' he murmured.

'You are the most beautiful boy in the whole wide world,' I said, leaning down to kiss his forehead. He giggled, as always.

When John came home that night I told him what had happened. He just stood there and said nothing.

'Adam could have been blinded or suffocated today,' I said, trying to drive home the seriousness of the situation.

'I'm sorry,' John said, looking genuinely contrite.

By April Adam had really found his legs. He'd climb onto the front gate to watch the trains. 'Choo-choo!' he'd squeal whenever a train went past.

One morning Adam was fully occupied playing with his little

dinky. I turned to get another sheet out of the basket, and he was gone. I looked down the side of the house. I checked the toilet and the shed, but he was nowhere to be found.

'Adam, my baby, where are you?' I kept on calling, trying not to panic.

Not the railway line, I prayed. *Holy Mary, please don't let my baby be on the railway line.* I ran across the street. A freight train was roaring past. *Thank God, he's not here.* I ran to the corner of the street. *How could a little baby get away so fast? Someone has taken him*, I thought.

'Adam! Adam!'

By this time I was hysterical, making enough noise to raise the dead. 'Help me! Help me!' I screamed until I was hoarse, but no one came to see what was wrong. *What kind of a neighbourhood is this? Are all these houses are empty?*

I ran two blocks to the local shop to phone the police. My knees almost gave way with relief when I saw Adam sitting on the front step of the shop, smiling as if he had been waiting for me.

'Darling,' I said, collapsing onto the concrete next to him. 'You gave Mummy such a fright.'

'Mum, Mum,' he said and smiled, oblivious to what he had put me through.

I picked him up and hugged and kissed his little face all the way home.

When John came home I told him what had happened, but not even this incident motivated him to fix the holes in the fences.

From then on, whenever Adam and I were in the backyard and I was caught up with chores, I tied a rope around his waist and tethered him to the Hills hoist. He was crying and tugging on the rope one morning when Harry Mack came down the side passageway.

'Why's the baby tied to the clothesline?' he asked sternly, picking Adam up to comfort him.

After I explained that John hadn't yet fixed the gates and I was terrified that Adam would wander across the road to the railway line, Harry went out to his car. He came back with a tape measure and took some measurements.

'I'll fix the gates,' he said, putting his arm around me as my tears welled up.

'Do you think we could get some kind of a catch or lock on the back door too, and the fridge?' I asked.

Not having a lock on the back door had always been a concern. I felt very vulnerable, especially taking a bath in the afternoon, and it was worse when John worked overtime. He was a compositor and often worked late to meet printing deadlines. When it grew dark I'd push the washing machine across the back door so I had a chance of hearing it if someone tried to come in. I was on edge every night until I heard John's car pull up.

'A lock on this door isn't going to be much help,' Harry said, having checked it. 'The timber's rotten. You could kick it in.'

Apart from the local news in the weekly paper, which John brought home from work every Wednesday, watching the nightly news on television was the only way I learned anything of what was happening in the world. As the death toll of Aussie soldiers went into triple digits, the momentum of the anti-Vietnam movement grew. Robbie was with the 5th RAR and had been wounded in action, and I feared for what might have happened to Peter. Not knowing ate at me.

The Vietnam conflict wasn't the only news item of interest. A referendum was set for 27 May. Australians would be asked to vote yes or no about giving Aboriginal people full citizenship rights. Imagine that, having to be asked if you wanted to give the original people of this country a fair go. But that was how it was.

The McNortons were not much unlike any other non-Aboriginal family I knew at that time. They were totally ignorant of the plight of Aboriginal people. Either that or they didn't care. There was no discussion around their dinner table about these historical events. I often thought about Aunty Lorna, and imagined that she probably wouldn't give a bugger about the referendum either. 'The gubbas can kiss my black arse,' she used to say.

The yes votes won. Aboriginal people would have the full citizenship rights that were taken for granted by the whitefellas. But ten per cent of the population actually voted no. At sixteen, my understanding of the profound injustices suffered by Aboriginal people in this country were limited. Still, I wondered if more Aboriginal people would now be able to own property and not have to live in dumps like Herne Bay.

'When I lived in the bush, my Aunty Lorna and I had to wait behind the white line in the shop to be served,' I told Mrs Mack one day.

She didn't look up from her sewing. 'Your grandmother mentioned that she was Aboriginal. But you'd only have a bit of Aboriginal blood, wouldn't you?'

John was grinning from ear to ear when he came through the door one night after work. *Perhaps he's had a pay rise and may give me some money*, I hoped.

'We're going on a steam train ride with Graham. Mum said she'll take care of Adam for the day.'

Graham was John's best mate, and, although I liked him, it annoyed me that all the arrangements had been made without speaking to me first. The flaw in the plan was that I had absolutely nothing to wear. Going to John's mother's looking like a scarecrow was one thing, but going out in public was another.

The next-door neighbour had a regular salesman from Walton's call at their house. He had a van full of clothes. You could pay off a bit each week, she told me. He usually came on Mondays, so when I heard his car I went out to catch him.

'Excuse me, may I have a look at some of the clothes?'

'Sure, love. What are you looking for?' He opened the back door of the van.

'I was thinking about a slack suit.'

He asked my size. It had been so long since I'd bought clothes off the rack, I really had no idea.

'XXSW, I think.'

He pulled out a pure wool, camel-coloured, two-piece slack suit with a fully lined jacket. I had never owned anything as smart. I tried it on, and, apart from having to chop about six inches from the legs, it was a perfect fit. And being a neutral colour meant I could team it with my orange shoes and the knitted top, which were still in reasonable condition.

'For you, love, five dollars,' he told me, when I asked the price.

'I'll have to ask my husband if we can afford it,' I said, feeling my heart sinking.

'Hang on to it and let him see it on you. That ought to clinch the deal.' He winked at me.

When John came home I put the suit on. He smiled and nodded approvingly. 'You look very nice.'

'It costs five dollars. Can we afford it?'

John opened his wallet and handed the money to me. Just like that, a crisp new five-dollar note.

On the day of the outing I became very self-conscious about my new suit. Adam was wearing an outfit that was my first improvised attempt at sewing with stretch fabric. It definitely looked homemade, but it was the only warm outfit he had, and it was a cold day. On his feet were the only shoes he owned, a pair of blue and grey tartan slippers. I felt so ashamed to be dolled up in something so smart while my baby was dressed so poorly.

Mrs Mack was watering the plants in the window boxes at the front of the house when we pulled up, and Adam waved frantically at his gran. As I got out of the car Mrs Mack looked me up and down, and then at Adam.

'Look at you,' she snapped, taking Adam by the hand. 'You ought to be ashamed of yourself. Dressed up to the nines with your baby in rags!'

My face flushed. I wanted to evaporate, I was so embarrassed.

'I have the ladies' card group coming over today. How am I going to face them with Adam dressed like this?' She walked away in a huff.

Adam began to cry. He wasn't used to people talking in aggressive tones. Mrs Mack softened and picked him up. 'You poor baby,' she cooed, which made me feel worse.

A few minutes later my fury kicked in. Mrs Mack had seen me wearing the same clothes every Saturday for the past eighteen months and most of Adam's clothes were made from old shirts and trousers John had discarded. In all that time she had never said a word or so much as offered to knit Adam a jumper, and she was always knitting something. Now, because she would be embarrassed in front of her friends, she had shamed me. I told John I wanted to go home.

He looked stunned. 'Why? What's wrong?'

Sometimes I wondered if John didn't have a hearing problem. Things just went right over his head. 'I want to go home,' I repeated.

He started to look agitated, then sulky. 'We'll be letting Graham down. He's already paid for the tickets.'

We went on the train ride but I was miserable all day. I just wanted the day to end so I could pick up Adam and go home. I spent most of the day asleep on the train so I didn't have to face the shame I was feeling.

When we got back to Mrs Mack's, Adam was wearing a red jumper and a pair of pure wool pants. He looked wonderful.

'Where did those clothes come from?' I asked.

'They were Sam's when he was a baby. I've thrown the rags Adam was wearing into the bin.'

Adam ran towards me. I scooped him up into my arms and hugged him and kissed him all over his face. He giggled and kissed me back.

'Mummy missed you so much today, and don't you look handsome in your beautiful red jumper,' I said, tickling his tummy. He rubbed his hand over the front of the lovely hand-knitted jumper.

As we drove home John was still keyed up about the thrill of having taken some great photographs of the steam engine. He couldn't wait to get the slides back.

When I told him I needed some money to buy Adam some clothes and that I never wanted to be humiliated like that again, he couldn't understand why I was so upset. He opened his wallet, though, and gave me ten dollars.

Bright and early on Monday morning I bathed and dressed Adam and walked into Granville shopping centre. I bought Adam some proper little boys' clothes, a pair of brown leather shoes and some white socks.

A week later John came home one night with another car – the FJ Holden he had fantasised about owning for a long time.

'Graham and I are going to do it up,' he announced, sounding very pleased with the purchase.

I was speechless for a moment and just stood there, staring at him. 'Are you serious? Can't you see how Adam and I have been living?'

34

The black dog

The depression crept up on me, on tiptoes, one step at a time. Like a silent thief, it plundered my strength and left me groping around in the dark for days on end. John would go to work and somehow I'd drag myself to my feet to feed Adam. I'd change his nappy, put him in his dark cold room and shut the door. I was totally exhausted and just had to sleep. I'd lie motionless on the bed, listening to my baby complaining to be let out of his room.

'Mum, Mum,' he'd whimper behind the closed door.

If I let him out, I'll have to watch him, I told myself. *And I just have to sleep.*

After about an hour the crying would stop.

He'll wake me up when he gets hungry.

For days I went without a bath. Adam would get a wash before his dinner, rather than the bath we used to share in the afternoon before John came home from work. I wasn't even trying to make nice meals for John anymore. If he was happy to have grilled chops, with carrots, peas and mashed potato every night, then I was happy to give it to him. Anything more interesting would take more effort, and I had lost all interest in everything. Some days I didn't even clean my teeth.

How John didn't notice the changes taking place around him is a mystery to me. Ordinarily I was very fastidious with both my personal grooming and the housekeeping. In fact, I bordered on being obsessive about having the house clean and tidy. Now piles of dirty nappies were left to get fly-blown in the laundry tubs. Dirty dishes cluttered the sink, and our bed, which usually had starched and ironed pillowcases, weren't changed for weeks. If John needed a shirt I had to iron it while he stood there waiting. Sometimes I went to bed at night fully clothed. I can't imagine how awful I must have smelled, not bathing daily and having no deodorant, powder or perfume to mask my body odour. My moods were very black. I got irritable and cranky at the slightest thing. There were moments when thought I'd be better off dead.

One night I lost control and smacked Adam's bottom. It was the first and last time I ever hit my son. He was just being a baby and, as babies do, he wanted to play when I wanted to get him fed and into bed. It was a hard slap, too hard. Adam's little face dissolved. I felt like a bully, and deeply ashamed.

'Mummy is so sorry, darling. I didn't mean to do that. Please forgive me,' I begged.

Of course he was too young to know what I meant but when I started crying he kissed my face as if to say, 'It's alright, I know you didn't mean it.'

I pulled out Peter's old letters and photographs from their hiding place, behind the dressing table. Sitting on the floor with Adam I'd go through the mementoes, reliving that glorious fleeting time between May and August 1966, before I had to go back to Dubbo and face Mamma. The days when I had friends and went dancing to live music, and sat around discussing politics and world affairs. Now I was trapped in a dark cave of almost total solitary confinement, as the black hole of despair got deeper and darker with every heartbeat. For hours I'd sob out of control, scaring the wits out of Adam, who cried in sympathy.

Resentment towards John grew worse each day. I was starting to dislike him with intensity. I was angry with Peter too, for all the flowery promises that amounted to nothing. There was no point in holding on to these letters and photographs. They'd helped keep me sane at St Margaret's Hospital, but now tortured and haunted me. One by one I ripped them into tiny little pieces. I handed some to Adam, who thought it was a great game.

Down and down I went; some days my thoughts were so dark I actually plotted how I could do away with John and be free. If only there was someone I could talk to. I thought about calling Aunty Daphne, even if it meant giving Uncle Jack the satisfaction of saying, 'I told you so.' But the nearest public phone box was two blocks away. I would have to get dressed and I didn't have the will for that. It was easier to stay in the dark.

One morning I looked at myself in the mirror. There was a stranger looking back at me. I looked like a puffer fish. John never said a word, yet anyone with eyes could have seen that I was very ill. Somehow, I still managed to tidy myself enough to go to his parents' place on Saturday nights. Mr Mack often gave me an odd look, but no one ever asked, 'Kay, are you alright?' And I was grateful that they didn't. I didn't want them to know I wasn't coping. When we came home I just wanted to stay in bed and never get up. It agitated John that he had to look after Adam on Sunday, and when a dirty nappy needed changing I had to find the strength to deal with it.

The turning point came one morning when I was just too weak

to get out of bed and make John's breakfast. I told him I couldn't get up and asked him to give Adam a bottle before he went to work. I could hear Adam laughing and chortling and rattling the sides of his cot.

'He's in his cot with the bottle. I'm going now,' John said, popping his head into the bedroom.

I pretended not to hear him. I had drifted away, not asleep, but not awake either, in a kind of twilight zone.

I heard Adam in the distance. Then the sides of his cot rattled. When I didn't respond, his calls grew louder. Then I heard a thump. I waited. Everything went quiet.

Good, he's gone back to sleep. I drifted into a coma-like state. I couldn't feel my arms and legs. It was as if I was outside my body somehow and couldn't find my way back. Adam started to cry. His cries intensified. *Why won't he let me sleep?* I asked myself. *Shut up! I'm so exhausted.* He cried for a long time, but I couldn't move. I just wanted to leave this miserable life.

Now it was a pitiful, pleading cry. Adam sounded as desperate as I was feeling. Finally my maternal instinct overcame the numbing paralysis. Like a crazy, drunken woman, I struggled to my feet and staggered to Adam's bedroom, bumping against the walls in the hallway. Adam was sitting hard against his door and it wouldn't open.

'It's Mummy, darling,' I said, hoping he would stand up so I could open the door.

'Mum, Mum,' he whimpered. The door still wouldn't open.

As I managed to inch the door open the stench hit me. Adam had soiled himself, several times judging by the amount of the excrement all over him and everything else he had touched in the room. There were marks from his little hands over the floor to the back of the door and on the walls. It was everywhere. He looked like he had rolled in it.

'Oh my God! What have I done to you, my darling?'

I picked him up and carried him to the bathroom. His little face was bright red and tears stained his cheeks from hours of distress. Now he was chuckling and I was crying. I ran a bath and stripped us both off. After washing the mess out of his hair I ran some clean water and scrubbed us both from head to foot. We played in the bathtub until the water grew cold. I dried myself and wrapped Adam in a towel and took him to the dining room, the only room that saw any sunshine. I yanked the venetian blinds up to the top and the warm sun flooded the room.

Adam giggled as I massaged his scalp and combed his hair. I felt so ashamed of myself for having neglected my baby. Perhaps Sister Anne was right after all. I was too young to take proper care of my son.

Adam was totally exhausted after his ordeal and before long he was asleep in my bed. After scrubbing the walls and floor in his room, I sat on the lounge staring at the ceiling. Desperation, shame, disgust and a feeling of total aloneness devoured me. I didn't even have any tears left; I was all dried up. Without any conscious thought, I heard myself praying. Just as I'd done at St Margaret's, I was chanting the Hail Mary over and over again. I had just enough sanity to know that I was in trouble – and that I wouldn't get any help if I didn't ask for it. I felt I had failed, that I had been selfish for not letting my baby go to a mother who could take better care of him. I was angry with John too. He must have seen the changes in me, but he carried on as if nothing was happening.

When John came home that night I poured my heart out to him. I left nothing out. He just sat there, staring straight ahead and saying nothing. *I've just told my husband that I've been plotting to kill him and he's said nothing! Am I married to a zombie?* I wasn't going to let him just shrug his shoulders and walk away this time.

'Did you hear what I just said?' My voice quavered. I wanted to scream at him, to make him understand my desperate need for help, but somehow I managed to stay calm. John looked pensive, as if he was trying to absorb what he was being told.

I went to bed but the pain in my chest was so sharp I could hardly breathe. When John finally joined me, he made no attempt to comfort me. Perhaps because I'd rejected him so many times he was afraid to reach out, but his impassivity told me that I was on my own.

I had to find a way out of this nightmare or perish.

35

Door to door

A few days later the Avon lady called. I could never afford to buy anything but she had left her catalogue, which always invited women to become Avon ladies. Then it struck me! I wasn't quite sure how I was going to manage this with Adam, but I had to try something.

I told John about my plan and he had no objections. After all, being an Avon lady wasn't a proper job. He didn't ask me who was going to take care of Adam; that was all up to me to organise.

Avon ladies wore hats and gloves. Mine would have to be orange, to team with the only pair of shoes I owned. John gave me the money I needed to get the accessories. I dressed Adam in an outfit I'd made and off we went 'Avon calling' in Harris Park. We could only go in a radius that was practical on foot. In two weeks I spoke to every lonely old pensioner and desperate house-wife within two miles. I sold one lipstick and a bottle of Rapture cream perfume. At that rate it would take me a year to pay for the demonstration kit.

272

One day I had a delivery to make to a customer three blocks away. I asked my neighbour if Adam could play with her son; I didn't like leaving Adam in that filthy house, but I knew I'd only be gone for fifteen minutes.

I put on my hat and gloves. 'Mummy won't be long, darling,' I reassured Adam.

I walked so fast I was almost running. I had to wait while the customer scratched around in her handbag to pay for the lipstick. She was a dollar short, which was my profit on the product.

On my way back I could hear Adam screaming. I started to run. My hat flew off and blew away.

'*Mum! Mum!*'

Then there was silence. I stopped to take off my shoes, gathered up my skirt and bolted for home.

When I reached my neighbour's gate Adam's face was blue. His mouth was open and nothing was coming out. The neighbour's son, about five years old, had bit into Adam's arm and had latched on, growling like a dog. Thinking only of making him let go, I clenched my fist and punched him in the face. When his mouth opened to scream I pulled Adam away, laid him on the ground and gave him mouth-to-mouth resuscitation, which I'd learned for the Bronze Medallion. He got his breath back and started to cry. My neighbour came out running out, abusing me for hitting her son. He did have a shiner. I really clobbered him.

'He's a little savage! Look what he did. I heard Adam screaming from three blocks away, you bitch!' She turned on her heels and ran inside.

Back home, Adam fought like crazy while I tried to hold a packet of frozen peas on his arm. The bite had nearly gone right through the skin. It took a long time to settle him, and when I did, I realised I was still wearing the orange gloves.

*

Selling Avon in Harris Park wasn't worth the effort. Then I heard Mrs Mack was holding a Tupperware party. *I could do that*, I thought. After I got the basic kit, I practised the demonstration of the new lettuce crisper, with Adam as my audience. He thought it was a great game.

At my first party, which John's Aunty Peggy had lined up, everything was going well. I could feel the ladies were ready to buy. Then our hostess screamed from the kitchen and we ran out to see what had happened.

Adam had climbed onto the table and taken a bite out of just about every cake, and was starting on the sandwiches. So much for the magnificent spread – and my short-lived career. I did get to keep the innovative lettuce crisper.

I sat on the grass scouring the positions vacant section in the local rag. There was a vacancy for a counter assistant at Granville station kiosk. It was part-time, four nights a week on the graveyard shift from ten until two in the morning. I would need to take John's car. I could hardly expect him to take me to work then stay awake to collect me at that hour. The problem was, I didn't have a driver's licence.

'What do you need to get a job for anyway?' John asked.

I was astounded and tried to explain that getting a job was not just about the money. I had to have some social interaction, hopefully even make a friend or two.

'Alright, you can take the VW,' he said.

The next day John came home with a new accessory for his FJ. While I was ravaged by depression, John had done up the Holden and had it registered. The VW was now our second car, which, although I didn't have a licence to drive, I could use take to get to a job in the middle of the night.

The interview for the job was arranged for a Saturday. I lied about my age so I would be paid as a twenty-one year old. Being married with a toddler, I knew they would never suspect I was only seventeen. I got the job on the spot and was asked to start the following week. I didn't know how I was going to juggle taking care of a toddler all day with work four nights a week. But I was so desperate; I knew I'd just have to work it out as I went along.

In those days railway station kiosks served alcohol. When the pub across the road from the station closed at ten o'clock, the insatiable drinkers staggered over to the kiosk. I started in July, so the doors and windows were kept closed to keep out the icy cold winds that blew down from the Blue Mountains. By midnight the kiosk would be full of drunks and thick with choking cigarette smoke, which made my eyes water. My shift didn't always finish on time. On the night when someone vomited on the floor, I didn't get away until two-thirty. By the time I'd arrived home and taken a bath, it was after three and I had to be up again at six-thirty to take care of Adam.

At the end of my first week I was almost delirious. It was tiredness like I had never experienced. Every night after dinner I'd fall asleep in front of the television. John would wake me as he was going to bed. I'd get up and go out in the freezing cold night to work for four hours.

Wednesday was pay day. I dressed Adam and we headed into Granville to pick up my first pay. As we crossed the Goode Street Bridge, I noticed a familiar face coming towards me. It was Robbie; he was still in uniform. He looked so handsome, and I could sense that the army and going to war had changed him.

'Hello, Katie,' he said, smiling. 'What did you call the baby? He's a cutie.' He bent down to shake Adam's hand.

I was still too hurt and angry with everyone in my family to find much to say to Robbie. He didn't look comfortable either, so our catch-up didn't take long.

After I picked up my pay, I bought Adam a beautiful knitted suit and a set of fleecy-lined pyjamas. For myself I bought some much-needed underwear, a yellow jumper and a pair of white shoes. On the way home we both had ice cream to celebrate my new financial independence. Just putting on fresh new underwear felt like I had won the lottery.

Not long after, a man from Bernie Studios came to our door offering studio-quality portraits taken at home. I made an appointment. I cut Adam's hair and dressed him in his new clothes. He looked wonderful, and he knew it. I ordered a large gilt-framed colour photograph, which I gave to Harry and Mrs Mack to hang on their wall with the photographs of John and his brothers – a reminder of how well I could take care of my son when I had the means to do so.

36

A terrible mistake

Although the job at the kiosk solved my financial crisis, there was no chance of making friends on the graveyard shift. I worked by myself and was desperate for someone to talk to.

John was taking his FJ to work, and, although I'd been driving the VW on the backstreets to and from Granville each night, I'd never driven on the main roads in the daytime. One day I was feeling so desperate for company I decided to risk it and visit Sandy. I'd only seen her and Michael's house once, from the outside, but I remembered where it was.

As I pulled up in front of the house I saw the front curtains stir. There was no car in the driveway, but someone was at home. I was praying that it wasn't Michael. I'd timed my visit for the middle of the day, when I figured he'd be at work.

Sandy opened the door, and, if not for the fact that she was about eight months pregnant, I could easily have mistaken her for her mother. She was haggard and thin.

She smiled, raising her hand up to her mouth to cover her

decaying front teeth. 'Hello, Kay,' she said warmly, looking very happy to see me.

A little blond-haired, blue-eyed clone peered at me shyly from behind her mother's skirt.

'What's your name?' I asked, placing Adam on the floor.

'It's Chanel,' Sandy said.

'What a lovely name. This is Adam.' I watched the babies size each other up.

Adam was very sociable and not at all shy. He put his arms around Sandy's little girl, calling her 'Bubba', and smothered her with kisses. I realised how deprived he'd been of the company of children his own age. The only time he'd played with another small child, the kid had tried to eat him. I'd brought some of Adam's toys and was pleased to see that he shared them with Sandy's little girl.

'When's your baby due?' I asked.

'About five weeks, and it won't come soon enough for me. I'm so sick of myself.'

Sandy made us a cup of tea. I was on edge most of the time, hoping that Michael wouldn't come home. Sandy told me about her miserable life married to Michael, and I could see from her home and appearance that she was doing it tough.

I told Sandy where I was working and living. Perhaps to make her feel better about her miserable life, I told her about the day I found Adam covered in his own shit. We hugged each other and cried.

Not wanting to turn the visit into a wake, I related my experiences as an Avon lady. There were some funny stories, and some so sad they made me feel like a whinger. We laughed until our ribs hurt when I recanted the Tupperware party story and Adam demolishing the afternoon tea.

When it felt like it was getting late, I got up to leave. 'It's been wonderful seeing you, Sandy. I want to miss the peak-hour traffic when the factories close.' I picked up Adam and walked towards the door.

'I hope you'll come over again sometime,' Sandy said, giving me a hug.

Just as I was putting Adam in the car, Michael pulled up. He smiled when he saw me. I hurried to the driver's side of the VW.

'Wait!' he said, grabbing the door. 'How have you been?'

'I've been fine.'

'I need to see you, Kay. I need to talk to you.'

'You're seeing me now, Michael. What do you want?'

Adam was getting impatient and had crawled across the seats. He was standing in front of the steering wheel, turning it in his hands, making *vroom-vroom* noises.

'He's great. He looks like you. And you look fabulous,' Michael said, smiling at Adam and giving me a penetrating look. 'I need to see you alone, Kay. I've made a terrible mistake.'

I was shocked. After talking with Sandy for three hours I knew the mistake was hers.

'I can't see you. I came over to see Sandy. But I won't be coming back,' I climbed into the car and started the engine.

'Please, Kay,' he pleaded.

'Goodbye, Michael,' I said and turned the key in the ignition.

I'd been brazen enough to drive to Sandy's, so it didn't take much more nerve to go the extra distance to Seven Hills to visit Aunty Daphne. I phoned to let her know I was coming.

Roberta would have been around three years old and wasn't as timid as Trudy was at the same age. Perhaps Uncle Jack didn't whip her little sister's legs with willow branches. Aunty Daphne was skin and bone, looking more drawn than ever, but at least her face wasn't black and blue. Maybe Uncle Jack had found a new punching bag, or realised that if he kept pounding Aunty Daphne night after night, he might actually kill her.

Aunty Daphne was very pleased to see us, and her affection for Adam was spontaneous. She balanced him on her knee and handed him a homemade biscuit. 'He's a gorgeous little fella.'

Seeing Aunty Daphne again, I felt a connectedness I thought I'd lost forever. But I could also see that not much had changed for her, and she would probably have laughed at me if I'd told her how awful my life was. She had known suffering and brutality I couldn't even relate to. I didn't have any news about the family, and her isolation seemed worse than mine. Aunty Daphne went through her cupboards and gave me jumpers and pants that Stevie had long grown out of and were still in good condition. It would be a while before they'd fit Adam, but I was very grateful.

I had to leave before Stevie and Trudy got home from school because the roads would be busy with too many police about. As I drove away that day I had no idea that I would never see Aunty Daphne again.

Walking to the car in the Granville station car park in the early hours of the morning was a heart-pounding experience. In the freezing conditions, the old VW never started the first time. 'Come on, start! You mongrel!' I'd curse, trembling, until I'd shifted it into gear and driven away. One night I nearly jumped out of my skin when someone spoke to me.

'Hello, Midnight.'

'Oh my God! Michael? What are you doing here?'

'I told you. I have to see you, Kay. Will you get into the car?'

'I really have to be getting home,' I told him.

'Ten minutes, Kay. Please, I just have to tell you something, then I'll go.'

He sounded very calm and sober, so I got into the passenger's seat. 'Is this a new car?' I asked, trying to keep the conversation light.

He told me he'd had it for a while. Even so, there was something familiar about it. Perhaps it was the roomy interior, the leather seats, the walnut dashboard. Maybe it was just that familiar smell that was so distinctly Michael's.

'You look beautiful, Kay,' he said, flashing that amazing smile. 'I've made a terrible mistake. Like I told you, I should never have let you go.'

What is the point of telling me this now? I thought.

I couldn't respond but that didn't deter Michael. 'I never stopped loving you. You are the only one I ever really loved. I'm sorry if I hurt you,' he said, sounding so sincere I thought he was going to burst into tears.

Suddenly I was fourteen again, wanting him to hold me and love me. All the bad stuff was forgotten. He really did love me all the time. Sandy tricked him.

'I wish Adam was mine,' he said.

That was it. I couldn't hold back the emotion. Tears stung my cheeks. 'This is pointless – Adam isn't yours and never will be,' I sobbed.

'I just wanted you to know how I felt.' He leaned forward, slowly, cautiously, reaching out to touch me.

I pulled away. 'It's late. I have to go,' I said, reaching for the doorhandle.

He didn't try to stop me, just sat in his car and waited for me to drive away.

When I got home, I took a bath as usual and got into bed. John stirred, wanting sex. I pulled away.

37

Fair game

All day Sunday I couldn't get Michael out of my mind – the way he looked, the way he smelled, the familiar tenderness in his voice, especially when he told me how sorry he was that he'd hurt me and how he wished that Adam had been his son.

Throughout the following week I kept fantasising about what it would be like to be married to a man who loved me, who said tender words and held me in his arms. I yearned for someone to take care of Adam and me, to care that we had at least the basic necessities of life. What would it be like to lie with such a man and want him to touch me, caress me?

At work the next week, I fully expected to see Michael's car parked next to mine, and was disappointed when it wasn't. When I left work on Sunday night he was there, waiting for me.

'Hello, Midnight. Can we talk?'

This time, without much hesitation, I got into his car.

He shook his head. 'This is driving me insane. I can't get you out of my mind.'

'Yes, I've thought a lot about you too,' I confessed.

'You have?' Michael sounded as happy as a puppy with two tails. 'That's wonderful,' he said, pulling me to towards him. 'I knew you still loved me.'

This time I didn't pull away. Michael's lips broke a long drought. The passion flooded me as I drank like a thirsty animal. He groaned with pleasure. I was pleasing him. Michael held me close and buried his face in my hair, taking deep breaths, as though he was trying to suck me in. Without a thought for the consequences, I surrendered to the warmth of his embrace.

'I love you,' Michael whispered.

I started to cry.

'What's wrong?'

'I've been so miserable,' I blurted out, before telling him what it was like being married to John.

'He only married you because he had to. I would have married you because I loved you,' he said. 'You don't have to stay with John. We can run away together.'

My mind started racing. I had been serving life in exile, a prisoner on a barren island. Suddenly a raft, with a sail, had drifted onto the shore. The thought of never having to wake up and face another day of my pathetic existence in Harris Park was almost more than I dared to think about. From that perspective, it was fairly easy for Michael to seduce me, and he had all the right moves. He knew exactly how to tune in to my vulnerabilities and he did it with precision. He whispered, coaxed and caressed me, and before I knew it we were in the back seat of his car with my pants down and my skirt up to my waist. Michael drew my legs into the air and unceremoniously drove himself deep into me.

'No! Stop!' I cried, as the realisation of what was happening shook me.

'I can't stop now,' he said, driving into me again.

Having had a child there was no searing pain this time, but Michael wasn't a small man and I was still not much older than a child. All the feigned tenderness had gone; he was growling and grunting, pounding me so hard my head was banging against the car door. My pleas were ignored.

'Oh God, you're still so tight,' Michael said, pushing on to his climax.

I had gone somewhere else, trying to block it all out, but I could hear my pitiful whimpering even if he couldn't.

Finally, he collapsed on top of me. I could hardly breathe. 'Get off me.'

Michael pulled back and smiled as he handed me a towel. What fair game I was – and how predictable. He had come prepared. I felt totally degraded, more ashamed of this than of anything else I had ever done. I buried my face in my hands.

'Didn't you enjoy making love?' Michael asked, sounding hurt.

That was making love?

As I wiped between my legs all my fantasies vanished. 'I have to go home,' I said, pulling on my pants.

'I want you to come away with me,' he whispered.

'I can't leave my son and run away with you.'

'Who said anything about you leaving your son?' He reached across the back of the seat to stroke my hair.

I shivered at his touch. 'Please, I can't talk about this.' I opened the car door.

'I thought you loved me?' Michael snapped angrily, grabbing his cigarettes from the dashboard.

'That's insane, Michael. Now, I have to go home.'

As I drove home sitting in the damp patch at the back of my skirt, Mamma's face came into focus. All the insults and predictions she'd hissed at me were ringing in my ears. At home, I buried my face in a towel, sobbing, trying not to wake John up as I ran a bath.

I filled the tub almost to the top. I took a deep breath and slid below the surface, wondering if drowning was a quick and painless death. The strains of the past four years had nearly driven me to insanity, leaving me more vulnerable at seventeen than I'd been as a naive and needy fourteen-year-old. I nearly scrubbed my skin raw, but when I crawled into bed it still felt like a part of Michael was inside me. Not even a bath could make me feel clean.

The following Tuesday I heard a car pull up outside our house. Sandy must have told Michael where I lived. My stomach knotted with fear and panic. Harry Mack could arrive at any time to cut the grass.

'What are you doing here?' I asked, trying to sound calm.

'Sandy had a baby girl last night,' he announced with a smile.

'That's wonderful. Congratulations. What have you called her?

'Angelique.'

It would have been appropriate to at least give Michael a hug on hearing this news, but I didn't want him touch me.

'Have you thought about what I said?' he asked, looking at me searchingly.

'Yes, but I need more time,' I lied. In truth, I just needed him to go before Harry arrived.

'I need some more time too, to sort a few things. I can get a job as a truck driver in Queensland, but I need to save a bit more cash before we can go.' He sounded pretty sure that I would go along with his whacky plan.

It was a relief to get through the next week without Michael turning up at work. I hoped the joy of a new baby girl had brought him to his senses. But one day when Adam was having his after-noon nap, I heard his car pull up. My heart was pounding as I watched him from behind the lace curtains.

Michael knocked on the door. I didn't answer it. If I pretended not to be at home perhaps he would leave.

'Kay!' he called out, loudly banging on the door.

The noise woke Adam and he started crying. There was no point in pretending any longer.

'What took you so long?' Michael asked as I opened the door.

'I was in Adam's room,' I muttered, trembling, but trying to sound normal

'We're nearly all set to go.'

I stepped back. 'Michael, I can't run away with you.'

His face contorted. He grabbed me by the shoulders and shoved me inside, slamming the door shut behind us. It was almost pitch black in the hallway. Michael towered over me. He tried to kiss me, digging his fingers into me and pinning me against the wall.

'You are coming with me,' he snarled.

I was frightened but had to keep my cool. He was acting and sounding like a madman, and I knew Michael was strong enough to snap my neck with his bare hands.

'This is crazy,' I pleaded.

'I'm going to Queensland and you are coming with me. If you don't, I'll tell John that I fucked you and he'll throw you onto the street.'

This prospect terrified me so much I couldn't respond. What Michael was saying was possible. If a woman committed adultery, she forfeited all property rights and custody of her children. She could be thrown onto the street with just her clothes and, if she owned one, a sewing machine. This had happened to a neighbour in Jeffrey Avenue. Ironically, the man involved was Michael's father.

'I'll be back in a month. Be ready to leave,' Michael commanded, before releasing his grip.

After he'd gone I opened Adam's door. He looked very

frightened. 'Mum, Mum, Mum,' he cried, patting my tear-stained face as I carried him out to the lounge.

I sat down with Adam on my lap and sobbed as I rocked him in my arms. Even my faith that there was a mother in heaven was gone. *There is no God*, I told myself. *God would not put me through so much pain and bring me to this place.* Losing my faith was one of the deepest cuts of all. I felt more abandoned than ever.

'My darling, what's Mummy going to do?'

38

A girl, a suitcase and a sewing machine

It was a Saturday and I had swapped a shift and was working the afternoon in the kiosk. I was serving at the platform counter. A train pulled in to the station, the door of a carriage was right in front of the counter.

'Peter!' I called out.

'Kay!'

The train pulled away from the platform. He was gone. *Perhaps I imagined it*, I thought. A few moments later I heard a familiar voice behind me. Peter Ashton was standing there, smiling, and looking as handsome as ever. I wanted to jump over the counter and throw my arms around him.

'You look good and all,' he winked, looking me up and down. 'What time do you get off?' I had another thirty minutes until the end of my shift and Peter said he'd wait.

As he walked me to the car, he took my left hand. 'What's this then?' he asked, turning my wedding ring between his fingers.

'I married John McNorton.'

'Why didn't you wait for me?'

'You didn't want my baby,' I reminded him, 'and I couldn't give him up.'

'But I wrote and told you I was sorry that I said that. You didn't get that letter?'

Perhaps, if indeed there was such a letter, it had gone to Uncle Les's place. One more juicy envelope would have been far too tempting for Shirl.

'Was it a boy?'

'Yes, I called him Adam Jon.'

'You broke my heart,' Peter said.

I let loose. 'I couldn't begin to tell you what I went through at that hospital. They tried everything short of killing me to get my baby. They didn't care a scrap what happened to us. How could you have helped? You were still in the army.' The tears streamed as I recalled that nightmare.

'You could have gone to live with Deanie until I got out.' Now he was crying too.

'There's no use telling me now what I could have done. I had no idea how to get in touch with Deanie.'

'When do you get a day off?'

'Not until Tuesday.'

'Would you like to come over and see the lads?'

It had turned out that Peter shared a house with Deanie at Merrylands, with another friend, Wally. I remembered all the fun times we used to have at O'Connell House. The thought of seeing Deanie again filled me with joy.

'Yes, but I'll have to bring Adam with me.'

'Great! I'd love to see him,' Peter said, putting his arms around me. 'Is it alright if I kiss you?'

'I'd be broken-hearted if you didn't.'

Peter gave me a peck on the lips, not long enough to be

passionate, but sweet enough to make me realise how needy I was for genuine affection.

That night I tried to work through my options. I didn't have much time before Michael would be back, and I feared what might happen. My dilemma was to figure out a way to leave John and be able to support Adam and myself. If we could share a house with Peter, Deanie and Wally, at least we'd have a roof over our heads. I could get a job and pay our way. But would Deanie and Wally agree to have a toddler living with them? Who'd take care of Adam while I worked?

One thing I was sure about was that going away with Michael was not one of my options. To run away with another woman's husband was a shame I couldn't bring upon myself, and after the threat Michael had made, I despised him. Whatever I deserved it was more than I could expect from him, and I didn't believe for an instant that he would love another man's child.

If I took Adam away and moved in with Peter, and John discovered where I was, I knew he could take Adam and I would be denied access. If I stayed and Michael made good on his threat, and I believed that he would, John could toss me out onto the street. I had no reason to think that he wouldn't. Living with Peter, Deanie and Wally, and not telling John where I was, seemed to be the only chance. It would mean leaving Adam behind until I could discuss arrangements for access with John. The thought of not seeing Adam every day for a while was difficult, but the thought of not seeing him again, ever, was inconceivable. I had made a mistake of such magnitude that I really didn't have any options. No matter what I did, I was going to be separated from my son.

I kept plotting and planning. I figured that if I went away and disappeared for a while, Michael would have no reason to cause trouble. After all, if he confessed he would also be exposing himself and Sandy could kick him out. I thought about going to Aunty

Daphne, but I couldn't tell her about Michael, and I knew she wouldn't understand how I could leave John after all his family had done for me. The same applied to Uncle Stan. And if Michael followed through with his threat, I worried that even Uncle Stan and Aunty Daphne might abandon me. I had no confidence that anyone would stand by me and help.

I didn't admit my infidelity with Michael to Peter, and let him believe that I cared enough for him to leave my son. That he accepted this showed how little he knew me. But this wasn't about me and Peter, it was about how to get out of this mess and not lose my son completely – or allow him to lose his mother. I had learned not to rely on Peter and I was prepared to use him without shame, until I could somehow have Adam back in my life.

Peter and I inspected a brand new, fully furnished duplex at Auburn, within easy walking distance to trains, buses and the shopping centre. It was a fabulous unit with large bright rooms. With the rent split four ways, it worked out to be very reasonable. The room I would share with Peter had a lovely view overlooking the park and the Auburn swimming pool.

We had about two weeks before we could move in, which was very close to the time Michael had threatened to be back. I quit my job at the kiosk to spend every possible moment I could with Adam, without feeling tired or cranky. We played in the yard every day. The weather was warming up, and I'd make a cubby house for him by folding his playpen into an A-frame and draping it with a blanket. Adam loved it.

It was 20 October 1967, the day that Lyndon B Johnson, president of the United States, visited Sydney, and the New South Wales premier, Sir Robert Askin, told his driver to 'run the bastards over', referring to the Vietnam War protesters blocking their cavalcade. It would be a day I would never forget.

Peter had arranged for a taxi to pick me up at eight-thirty that night. I had bought a new suitcase and packed in secret. The only things I took from the house were four plates from the Willow pattern dinner set that Uncle Stan had given us for a wedding gift. I knew that no one would appreciate their sentimental value.

If John had suspected anything that day, he never said a word. He went to work as usual. Adam and I played all morning. We watched Mr Squiggle come down in his rocket ship, telling Miss Gina to hurry up. One of Mr Squiggle's favourite sayings was, 'Everything's upside down these days.' It certainly applied to me.

It was a lovely sunny day so I made up Adam's cubby and we had a picnic lunch. When he was ready for his afternoon nap I carried him to my bed and lay down with him. As I watched him sleep I thought of everything we had gone through together. Twice in the past twenty-one months I had been driven to the very precipice of insanity, and it was only the profound love for this precious little person that had rescued me each time. The thought that I was planning to leave Adam for even a day was impossible to take in. Would John forgive me if I told him what had happened with Michael and admitted my terrible mistake? But I knew that whatever John felt for me had nothing to do with love. He hadn't invested anything, emotionally or financially, into our marriage and had no motive for trying to understand, let alone forgive, anything.

Adam woke up and gave me a big smile. 'Mum, Mum,' he gurgled, reaching over to kiss me.

I ran a bath and stripped us both off. We got in the tub and played and laughed until we looked like prunes and then I dressed him in his new pyjamas printed with little elephants. I turned on the television so he could watch the Bugs Bunny cartoons, while I made his favourite dinner of pasta with bolognaise sauce.

'Clever boy,' I said, praising him as he spooned the food into his mouth without dropping any.

John came home at the usual time. He must have sensed something was up because he was more aloof than ever. Maybe he'd noticed that I was wearing a new dress, I had make-up on and a rinse through my hair.

Usually I put Adam to bed at six-thirty, but I wanted to have him for as long as I could that night. By seven-thirty he was very tired. I made his bottle and nursed him in my lap. I knew this would be the last time I would hold my son in my arms for a little while. I just didn't want it to end until it had to. Adam was sound asleep when I carried him to his cot. I covered him and gave him his panda bear to snuggle.

As I stood there watching him sleep, my heart felt like it had been cut open and was bleeding all over the floor. We had been to hell and back, this little baby and me. No one else knew what we had gone through. I remembered the night I lay on my bed at the home for unwed mothers, his tiny feet kicking me in the ribs, making his presence felt. I promised him that I would never let anyone take him from me.

I tried to muffle my sobbing so I wouldn't wake him, but he stirred and looked up.

'You are the most beautiful boy in the whole wide world,' I said softly, bending over the side of the cot to kiss his forehead.

My tears fell like raindrops onto his hair. He gave me a sleepy grin and snuggled into his panda bear. Tomorrow he would wake up and ask for me and I'd be gone. I stood there watching him sleep. There was never a time before or since when I have known such depth of pain. It would become the yardstick by which all future unhappiness would be measured.

I went out to the lounge room. John was watching television. He turned his head. He seemed to be waiting for me to say something.

'I'm leaving tonight.'

He stood up and faced me, putting his hands in his pockets and nodding his head up and down, the way he had since I met him. 'Uh-huh,' he said, as if this was no big deal. 'But you're not taking Adam with you.'

'Believe me, I would if I could,' I said. 'I know I can't take him but I'm not leaving him either. When I get settled I'll call you at work to discuss access.'

I had nearly died having this baby and felt as though I'd had to fight the devil to keep him. *Who does he think he is telling me I can't take my son?* John hadn't cared enough about either of us to even contact me when he knew I was carrying his child. For the past two years he'd squandered money on his cars and hobbies while Adam and I walked around in rags. He never gave me a penny I didn't have to ask for. Not once did he hand me a few unsolicited dollars and say, 'Here, go buy the baby a new pair of shoes.' Now he was telling me I couldn't take him?

I wanted to pick Adam up right then and there and scream into John's face, as I once screamed into Sister Anne's, 'You are not getting my baby!'

John's reaction suddenly made me wonder whether the past two years of my life had been a set-up. *Did the McNortons put us into this dump thinking that I would eventually crack and run away and they'd get to keep the baby?* This may have been crazy thinking, but I still wasn't sure whether Mamma had told them how my mother had abandoned me and how I was just like her. John's reaction was so cold it seemed premeditated. He showed no shock or surprise about my leaving; it was as if he'd been expecting it, sooner or later. And he never asked why.

John followed me to Adam's room and stood beside the cot. The urge to pick up my baby and run out the door with him was overwhelming. But I knew that walking out alone was my only option if I ever hoped to see him again. I knew Adam would be in good hands with Mrs Mack and, especially, Harry. I had considered how heartbroken Harry would have been if I'd taken his grandson away, and how Adam would have missed his pa.

'Where are you going?' John finally asked.

'Queensland,' I said stupidly. 'When I get a job and get settled I'll contact you.'

Adam stirred. I pulled the blanket up and tucked him in. His blond curls framed his angelic little face. People had always told me he was too pretty to be a boy.

My beautiful boy, how am I going to breathe tomorrow, knowing that you'll be missing me? What am I going to do without you? One stupid mistake and all the fights we have fought and won have come to this, a total defeat.

I had let my darling son down. Would he ever forgive me?

Knowing that John would have no idea what to do in the morning before he took Adam to his mother's place, I had everything ready.

'His clothes are on a hanger on his wardrobe door,' I said. 'He likes egg soldiers for breakfast, with tomato sauce.' I could hardly make myself understood through the tears.

John just stood there, not moving a muscle, not saying a word, as if he had a script to follow and saying and doing nothing was how to play it.

The taxi honked its horn. After giving Peter my share of the costs to take the flat, I had only a few dollars in my purse. I asked John whether he could lend me some money until I found a job. He opened his wallet and took out forty dollars. It would have taken me three weeks to earn that much. He was walking around with it in his pocket.

'Goodbye,' I said, leaning over to kiss Adam on the cheek one last time.

'How can you do this after all my family has done for you?'

The taxi honked its horn a second time. If I'd been taking Adam with me I could have almost understood that question. *How is leaving my son showing a lack of gratitude towards his family?* If he'd said, 'Kay, don't leave. Can we talk about this?' I would have let the taxi go.

John really was out of touch with reality if he thought that leaving my son with his family was going to hurt them more than it would hurt Adam and me. Or that I ought to be grateful for all that his family had done for me.

At seventeen years old, I lacked the maturity to comprehend the danger of isolation. But John's parents should have known. Perhaps John thought I should have been grateful for having to work in the middle of the night to put decent clothes on my baby. But as much as anything, it was John's tone and manner that incensed me. He had never asked about my time at St Margaret's, and what I had been through to keep Adam. If he had, he'd have known that I couldn't just walk out and leave my son. Nothing the McNortons did for me would have been a fair trade for Adam.

'How can I do this after all your family has done for me?' I said, as the taxi blasted three more impatient honks. 'I have no choice.' I picked up my suitcase in one hand and the old hand-me-down sewing machine in the other, and walked out the door.

Epilogue

A plea to John for forgiveness and reconciliation was rejected. A request for regular access to my son was also rejected. I sought legal advice, but the solicitor nearly threw me out of his office when I told him my position. As a confessed adulteress I had no recourse at all. It was almost more than I could bear.

Today this kind of heartless behaviour – denying a child access to his mother – would not be condoned by the law. But it took me decades to realise that I wasn't an adulteress in the true sense. I had not given myself willingly to someone who was not my husband. It appeared to everyone that I had run away with another man. In fact, I had run away *from* a man – one who made good his threat even after I'd gone. I was well into the task of writing this book before I saw Michael for the sexual predator he was and how my vulnerability enabled him to control me, even long after I'd stopped thinking about him.

At seventeen, I was deeply traumatised. I did what all survivors of trauma do and manifested a false self to preserve my sanity. The ghosts and shadows of my past went into a locked space, tied up with rope, and there they stayed, waiting for that inevitable trigger event that would make it possible to speak about the previously unspeakable.

For the next fourteen years I was driven to succeed. I felt totally responsible for everything that had happened to me, a burden of guilt that crushed my self-esteem.

Any true sense of self was almost undetectable, hidden behind the façade of an outgoing, self-assured woman who seemed capable of taking on the world.

My formal education had been cut short before I completed high school, so I had much catching up to do. Libraries and second-hand bookshops were my favourite haunts. I became work obsessed. So long as I was immersed in my job, I didn't think about that little face smiling back at me from his cot. In my private life I was a jumble of contradictions – living on impulse and reacting to situations, rather than taking a reasoned, thoughtful approach.

Despite myself, my career took off. By 1982, I was co-owner of a company that had gone from being a hole in the wall in Hunter Street in downtown Sydney to a leader in the field of personnel management. Our business was the precursor to what today is the largest company of its kind in Australia, with an IT division that takes care of Australian Defence Force contracts. I could look back and say, 'I did that.' But the most important job was still to be done.

By the time my son was sixteen, an unusual event resulted in my reunion with Uncle Stan and Aunty Shirley. Meanwhile, the laws that had kept Adam and me apart had been amended, and I sensed the time was right to attempt to find a way back into his life. Naturally, I felt trepidatious. Would he want to know me? How had my long absence been explained to him?

I started by writing him a letter. I told my son that I would call him at precisely four o'clock on a certain day, and if he wanted to speak to me, all he had to do was come to the phone.

He answered.

Hearing him call me 'Mum' for the first time in nearly a decade and a half took my legs from underneath me.

On a stinking hot day in December I went to his grandmother's home, where my son had been living with his father, who had never remarried. Mrs Mack tried to rewrite history, telling me how hard life had been raising my son, and what a difficult and angry child he had been. By this time she was an old lady and I had not gone there to beat her up. I only wanted to go forward and reconnect with my son; I wanted the past to stay in the past. But I could not let her words go unanswered. After some very uncomfortable moments I brought her back to reality. I reminded her of what had really happened. I had not abandoned my son, I had been denied access.

When Adam came crashing through the door, as boys do, he walked up without hesitation and put his arms around me, like we'd only seen each other that morning. He kissed my cheek and said, 'Hello, Mum.'

'Hello, Toes,' I said, using the pet name I called him when he was a baby.

He turned to his grandmother, and what he said next blew me away.

'My mother thinks I'm the most beautiful boy in the whole wide world.'

These were the very last words I had spoken to him fourteen years earlier, a few months before his second birthday, when I'd tucked him into bed with his panda bear.

*

Having reconnected with my son, and Uncle Stan, I was now ready to reconcile with my long-estranged family and make my way back home. I discovered that I was too late for Mamma, Aunty Daphne, Uncle Jack and Phyllis and others, who had died, but not for Aunty Lorna. She had carried the guilt of my banishment from Nudgawalla for a long time, and just before she died she asked me to forgive her. Uncle Les and Shirl also asked for my forgiveness. We hugged and cried for the pain that was caused by a backward-thinking society.

Shortly after Robbie and I reconciled, he was diagnosed with lung cancer. At that time Vietnam veterans were still waiting for their welcome home parade, and fighting the government to acknowledge the lethal legacy of Agent Orange. Robbie called family from across the state for a day of healing. Here I was delighted to put my arms around my cousin Trudy. Her abuse at the hands of her father, my Uncle Jack, escalated after I left, and I will always regret that I didn't insist that she open the door that night I heard her whimpering from the bathroom.

On the night Robbie died, I sat with him and held his hand as we reminisced about the fun we'd had at Mitchell Farm. All the bad times were assigned to the past – 'I always loved you, Katie,' he said, and we parted with a kiss.

Uncle Stan and Aunty Shirley are alive and well, and although he is now in his eighties, Christmas at Uncle Stan's is still a grand affair.

In February 2007, when the Australian government made the long-overdue apology to Aboriginal Australians for past practices, Prime Minister Kevin Rudd asked stolen generation survivor Nana Nungala Fejo, 'What would you have me say?'

She replied simply, 'All mothers are important.'

Epilogue

In December 2000, in the final report *Releasing the Past*, the standing committee conducting the Parliamentary Inquiry into Adoption Practices 1950–1998 made, among others, two recommendations. Recommendation sixteen of the report states:

> The NSW Government should issue a statement of public acknowledgment that past adoption practices were misguided, and that on occasions unethical or unlawful practices may have occurred causing lasting suffering for many mothers, fathers, adoptees and their families.

Recommendation seventeen of the report states:

> The departments, private agencies, churches, hospitals, professional organisations and individuals involved in past adoption practices should be encouraged to issue a formal apology to the mothers, fathers, adoptees and their families who have suffered as a result of past adoption practices.

To date, no such formal apology or acknowledgment has been issued by the New South Wales government. With the exception of the apologies from adoption agencies Centacare and Anglicare, and expressions of regret and sorrow offered by other agencies and individual practitioners, the matter of an apology and redress for the victims of past adoption practices remains unresolved.

Although I didn't relinquish my son for adoption, he didn't come away unscathed. When I finally retrieved my medical records from St Margaret's archives, forty years after the birth, my distress was immense when I noted Adam's feeding chart. He received no feeds on 29 January, the day he was born, and 30 January. On 31 January he received three ounces for the whole day, supplemented with boiled water. In that time his weight plummeted, in today's scales, from 3.88 kilograms to 3.66 kilograms. His feeding pattern was kept at the bare minimum for the next ten days, in which time he didn't regain a milligram of weight. They had in fact starved my baby. His cries for help are as vivid today as they were then.

Still, I consider myself one of the lucky ones. I survived a shameful time in Australia's past and lived to write about it. For the mothers less fortunate or whose lives were totally shattered by these adoption practices, and for the 'stolen children', many of whom were never reconnected with their mothers, my hope is that you receive the acknowledgment, compensation and apology you deserve, so you may finally begin to release the past.

My last thoughts are for Dian Wellfare, former secretary of Origins Inc. New South Wales, who passed away in 2008. She was a brave female warrior for justice and a victim of past adoption practices for whom, like too many before her, an apology will come too late.

Acknowledgments

My thanks go firstly to two women whose names I never knew. The lady in the opposite bed to mine in St Margaret's, who saw how we were suffering and spoke up. And the nurse, or perhaps nun, who took a great risk to help us. To a dear departed friend, John Scipione. To Edward Hamala, Keith Adlam and Dennis Spruille, all of whom, in various ways, provided inspiration and encouragement. To a network of deadly women, Sarah-Jane Norman, Marti Young, Dr Cathy Cole, Dr Larissa Behrendt, Dr Keri Glastonbury and Dr Anita Heiss, who saw merit in a rough manuscript and spurred me on to keep working.

A special thanks to my editor, Dr Janet Hutchinson, who prompted me to enter the David Unaipon Award in 2008. Janet helped me to dig deeper for the details that would take the reader to the places in my life that had been locked for decades.

To the genius women at University of Queensland Press, Wendy Sanderson, Madonna Duffy and Rebecca Roberts, who were instrumental in getting this story to the reader.

To Uncle Stan and Aunty Shirley, who are the best role models anyone could ever hope to have.

Last, but never least, my children, you are and always will be the light of my life. And to Kate, my granddaughter, your very existence tells me that I am blessed.